2nd Workshop on Cognitive Modeling and Computational Linguistics 2011

(CMCL 2011)

Held at ACL HLT 2011

Portland, Oregon, USA
23 June 2011

ISBN: 978-1-61839-230-5

Printed from e-media with permission by:

Curran Associates, Inc.
57 Morehouse Lane
Red Hook, NY 12571

Some format issues inherent in the e-media version may also appear in this print version.

Printed by Curran Associates, Inc. (2011)

Association for Computational Linguistics
209 N. Eighth Street
Stroudsburg, Pennsylvania 18360

Phone: 1-570-476-8006
Fax: 1-570-476-0860

acl@aclweb.org

Additional copies of this publication are available from:

Curran Associates, Inc.
57 Morehouse Lane
Red Hook, NY 12571 USA
Phone: 845-758-0400
Fax: 845-758-2634
Email: curran@proceedings.com
Web: www.proceedings.com

Introduction

The papers in these proceedings were presented at the *2nd Workshop on Cognitive Modeling and Computational Linguistics* (CMCL), held at ACL HLT in Portland, Oregon on 23 June 2011.

The aim of the CMCL workshop series is to provide a forum for research that applies methods from computational linguistics to problems in the cognitive modeling of human language. It is the ambition of CMCL to encompass a broad spectrum of work in the cognitive science of language. This is reflected in the program of this year's CMCL, which includes work modeling morphological, phonological, syntactic, semantic, and discourse processing. A similarly broad range of cognitive processes is represented by the papers in the workshop, including models of the comprehension, production, and acquisition of language, as well as work on perceptual aspects of language (such as reading and color associations), and on atypical language.

We were pleased to receive 27 submissions, of which we accepted twelve papers for presentation at the workshop. We would like to thank the program committee for the excellent job they did in reviewing the submissions.

Frank Keller
David Reitter

Organizers:

Frank Keller, University of Edinburgh
David Reitter, Carnegie Mellon University

Program Committee:

Steven Abney, Michigan
Matthew Crocker, Saarland
Vera Demberg, Saarland
Robert Daland, Northwestern
Amit Dubey, Edinburgh
Mike Frank, Stanford
Ted Gibson, MIT
John Hale, Cornell
Keith Hall, Google
Jeff Heinz, Delaware
Florian Jaeger, Rochester
Gaja Jarosz, Yale
Roger Levy, San Diego
Richard Lewis, Michigan
Brian Murphy, Trento
Stephan Oepen, Oslo
Tim O'Donnell, Harvard
Ulrike Pado, VICO Research
Sebastian Pado, Heidelberg
Amy Perfors, Adelaide
Douglas Roland, Buffalo
William Schuler, Ohio State
Mark Steedman, Edinburgh
Patrick Sturt, Edinburgh
Shravan Vasishth, Potsdam

Table of Contents

Conference Program

June 23, 2011

08:50-09:00 Opening Remarks by Frank Keller, David Reitter

09:00–09:30 *Testing the Robustness of Online Word Segmentation: Effects of Linguistic Diversity and Phonetic Variation*
Luc Boruta, Sharon Peperkamp, Benoît Crabbé and Emmanuel Dupoux

09:30–10:00 *A Bayesian Belief Updating Model of Phonetic Recalibration and Selective Adaptation*
Dave Kleinschmidt and T. Florian Jaeger

10:00–10:30 *Unsupervised Syntactic Chunking with Acoustic Cues: Computational Models for Prosodic Bootstrapping*
John Pate and Sharon Goldwater

10:30-11:00 Morning Break

11:00–11:30 *A Statistical Test for Grammar*
Charles Yang

11:30–12:00 *Top-Down Recognizers for MCFGs and MGs*
Edward Stabler

12:00–12:30 *Exploring the Relationship Between Learnability and Linguistic Universals*
Anna N. Rafferty, Thomas L. Griffiths and Marc Ettlinger

12:30-14:00 Lunch Break

14:00–14:30 *Composing and Updating Verb Argument Expectations: A Distributional Semantic Model*
Alessandro Lenci

14:30–15:00 *WM Load Influences the Interpretation of Referring Expressions*
Jacolien van Rij, Hedderik van Rijn and Petra Hendriks

15:00–15:30 *Chameleons in Imagined Conversations: A New Approach to Understanding Coordination of Linguistic Style in Dialogs*
Cristian Danescu-Niculescu-Mizil and Lillian Lee

15:30-16:00 Afternoon Break

June 23, 2011 (continued)

16:00–16:30 *Classification of Atypical Language in Autism*
Emily T. Prud'hommeaux, Brian Roark, Lois M. Black and Jan van Santen

16:30–17:00 *Colourful Language: Measuring Word-Colour Associations*
Saif Mohammad

17:00–17:30 *A Survival Analysis of Fixation Times in Reading*
Mattias Nilsson and Joakim Nivre

Testing the Robustness of Online Word Segmentation: Effects of Linguistic Diversity and Phonetic Variation

Luc Boruta[1,2], **Sharon Peperkamp**[2], **Benoît Crabbé**[1], and **Emmanuel Dupoux**[2]
[1] Univ. Paris Diderot, Sorbonne Paris Cité, ALPAGE, UMR-I 001 INRIA, F-75205, Paris, France
[2] LSCP–DEC, École des Hautes Études en Sciences Sociales, École Normale Supérieure, Centre National de la Recherche Scientifique, F-75005, Paris, France
luc.boruta@inria.fr, peperkamp@ens.fr, benoit.crabbe@inria.fr, emmanuel.dupoux@gmail.com

Abstract

Models of the acquisition of word segmentation are typically evaluated using phonemically transcribed corpora. Accordingly, they implicitly assume that children know how to undo phonetic variation when they learn to extract words from speech. Moreover, whereas models of language acquisition should perform similarly across languages, evaluation is often limited to English samples. Using child-directed corpora of English, French and Japanese, we evaluate the performance of state-of-the-art statistical models given inputs where phonetic variation has not been reduced. To do so, we measure segmentation robustness across different levels of segmental variation, simulating systematic allophonic variation or errors in phoneme recognition. We show that these models do not resist an increase in such variations and do not generalize to typologically different languages. From the perspective of early language acquisition, the results strengthen the hypothesis according to which phonological knowledge is acquired in large part before the construction of a lexicon.

1 Introduction

Speech contains very few explicit boundaries between linguistic units: silent pauses often mark utterance boundaries, but boundaries between smaller units (e.g. words) are absent most of the time. Procedures by which infants could develop word segmentation strategies have been discussed at length, from both a psycholinguistic and a computational point of view. Many models relying on statistical information have been proposed, and some of them exhibit satisfactory performance: MBDP-1 (Brent, 1999), NGS-u (Venkataraman, 2001) and DP (Goldwater, Griffiths and Johnson, 2009) can be considered state-of-the-art. Though there is evidence that prosodic, phonotactic and coarticulation cues may count more than statistics (Johnson and Jusczyk, 2001), it is still a matter of interest to know how much can be learned without linguistic cues. To use Venkataraman's words, we are interested in "the performance of *bare-bones* statistical models."

The aforementioned computational simulations have two major downsides. First, all models of language acquisition should generalize to typologically different languages; however, the word segmentation experiments mentioned above have never been carried out on phonemically transcribed, child-directed speech in languages other than English. Second, these experiments use phonemically transcribed corpora as the input and, as such, make the implicit simplifying assumption that, when children learn to segment speech into words, they have already learned phonological rules and know how to reduce the inherent variability in speech to a finite (and rather small) number of abstract categories: the phonemes. Rytting, Brew and Fosler-Lussier (2010) addressed this issue and replaced the usual phonemic input with probability vectors over a finite set of symbols. Still, this set of symbols is limited to the phonemic inventory of the language: the reduction of phonetic variation is taken for granted. In other words, previous simulations evaluated the performance of the models given idealized input but offered no guarantee as to the performance of the models on realistic input.

We present a comparative survey that evaluates the extent to which state-of-the-art statistical models of word segmentation resist segmental variation. To do so, we designed a parametric benchmark where more and more variation was gradually introduced into phonemic corpora of child-directed speech. Phonetic variation was simulated applying context-dependent allophonic rules to phonemic corpora. Other corpora in which noise was created by random phoneme substitutions were used as controls. Furthermore, to draw language-independent conclusions, we used corpora from three typologically different languages: English, French and Japanese.

2 Robustness benchmark

2.1 Word segmentation models

The segmentation task can be summarized as follows: given a corpus of utterances in which word boundaries have been deleted, the model has to put them back. Though we did not challenge the usual idealization that children are able to segment speech into discrete, phoneme-sized units, modeling language acquisition imposes significant constraints on the models (Brent, 1999; Gambell and Yang, 2004): they must generalize to different (if not all) languages, start without any knowledge specific to a particular language, learn in an unsupervised manner and, most importantly, operate incrementally.

Online learning is a sound desideratum for any model of language acquisition: indeed, human language-processors do not wait, in Brent's words, "until the corpus of all utterances they will ever hear becomes available". Therefore, we favored an 'infant-plausible' setting and only considered online word segmentation models, namely MBDP-1 (Brent, 1999) and NGS-u (Venkataraman, 2001). Even if DP (Goldwater et al., 2009) was shown to be more flexible than both MBDP-1 and NGS-u, we did not include Goldwater et al.'s batch model, nor recent online variants by Pearl et al. (in press), in the benchmark. All aforementioned models rely on word n-grams statistics and have similar performance, but MBDP-1 and NGS-u are minimally sufficient in providing an quantitative evaluation of how cross-linguistic and/or segmental variation impact the models' performance. We added two random segmentation models as baselines. The four models are described below.

2.1.1 MBDP-1

The first model is Heinz's implementation of Brent's MBDP-1 (Brent, 1999; Heinz, 2006). The general idea is that the best segmentation of an utterance can be inferred from the best segmentation of the whole corpus. However, explicitly searching the space of all possible segmentations of the corpus dramatically increases the model's computational complexity. The implementation thus uses an incremental approach: when the ith utterance is processed, the model computes the best segmentation of the corpus up to the ith utterance included, assuming the segmentation of the first $i-1$ utterances is fixed.

2.1.2 NGS-u

This unigram model was described and implemented by Venkataraman (2001). MBDP-1's problems of complexity were circumvented using an intrinsically incremental n-gram approach. The strategy is to find the most probable word sequence for each utterance, according to information acquired while processing previous utterances. In the end, the segmentation of the entire corpus is the concatenation of each utterance's best segmentation. It is worth noting that NGS-u satisfies all three constraints proposed by Brent: strict incrementality, non-supervision and universality.

2.1.3 Random

This dummy model rewrites its input, uniformly choosing after each segment whether to insert a word boundary or not. It defines a chance line at and below which models can be considered inefficient. The only constraint is that no empty word is allowed, hence no consecutive boundaries.

2.1.4 Random$^+$

The second baseline is weakly supervised: though each utterance is segmented at uniformly-chosen random locations, the correct number of word boundaries is given. This differs from Brent's baseline, which was given the correct number of boundaries to insert in the entire corpus. As before, consecutive boundaries are forbidden.

	English		French		Japanese	
	Tokens	Types	Tokens	Types	Tokens	Types
U	9,790	5,921	10,000	7,660	10,000	6,315
W	33,399	1,321	51,069	1,893	26,609	4,112
P	95,809	50	121,486	35	102,997	49

Table 1: Elementary corpus statistics, including number of utterances (U), words (W) and phonemes (P).

2.2 Corpora

The three corpora we used were derived from transcribed adult-child verbal interactions collected in the CHILDES database (MacWhinney, 2000). For each sample, elementary textual statistics are presented in Table 1. The English corpus contains 9790 utterances from the *Bernstein–Ratner* corpus that were automatically transcribed and manually corrected by Brent and Cartwright (1996). It has been used in many word segmentation experiments (Brent, 1999; Venkataraman, 2001; Batchelder, 2002; Fleck, 2008; Goldwater et al., 2009; among others) and can be considered a *de facto* standard. The French and the Japanese corpora were both made by Le Calvez (2007), the former by automatically transcribing the *Champaud*, *Leveillé* and *Rondal* corpora, the latter by automatically transcribing the *Ishii* and *Noji* corpora from rōmaji to phonemes. To get samples comparable in size to the English corpus, 10,000 utterances were selected at random in each of Le Calvez's corpora. All transcription choices made by the authors in terms of phonemic inventory and word segmentation were respected.[1]

2.3 Variation sources

The main effect of the transformations we applied to the phonemic corpora was the increase in the average number of word forms per word. We refer to this quantity, similar to a type-token ratio, as the corpora's *lexical complexity*. As allophonic variation is context-dependent, the increase in lexical complexity is, in this condition, limited by the phonotactic constraints of the language: the fewer contexts a phoneme appears in, the fewer contextual allophones it can have. By contrast, the upper limit is much higher in the control condition, as phoneme substitutions are context-free.

From a computational point of view, the application of allophonic rules increases both the number of symbols in the alphabet and, as a byproduct, the lexical complexity. Obviously, when any kind of noise or variation is added, there is less information in the data to learn from. We can therefore presume that the probability mass will be scattered, and that as a consequence, statistical models relying on word n-grams statistics will do worse than with phonemic inputs. Yet, we are interested in quantifying how such interference impacts the models' performance.

2.3.1 Allophonic variation

In this experiment, we were interested in the performance of online segmentation models given rich phonetic transcriptions, i.e. the input children process before the acquisition of allophonic rules. Consider the following rule that applies in French:

$$/\mathrm{r}/ \rightarrow \begin{cases} [\chi] & \text{before a voiceless consonant} \\ [\text{ʁ}] & \text{otherwise} \end{cases}$$

The application of this rule creates two contextual variants for /kanar/ (*canard*, 'duck'): [kanaʁ‿ʒon] (*canard jaune*, 'yellow duck') and [kanaχ‿flotɑ̃] (*canard flottant*, 'floating duck'). Before learning the rule, children have to store both [kanaʁ] and [kanaχ] in their emerging lexicon as they are not yet able to undo allophonic variation and construct a single lexical entry: /kanar/.

Daland and Pierrehumbert (2010) compared the performance of a phonotactic segmentation model using canonical phonemic transcripts and transcripts implementing conversational reduction processes. They found that incorporating pronunciation variation has a mild negative impact on performance. However, they used adult-directed speech. Even if, as they argue, reduced adult-directed speech may present a worst-case scenario for infants (compared to hyperarticulated child-direct speech), it offers no quantitative evaluation of the models' performance using child-directed speech.

Because of the lack of phonetically transcribed child-directed speech data, we emulated rich transcriptions applying allophonic rules to the phonemic corpora. To do so, we represented the internal structure of the phonemes in terms of articulatory features and used the algorithm described by Boruta

[1]Some transcription choices made by Brent and Cartwright are questionable (Blanchard and Heinz, 2008). Yet, we used the canonical version of the corpus for the sake of comparability.

(2011) to create artificial allophonic grammars of different sizes containing assimilatory rules whose application contexts span phonologically similar contexts of the target phoneme. Compared to Daland and Pierrehumbert's manual inspection of the transcripts, this automatic approach gives us a finer control on the degree of pronunciation variation. The rules were then applied to our phonemic corpora, thus systematizing coarticulation between adjacent segments. We made two simplifying assumptions about the nature of the rules. First, all allophonic rules we generated are of the type $p \rightarrow a\ /\ \_\ c$ where a phoneme p is realized as its allophone a before context c. Thus, we did not model rules with left-hand or bilateral contexts. Second, we ensured that no two allophonic rules introduced the same allophone (as in English flapping, where both /t/ and /d/ have an allophone [ɾ]), using parent annotation: each phone is marked by the phoneme it is derived from (e.g. $[\text{ɾ}]^{/t/}$ and $[\text{ɾ}]^{/d/}$). This was done to avoid probability mass derived from different phonemes merging onto common symbols.

The amount of variation in the corpora is determined by the average number of allophones per phoneme. We refer to this quantity as the corpora's *allophonic complexity*. Thus, at minimal allophonic complexity, each phoneme has only one possible realization (i.e. phonemic transcription), whereas at maximal allophonic complexity, each phoneme has as many realizations as attested contexts. For each language, the range of attested lexical and allophonic complexities obtained using Boruta's (2011) algorithm are reported in Figure 1.

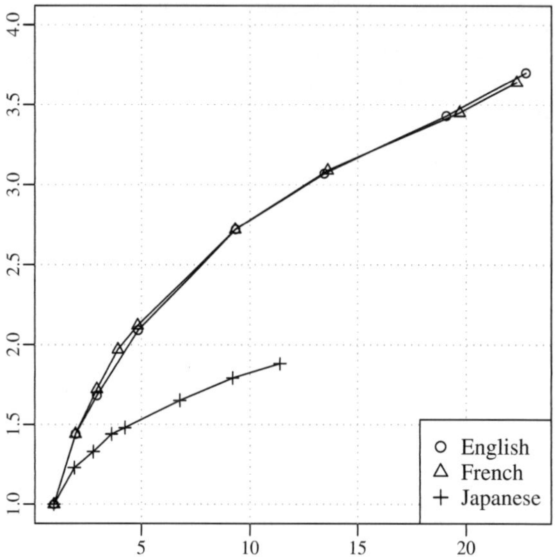

Figure 1: Lexical complexity (the average number of word forms per word) as a function of allophonic complexity (the average number of allophones per phoneme).

2.3.2 Phoneme substitutions

Allophonic variation is not the only type of variation that may interfere with word segmentation. Indeed, the aforementioned simulations assumed that all phonemes are recognized with 100% accuracy, but —due to factors such as noise or speech rate— human processors may mishear words. In this control condition, we examined the models' performance on corpora in which some phonemes were replaced by others. Thus, substitutions increase the corpus' lexical complexity without increasing the number of symbols: phoneme misrecognitions give a straightforward baseline against which to compare the models' performance when allophonic variation has not been reduced. Such corpora can be considered the output of a hypothetical imperfect speech-to-phoneme system or a winner-take-all scalar reduction of Rytting et al.'s (2010) probability vectors.

We used a straightforward model of phoneme misrecognition: substitutions are based neither on a confusion matrix (Nakadai et al., 2007) nor on phoneme similarity. Starting from the phonemic corpus, we generated 10 additional corpora controlling the proportion of misrecognized phonemes, ranging from 0 (perfect recognition) to 1 (constant error) in increments of 0.1. A noise intensity of n means that each phoneme has probability n of being rewritten by another phoneme. The random choice of the substitution phoneme is weighted by the relative frequencies of the phonemes in the corpus. The probability $P(p \rightarrow x)$ that a phoneme x rewrites a phoneme p is defined as

$$P(p \rightarrow x) = \begin{cases} 1 - n & \text{if } p = x \\ n\left(f(x) + \dfrac{f(p)}{|\mathcal{P}| - 1}\right) & \text{otherwise} \end{cases}$$

where n is the noise intensity, $f(x)$ the relative frequency of phoneme x in the corpus and $\mathcal{P}$ the phonemic inventory of the language.

2.4 Evaluation

We used Venkataraman's (2001) implementation of the now-standard evaluation protocol proposed by Brent (1999) and then extended by Goldwater et al. (2009). Obviously, orthographic words are not the optimal target for a model of language acquisition. Yet, in line with previously reported experiments, we used the orthographic segmentation as the standard of correct segmentation.

2.4.1 Scoring

For each model, we report (as percentages) the following scores as functions of the lexical complexity of the corpus:

- P_s, R_s, F_s: precision, recall and F-score on word segmentation as defined by Brent;
- P_l, R_l, F_l: precision, recall and F-score on the induced lexicon of word types: let L be the standard lexicon and L' the one discovered by the algorithm, we define $P_l = |L \cap L'|/|L'|$, $R_l = |L \cap L'|/|L|$ and $F_l = 2 \cdot P_l \cdot R_l/(P_l + R_l)$.

The difference between scoring the segmentation and the lexicon can be exemplified considering the utterance [əwʊdʧʌkwʊdʧʌkwʊd] (*a woodchuck would chuck wood*). If it is segmented as [ə˽wʊdʧʌk˽wʊd˽ʧʌk˽wʊd], both the segmentation and the induced lexicon are correct. By contrast, if it is segmented as [ə˽wʊd˽ʧʌk˽wʊdʧʌk˽wʊd], the lexicon is still accurate while the word segmentation is incorrect. A good segmentation inevitably yields a good lexicon, but the reverse is not necessarily true.

2.4.2 *k*-shuffle cross-validation

As the segmental variation procedures and the segmentation baselines are non-deterministic processes, all scores were averaged over multiple simulations. Moreover, as MBDP-1 and NGS-u operate incrementally, their output is conditioned by the order in which utterances are processed. To lessen the influence of the utterance order, we shuffled the corpora for each simulation. Testing all permutations of the corpora for each combination of parameter values is computationally intractable. Thus, scores reported below were averaged over three distinct simulations with shuffled corpora.

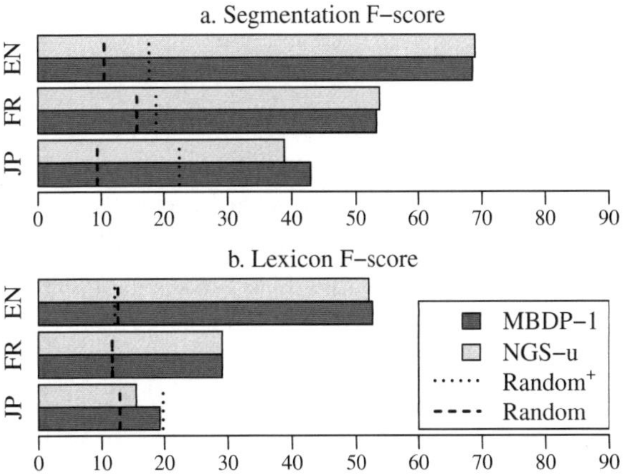

Figure 2: Cross-linguistic performance of MBDP-1 and NGS-u on child-directed phonemic corpora in English (EN), French (FR) and Japanese (JP).

3 Results and discussion

3.1 Cross-linguistic evaluation

Performance of the segmentation models[2] on phonemic corpora is presented in Figure 1 in terms of F_s- and F_l-score (upper and lower panel, respectively). We were able to replicate previous results on English by Brent and Venkataraman almost exactly; the small difference, less than one percent, was probably caused by the use of different implementations.

From a cross-linguistic point of view, the main observation is that these models do not seem to generalize to typologically different languages. Whereas MBDP-1 and NGS-u's F_s value is 69% for English, it is only 54% for French and 41% for Japanese. Similar observations can be made for F_l. Purely statistical strategies seem to be particularly ineffective on our Japanese sample: inserting word boundaries at random yields a better lexicon than using probabilistic models.

A crude way to determine whether a word segmentation model tends to break words apart (over-segmentation) or to cluster various words in a single chunk (under-segmentation) is to compare the average word length (AWL) in its output to the AWL in the standard segmentation. If the output's AWL is greater than the standard's, then the output is under-segmented, and *vice versa*. Even if NGS-u produces

[2]The full table of scores for each language, variation source, and segmentation model was not included due to space limitations. It is available upon request from the first author.

shorter words than MBDP-1, both models exhibit, once again, similar within-language behaviors. English was slightly under-segmented by MBDP-1 and over-segmented by NGS-u: ouputs' AWL are respectively 3.1 and 2.7, while the standard is 2.9. Our results are consistent with what Goldwater et al. (2009) observed for DP: error analysis shows that both MBDP-1 and NGS-u also break off frequent English morphological affixes, namely /ɪŋ/ (*-ing*) and /s,z/ (*-s*). As for French, AWL values suggest the corpus was under-segmented: 3.1 for MBDP-1's output and 2.9 for NGS-u's, while the standard is 2.4. On the contrary, Japanese was heavily over-segmented: many monophonemic words emerged and, whereas the standard AWL is 3.9, the ouputs' AWL is 2.7 for both models.

Over-segmentation may be correlated to the number of syllable types in the language: English and French phonotactics allow consonantal clusters, bringing the number of syllable types to a few thousands. By contrast, Japanese has a much simpler syllabic structure and less syllable types which, as a consequence, are often repeated and may (incorrectly) be considered as words by statistical models. The fact that the models do worse for French and Japanese is not especially surprising: both languages have many more affixal morphemes than English. Consider French, where the lexical autonomy of clitics is questionable: whereas /s/ (*s'* or *c'*) or /k/ (*qu'*) are highly frequent words in our orthographic standard, many errors are due to the agglutination of these clitics to the following word. These are counted as segmentation errors, but should they?

Furthermore, none of the segmentation models we benchmarked exhibit similar performance across languages: invariably, they perform better on English. There may be a correlation between the performance of segmentation models and the percentage of word hapaxes, i.e. words which occur only once in the corpus: the English, French and Japanese corpora contain 31.7%, 37.1% and 60.7% of word hapaxes, respectively. The more words tend to occur only once, the less MBDP-1, NGS-u and DP perform on segmentation. This is consistent with the usual assumption that infants use familiar words to find new ones. It may also be the case that these models are not implicitly tuned to English, but that the contribution of statistical cues to word segmentation differs across languages. In French, for example, stress invariably marks the end of a word (although the end of a word is not necessarily marked by stress). By contrast, there are languages like English or Spanish where stress is less predictable: children cannot rely solely on this cue to extract words and may thus have to give more weight to statistics.

3.2 Robustness to segmental variation

The performance of MBDP-1, NGS-u and the two baselines on inputs altered by segmental variation is presented in Figure 2.[3] The first general observation is that, as predicted, MBDP-1 and NGS-u do not seem to resist an increase in lexical complexity. In the case of allophonic variation, their performance is inversely related to the corpora's allophonic complexity. However, as suggested by the change in the graphs' slope, performance for English seems to stabilize at 2 word forms per word. Similar observations can be made for French and Japanese on which the performance of the models is even worse: F_l values are below chance at 1.7 and 3 variants per word for Japanese and French, respectively; likewise, F_s is below chance at 1.5 for Japanese and 2.5 for French. Phoneme substitutions also impede the performance of MBDP-1 and NGS-u: the more phonemes are substituted, the more difficult it becomes for the algorithms to learn how to insert word boundaries. Furthemore, F_l is below chance for complexities greater than 4 for French, and approximately 2.5 for Japanese. It is worth noting that, in both conditions, the models exhibit similar within-language performance as the complexity increases.

The potential lexicon that can be built by combining segments into words may account for the discrepancy between the two conditions, as it is in fact the models' search space. In the control condition, substituting phonemes does not increase its size. However, the likelihood of a given phoneme in a given word being replaced by the same substitution phoneme decreases as words get longer. Thus, the proportion of hapax increases, making statistical segmentation harder to achieve. By contrast, the

[3]For the control condition, we did not graph scores for noise intensities greater than 0.2: 80% accuracy is comparable to the error rates of state-of-the-art systems in speaker-independent, continuous speech recognition (Makhoul and Schwartz, 1995).

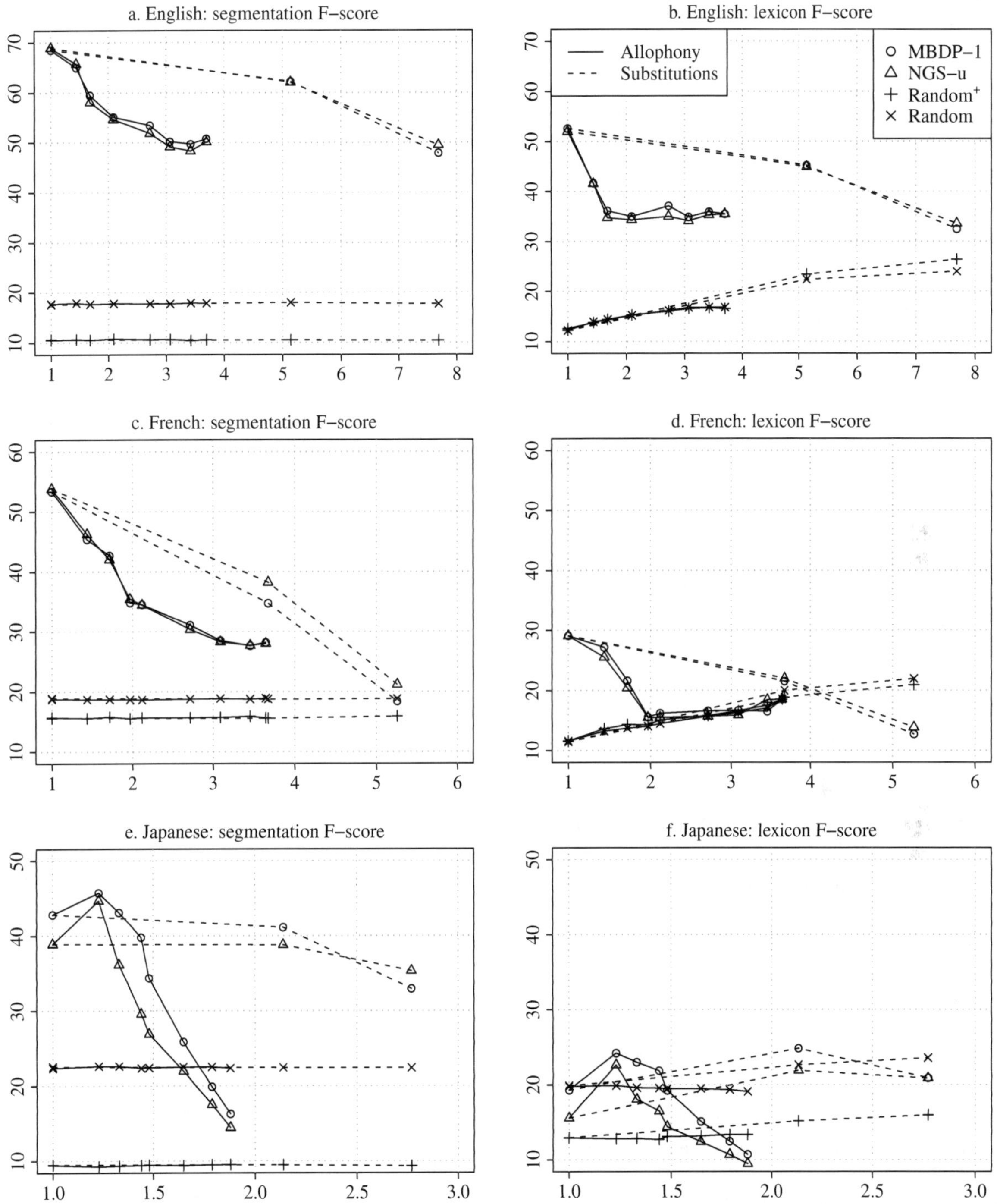

Figure 3: F_s-score (left column) and F_l-score (right column) as functions of the lexical complexity, i.e. the number of word forms per word, in the English (top row), French (middle row) and Japanese (bottom row) corpora.

application of allophonic rules increases the number of objects to build words with; as a consequence, the size of the potential lexicon explodes.

As neither MBDP-1 nor NGS-u is designed to handle noise, the results are unsurprising. Indeed, any word form found by these models will be incorporated in the lexicon: if [læŋgwɪʧ] and [læŋgwɪʤ] are both found in the corpus, these variants will be included as is in the lexicon. There is no mechanism for 'explaining away' data that appear to have been generated by systematic variation or random noise. It is an open issue for future research to create robust models of word segmentation that can handle segmental variation.

4 Conclusions

We have shown, first, that online statistical models of word segmentation that rely on word n-gram statistics do not generalize to typologically different languages. As opposed to French and Japanese, English seems to be easier to segment using only statistical information. Such differences in performance from one language to another emphasize the relevance of cross-linguistic studies: any conclusion drawn from the monolingual evaluation of a model of language acquisition should be considered with all proper reservations. Second, our results quantify how imperfect, though realistic, inputs impact MBDP-1's and NGS-u's performance. Indeed, both models become less and less efficient in discovering words in transcribed child-directed speech as the number of variants per word increases: though the performance drop we observed is not surprising, it is worth noting that both models are less efficient than random procedures at about twenty allophones per phoneme. However, the number of context-dependent allophones we introduced is far less than what is used by state-of-the-art models of speech recognition (Makhoul and Schwartz, 1995).

To our knowledge, there is no computational model of word segmentation that both respects the constraints imposed on a human learner and accommodates noise. This highlights the complexity of early language acquisition: while no accurate lexicon can be learned without a good segmentation strategy, state-of-the-art models fail to deliver good segmentations in non-idealized settings. Our results also emphasize the importance of other cues for word segmentation: statistical learning may be helpful or necessary for word segmentation, but it is unlikely that it is sufficient.

The mediocre performance of the models strengthens the hypotheses that phonological knowledge is acquired in large part before the construction of a lexicon (Jusczyk, 1997), or that allophonic rules and word segmentations could be acquired jointly (so that neither is a prerequisite for the other): children cannot extract words from fluent speech without knowing how to undo at least part of contextual variation. Thus, the knowledge of allophonic rules seems to be a prerequisite for accurate segmentation. Recent simulations of word segmentation and lexical induction suggest that using phonological knowledge (Venkataraman, 2001; Blanchard and Heinz, 2008), modeling morphophonological structure (Johnson, 2008) or preserving subsegmental variation (Rytting et al., 2010) invariably increases performance. *Vice versa*, Martin et al. (submitted) have shown that the algorithm proposed by Peperkamp et al. (2006) for undoing allophonic variation crashes in the face of realistic input (i.e. many allophones), and that it can be saved if it has approximate knowledge of word boundaries. Further research is needed, at both an experimental and a computational level, to explore the performance and suitability of an online model that combines the acquisition of allophonic variation with that of word segmentation.

References

E. Batchelder. 2002. Bootstrapping the lexicon: a computational model of infant speech segmentation. *Cognition*, 83:167–206.

D. Blanchard and J. Heinz. 2008. Improving word segmentation by simultaneously learning phonotactics. In *Proceedings of the Conference on Natural Language Learning*, pages 65–72.

L. Boruta. 2011. A note on the generation of allophonic rules. Technical Report 0401, INRIA.

M. R. Brent and T. A. Cartwright. 1996. Distributional regularity and phonotactic constraints are useful for segmentation. *Cognition*, 61:93–125.

M. R. Brent. 1999. An efficient, probabilistically sound algorithm for segmentation and word discovery. *Machine Learning*, 34(1–3):71–105.

R. Daland and J. B. Pierrehumbert. 2010. Learning diphone-based segmentation. *Cognitive Science*, 35(1):119–155.

M. Fleck. 2008. Lexicalized phonotactic word segmentation. In *Proceedings of ACL-2008*, pages 130–138.

T. Gambell and C. Yang. 2004. Statistics learning and universal grammar: Modeling word segmentation. In *Proceedings of the 20th International Conference on Computational Linguistics*.

S. Goldwater, T. L. Griffiths, and M. Johnson. 2009. A bayesian framework for word segmentation: exploring the effects of context. *Cognition*, 112(1):21–54.

J. Heinz. 2006. MBDP-1, OCaml implementation. Retrieved from http://phonology.cogsci.udel.edu/∼heinz/ on January 26, 2009.

E. K. Johnson and P. W. Jusczyk. 2001. Word segmentation by 8-month-olds: When speech cues count more than statistics. *Journal of Memory and Language*, 44:548–567.

M. Johnson. 2008. Unsupervised word segmentation for Sesotho using adaptor grammars. In *Proceedings of the 10th Meeting of ACL SIGMORPHON*, pages 20–27.

P. Jusczyk. 1997. *The Discovery of Spoken Language*. MIT Press.

R. Le Calvez. 2007. *Approche computationnelle de l'acquisition précoce des phonèmes*. Ph.D. thesis, UPMC.

B. MacWhinney. 2000. *The CHILDES Project: Tools for Analyzing Talk*. Lawrence Elbraum Associates.

J. Makhoul and R. Schwartz. 1995. State of the art in continuous speech recognition. *PNAS*, 92:9956–9963.

A. Martin, S. Peperkamp, and E. Dupoux. Submitted. Learning phonemes with a pseudo-lexicon.

K. Nakadai, R. Sumiya, M. Nakano, K. Ichige, Y. Hirose, and H. Tsujino. 2007. The design of phoneme grouping for coarse phoneme recognition. In *IEA/AIE*, pages 905–914.

L. Pearl, Sh. Goldwater, and M. Steyvers. In press. Online learning mechanisms for bayesian models of word segmentation. *Research on Language and Computation*.

S. Peperkamp, R. Le Calvez, J. P. Nadal, and E. Dupoux. 2006. The acquisition of allophonic rules: statistical learning with linguistic constraints. *Cognition*, 101(3):B31–B41.

C. A. Rytting, C. Brew, and E. Fosler-Lussier. 2010. Segmenting words from natural speech: subsegmental variation in segmental cues. *Journal of Child Language*, 37:513–543.

A. Venkataraman. 2001. A statistical model for word discovery in transcribed speech. *Computational Linguistics*, 27(3):351–372.

A Bayesian belief updating model of phonetic recalibration and selective adaptation

Dave Kleinschmidt[1] and **T. Florian Jaeger**[1,2]
Departments of [1]Brain and Cognitive Sciences and [2]Computer Science
University of Rochester
Rochester, NY, USA
{dkleinschmidt,fjaeger}@bcs.rochester.edu

Abstract

The mapping from phonetic categories to acoustic cue values is highly flexible, and adapts rapidly in response to exposure. There is currently, however, no theoretical framework which captures the range of this adaptation. We develop a novel approach to modeling phonetic adaptation via a belief-updating model, and demonstrate that this model naturally unifies two adaptation phenomena traditionally considered to be distinct.

1 Introduction

In order to understand speech, people map a continuous, acoustic signal onto discrete, linguistic categories, such as words. Despite a long history of research, no invariant mapping from acoustic features to underlying linguistic units has yet been found. Some of this lack of invariance is due to random factors, such as errors in production and perception, but much is due to systematic factors, such as differences between speakers, dialects/accents, and speech conditions.

The human speech perception system appears to deal with the lack of invariance in two ways: by storing separate, speaker-, group-, or context-specific representations of the same categories (Goldinger, 1998), and by rapidly adapting phonetic categories to acoustic input. Even though a person's inventory of native language phonetic categories is generally fixed from an early age (Werker and Tees, 1984), the mapping between these categories and their acoustic realizations is flexible. Listeners adapt rapidly to foreign-accented speech (Bradlow and Bent, 2008) and acoustically distorted speech (Davis et al., 2005), showing increased comprehension after little exposure. Such adaptation results in temporary and perhaps speaker-specific changes in phonetic categorization (Norris et al., 2003; Vroomen et al., 2007; Kraljic and Samuel, 2007).

To our knowledge, there is no theoretical framework which explains the range and specific patterns of adaptation of phonetic categories. In this paper, we propose a novel framework for understanding phonetic category adaptation—rational belief updating—and develop a computational model within this framework which straightforwardly explains two types of phonetic category adaptation which are traditionally considered to be separate.

While phonetic category adaptation has not thus far been described in this way, it nevertheless shows many hallmarks of rational inference under uncertainty (Jacobs and Kruschke, 2010). When there is another possible explanation for strange pronunciations (e.g. the speaker has a pen in her mouth), listeners do not show any adaptation (Kraljic et al., 2008). Listeners are more willing to generalize features of a foreign accent to new talkers if they were exposed to multiple talkers initially, rather than a single talker (Bradlow and Bent, 2008). Listeners also show rational patterns of generalizations of perceptual learning for specific phonetic contrasts, generalizing to new speakers only when the adapted phonetic categories of the old and new speakers share similar acoustic cue values (Kraljic and Samuel, 2007).

While it is not conclusive, the available evidence suggests that listeners update their beliefs about pho-

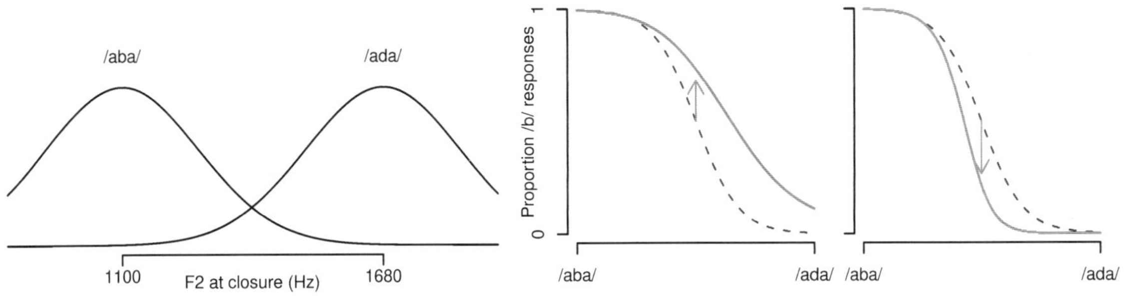

Figure 1: Left: approximate distribution of acoustic cue values for /aba/ and /ada/ stimuli from Vroomen et al. (2007). Right: exposure to acoustically ambiguous /aba/ tokens results in recalibration of the /aba/ category, with the classification boundary shifting towards /ada/ (center-right), while exposure to unambiguous /aba/ tokens results in selective adaptation of the /aba/ category, where the classification boundary shifts towards /aba/ (far right).

netic categories based on experience in a rational way. We propose that Bayesian belief updating can provide a principled computational framework for understanding rapid adaptation of phonetic categories as optimal inference under uncertainty. Such a framework has the appeal of being successfully applied in other domains (Brenner et al., 2000; Fine et al., 2010). In addition, rational models have also been used within the domain of speech perception to model acquisition of phonetic categories (Vallabha et al., 2007; Feldman et al., 2009a; McMurray et al., 2009), the perceptual magnet effect (Feldman et al., 2009b), and how various cues to the same phonetic contrast can be combined (Toscano and McMurray, 2010).

2 The Phenomena: Perceptual recalibration and selective adaptation

The flexibility of phonetic categories has been demonstrated through studies which manipulate the distribution of acoustic cues associated with a particular category. These studies take advantage of the natural variability of acoustic cues. Take, for example, the consonants /b/ and /d/. These two consonants can be distinguished largely on the basis of the trajectory of the second formant before and after closure (Iskarous et al., 2010). Like all acoustic-phonetic cues, there is natural variability in the F2 locus for productions of each category (depicted schematically in Figure 1, left). Listeners react to subtle changes in the distributions of acoustic cues, and adjust their phonetic categories for a variety of contrasts and manipulations (Kraljic and Samuel, 2006). In this paper, we model the effects of the two most common types of manipulation studied thus far, which produce opposite changes in phonetic classification.

The first of these is repeated exposure to acoustically ambiguous tokens, which results in a change in classification termed "perceptual learning" (Norris et al., 2003) or "perceptual recalibration" (Bertelson et al., 2003) in which the initially-ambiguous token becomes an accepted example of one phonetic category. Such ambiguous cue values are not uncommon because of the natural variability in normal speech. It is thus possible to generate a synthetic production /?/ which is acoustically intermediate between /b/ and /d/, and which is phonetically ambiguous in the absence of other cues but nevertheless sounds like a plausible production. When paired with another cue which implies /b/, subjects reliably classify /?/ as /b/. Disambiguating information could be provided by a video of a talker producing /b/ (Vroomen et al., 2007), or a word such as *a?out*, where a /b/ has been replaced with /?/ (Norris et al., 2003). When /?/ is repeatedly paired in this way with information biasing a /b/ interpretation, subjects begin to interpret /?/ as /b/ in general, classifying more items on a /b/-to-/d/ continuum as /b/ (Figure 1, center-right, red curve).

A second manipulation is repeated exposure to the same, acoustically unambiguous token. Repeated exposure to /b/ causes "selective adaptation" of this category, where listeners are less likely to classify items as /b/, indicated by a shift in the /b/-/d/ classification boundary towards /b/ (Figure 1, far-right).

Traditionally, recalibration and selective adaptation have been analyzed as separate processes, driven by separate underlying mechanisms (Vroomen et al., 2004), since they arise under different circumstances and produce opposite effects on classification. They also show different time courses. Vroomen et al. (2007) found that, on the one hand, strong recalibration effects occur after just a few exposures to ambiguous tokens, but fade with further exposure (Figure 3, upper curve). On the other, selective adaptation is present after a few exposures to unambiguous tokens, but grows steadily stronger with further exposure (Figure 3, lower curve).

We will show that these two superficially different adaptation phenomena are actually closely related, and will provide a unified account by appealing to principles of Bayesian belief updating. These principles are used to construct two models. The first, a unimodal model, treats phonetic categories as distributions over acoustic cue dimensions. The second, a multimodal model, treats phonetic categories as distributions over *phonetic* cue dimensions, which integrate information from both audio and visual cues. Both models capture the general effect directions of selective adaptation and recalibration, but only the multimodal model captures their distinct time courses.

The next section provides a high-level descriptions of these models, and how they might describe the selective adaptation and recalibration data of Vroomen et al. (2007). Section 4 describes this data and the methods used to collect it in more details. Section 5 describes the general modeling framework, how it was fit to the data, and the results, and Section 6 describes the multimodal model and its fit to the data.

3 Phonetic category adaptation via belief updating

In our proposed framework, the listener's classification behavior can be viewed as arising from their beliefs about the distribution of acoustic cues for each phonetic category. Specifically, as we will develop

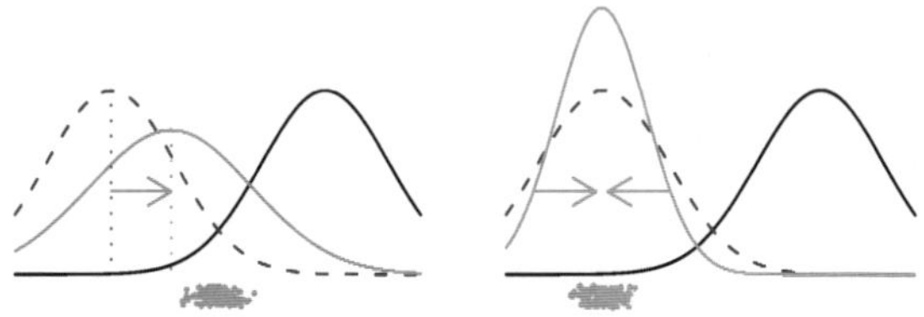

Figure 2: An incremental belief-updating model for phonetic recalibration and selective adaptation. These distributions correspond to the classification functions in Figure 1. Left: ambiguous stimuli labeled as /b/ cause a shift of the /b/ category towards those stimuli. Right: repeated unambiguous stimuli correspond to a narrower distribution than expected.

more rigorously below, the probability of classifying a given token x (which is the value of either an acoustic cue or a multimodal, phonetic cue) as /b/ is proportional to the relative likelihood of the cue value x arising from /b/ (relative to the overall likelihood of observing tokens like x, regardless of category). Thus, changes in the listener's beliefs about the distribution of cue values of category /b/ will result in changes in their willingness to classify tokens as /b/.

A belief-updating model accounts for recalibration and selective adaptation in the following way. When, on the one hand, a listener encounters many tokens that they consider to be /b/ but which are all acoustically intermediate between /b/ and /d/, they will change their beliefs about the distribution of /b/, shifting it to better align with these ambiguous cue values (Figure 2, left). This results in increased categorization of items on a /b/-to-/d/ continuum as /b/, since the range on the continuum over which the likelihood associated with /b/ is higher than that of /d/ is extended.

On the other hand, when a listener encounters repeated, tightly-clustered and highly prototypical /b/ productions, they update their beliefs about the distribution of /b/ to reflect that /b/ productions are more precise than they previously believed (Figure 2, right). They consequently assign lower likelihood to intermediate, ambiguous cue values for /b/, causing them to classify fewer /b/-/d/ continuum items as /b/.

Modeling the time course of selective adaptation

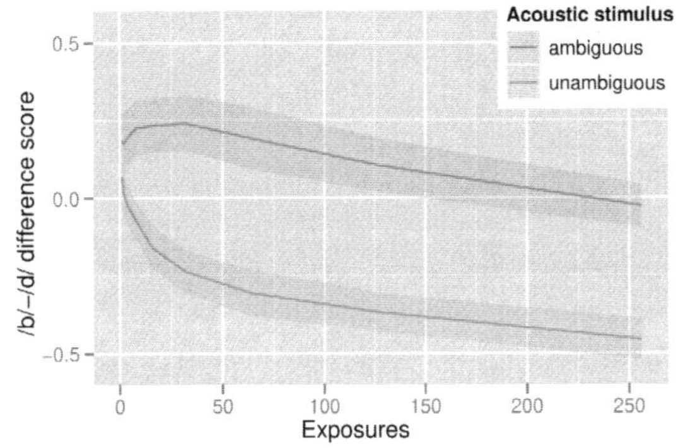

Figure 3: The results of Vroomen et al. (2007), showing the build-up time course of selective adaptation (as a function of unambiguous exposure trials) and recalibration (as a function of ambiguous exposure trials).

is straightforward: the more observations are made, the narrower the distribution becomes, and the more the classification boundary shifts towards the adapting category. However, modeling the time course of recalibration, as measured by Vroomen et al. (2007), is more complicated. Recalibration comes on quickly, but fades gradually with many exposures (Figure 3). As discussed below in Section 5.3, the unimodal model cannot account for this pattern, because it consideres the acoustically-similar exposure and test stimuli the same. The multimodal model, by integrating audio and visual cues to form the adapting percept, dissociates the adapting stimulus from the test stimuli and does not suffer from this problem. It is thus in principle capable of reproducing the empirical time course of recalibration observed by Vroomen et al. (2007). In practice, this model does indeed provide a good qualitative fit to human data, as discussed in Section 6.

4 Behavioral data: Vroomen et al. (2007)

Vroomen et al. (2007) investigated the time course of adaptation to audio-visual speech stimuli. In each block, subjects were repeatedly exposed to a single type of stimulus. The visual stimulus was either /aba/ or /ada/, and the audio stimulus was either an unambiguous match of the visual stimulus or was an ambiguous production. Throughout exposure, subjects were tested with unimodal acoustic test stimuli in order to measure the effect of exposure thus far.

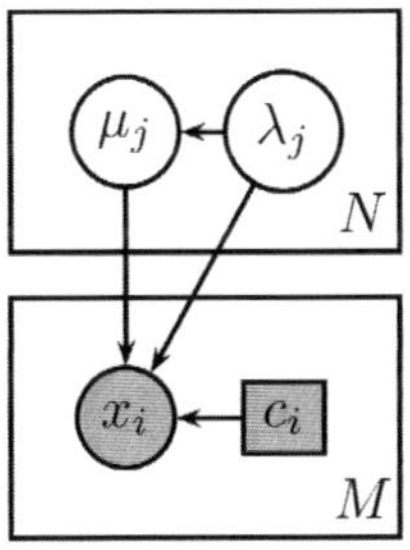

$$\mu_j \sim \textsc{Normal}(\mu_j^0, \kappa\lambda_j)$$
$$\lambda_j \sim \textsc{Gamma}(\alpha, \beta)$$

$$c_i \sim \textsc{Categorical}(\pi)$$
$$x_i \sim \textsc{Normal}(\mu_{c_i}, \lambda_{c_i})$$

Figure 4: Graphical model for the mixture of Gaussians with normal-gamma prior model. See text for description.

The overall effect of exposure to unambiguous stimuli was computed by comparing classification between unambiguous-/b/ and unambiguous-/d/ exposure, and likewise for the effect of exposure to ambiguous stimuli.

The acoustic stimuli used in exposure and test were drawn from a nine-item continuum (denoted $x = 1, \ldots, 9$) from /aba/ to /ada/, formed by manipulating the second formant frequency before and after the stop consonant (Vroomen et al., 2004). The most /aba/-like item $x = 1$ was synthesized using the formant values from a normal /aba/ production, and the most /ada/-like item $x = 9$ was derived from an /ada/ production. The maximally ambiguous item was determined for each subject via a labeling function (percent-/aba/ classification for each token) derived from pre-test classification data (98 trials from across the entire continuum). All subjects' maximally ambiguous tokens were one of $x = 4, 5$ or 6.

Each exposure block consisted of 256 repetitions of the bimodal exposure stimulus. After 1, 2, 4, 8, 16, 32, 64, 128, and 256 exposure trials subjects completed a test block, of six classification trials. They were asked to classify as /aba/ or /ada/ the three most ambiguous stimuli from the continuum (the most ambiguous stimulus and the two neighboring stimuli) twice each. For each ambiguity condition, the aggregate effect of exposure across categories was a difference score, calculated by subtracting the percent /aba/-classification after /d/-exposure from the percent after /b/-exposure. This /b/-/d/ difference score, as a function of cumulative exposure trials, is plotted in Figure 3.

5 The unimodal model

We implemented an incremental belief-updating model using a mixture of Gaussians as the underlying model of phonetic categories (Figure 4), where each phonetic category $j = 1 \ldots M$ corresponds to a normal distribution over percepts x with mean μ_j and precision (inverse-variance) λ_j (e.g. Figure 1, left).

$$p(x_i \mid c_i) = \mathcal{N}(\mu_{c_i}, \lambda_{c_i}) \tag{1}$$

The listener's beliefs about phonetic categories are captured by additionally assigning probability distributions to the means μ_j and precisions λ_j of each phonetic category. The prior distribution $p(\mu_j, \lambda_j)$ represents the listener's beliefs before exposure to the experimental stimuli, and the posterior $p(\mu_j, \lambda_j \mid X)$ captures the listener's beliefs after exposure to stimuli X from category j. These two distributions are related via Bayes' Rule:

$$p(\mu_j, \lambda_j \mid X) \propto p(X \mid \mu_j, \lambda_j) p(\mu_j, \lambda_j) \tag{2}$$

In order to quantitatively evaluate such a model, the form of the prior distributions needs to be specified. A natural prior to use in this case is known as a Normal-Gamma prior.[1] This prior factorizes the joint prior into

$$\begin{aligned} p(\mu_j, \lambda_j) &= p(\mu_j \mid \lambda_j) p(\lambda_j) \\ p(\mu_j \mid \lambda_j) &= \mathcal{N}(\mu_j^0, \kappa\lambda_j) \\ p(\lambda_j) &= \mathcal{G}(\alpha, \beta) \end{aligned}$$

where $\mathcal{N}(\mu_j^0, \kappa\lambda_j)$ is a Normal distribution with mean μ_j^0 and precision $\kappa\lambda_j$, and $\mathcal{G}(\alpha, \beta)$ is a Gamma distribution with shape α and rate β (Figure 4).

5.1 Identifying individual subjects' prior beliefs

In order to pick the most ambiguous token for each subject, Vroomen et al. (2007) collected calibration data from their subjects, which consisted of 98 two-alternative forced choice trials on acoustic tokens spanning the entire /aba/-to-/ada/ continuum. As revealed by this pre-test data, each subject's phonetic categories are different, and so we chose to estimate the prior beliefs about the nature of the exposure categories on a subject-by-subject basis. We fit each subject's classification function using logistic regression. The logistic function is closely related to the distribution over category labels given observations in a mixture of Gaussians model. Specifically, when there are only two categories (as in our case), the probability that an observation at x will be labeled c_1 is[2]

$$p(c_1 \mid x) = \frac{p(x \mid c_1) p(c_1)}{p(x \mid c_1) p(c_1) + p(x \mid c_2) p(c_2)} \tag{3}$$

Further assuming that the categories have equal precision λ and equal prior probability $p(c_1) = p(c_2) = 0.5$[3], this reduces to a logistic function of the form $p(c_1 \mid x) = (1 + \exp(-gx + b))^{-1}$, where

$$g = (\mu_1 - \mu_2)\lambda \quad \text{and} \quad b = (\mu_1^2 - \mu_2^2)\lambda$$

Even when b and g can be estimated from the subject's pre-test data, one additional degree of freedom needs to be fixed, and we chose to fix the distance between the means, $\mu_1 - \mu_2$. Given these values, the values for $(\mu_1 + \mu_2)/2$ (the middle of the subject's continuum) and λ can be calculated using

$$\frac{\mu_1 + \mu_2}{2} = \frac{b}{g} \quad \text{and} \quad \lambda = \frac{g}{\mu_1 - \mu_2} \tag{4}$$

We chose to use $\mu_1 - \mu_2 = 8$, the length of the acoustic continuum, which stretches from $x = 1$ (derived from a natural /aba/) to $x = 9$ (from a natural /ada/). This is roughly equivalent to assuming that all subjects would accept these tokens as good productions of /aba/ and /ada/, which indeed they do (Vroomen et al., 2004).

So far, we have accounted for the expected values of category means and precisions. The strength of these prior beliefs, however, has yet to be specified, and unfortunately there is no way to estimate this based on the pre-test data of Vroomen et al. (2007). The model parameters corresponding to the

[1] It is natural in that the Normal-Gamma distribution is the conjugate prior for a Gaussian distribution where there is some uncertainty about both the mean and the precision. Using the conjugate prior ensures that the posterior distribution has the same form as the prior.

[2] Here we are abusing notation a bit by using c_1 as a shorthand for $c = 1$.

[3] This assumption is not strictly necessary, but for this preliminary model we chose to make it in order to keep the model as simple as possible.

subject's confidence in their prior beliefs are κ and α for the means and variances, respectively. Given the specific form of the prior we use here, these two parameters are closely related to the number of observations that are required to modify the subject's belief about a phonetic category (Murphy, 2007).

5.2 Model fitting

In order to evaluate the performance of this model relative to human subjects, four simulations were run per subject, corresponding to the four conditions used by Vroomen et al. (2007): ambiguous /d/ and /b/, and unambiguous /d/ and /b/. For each subject, the hyper-parameters $(\mu_j^0, \kappa, \alpha, \beta)$ were set according to the methods described above: values were chosen for the free parameters α and κ, and β and μ_j^0 were set based on the subject's pre-test data.

To model the effect of n exposure trials in a given condition, the stimuli used by Vroomen et al. (2007) were input into the model in the following way. For ambiguous blocks, the observations X were n repetitions of that subject's most ambiguous token, and for unambiguous blocks they were n repetitions of the $x = 1$ for /b/ or $x = 9$ for /d/. For /b/ exposure blocks, the category labels C were set to 1, and for /d/ they were set to 2, corresponding to the disambiguating effect of the visual cues.

For each subject, condition, and number of exposures, the posterior distribution over category means and precisions $p(\mu_j, \lambda_j \mid X, C)$ was sampled using numerical MCMC techniques.[4]

To compare the simulation results with the test data of Vroomen et al. (2007), it was necessary to find the classification function, $p(c_{\text{test}} = 1 \mid x_{\text{test}}, X)$, which is the probability that acoustic test stimulus x_{test} will be categorized as /b/ ($c_{\text{test}} = 1$) given the training data X. Based on (3), it suffices to find the predictive distributions

$$p(x_{\text{test}} \mid c_{\text{test}} = 1, X) = \iint p(x_{\text{test}} \mid \mu_1, \lambda_1) p(\mu_1, \lambda_1 \mid X) \mathrm{d}\mu_1 \mathrm{d}\lambda_1$$

and, analogously, $p(x_{\text{test}} \mid c_{\text{test}} = 2, X)$. These integrals can be approximated numerically, by averaging over the individual likelihoods corresponding to each individual pair of means and variances drawn from the posterior $p(\mu_j, \lambda_j \mid X)$.

[4]Specifically, 1 000 samples for each parameter were obtained after burn-in using JAGS, an open-source implementation of the BUGS language for Gibbs sampling of graphical models: `https://sourceforge.net/projects/mcmc-jags`

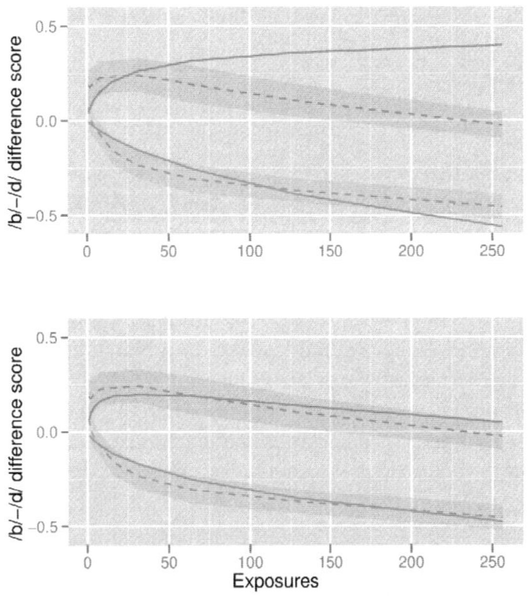

Figure 5: Overall fit of the acoustic-only (top, $R^2 = 0.14$) and bimodal model (bottom $R^2 = 0.67$). Solid lines correspond to the best fit averaged over subjects, and dashed lines correspond to empirical difference scores, with shaded regions corresponding to the 95% confidence interval on the empirical subject means.

Once this labeling function is obtained, the dependent measure used by Vroomen et al. (2007)—average percentage categorized as /b/—can be calculated, by averaging the value of $p(c_{\text{test}} = 1 \mid x_{\text{test}}, X)$ for the test stimuli x_{test} used by Vroomen et al. (2007). These were the subject's maximally ambiguous stimulus ($x = 4, 5$ or 6, depending on the subject), and its two neighbors on the continuum. The difference score used by Vroomen et al. (2007) was computed by subtracting the average probability of /b/ classification after /b/ ($c = 1$) exposure from the probability of /b/ classification after /d/ ($c = 2$) exposure. The best fitting confidence parameters α and κ were those which minimized mean squared error between the empirical and model difference scores.

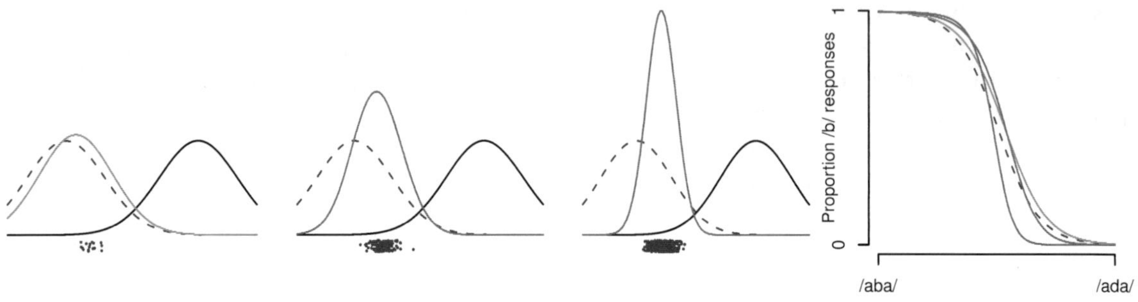

Figure 6: When audio and visual cues are integrated before categorization, a small number of ambiguous tokens still produces a shift in the category mean, and thus recalibration (left, bright red). However, a large number of ambiguous tokens produces both a shift of the category mean and an increase in precision (center-right, dark blue). If the audio-visual percept is located away from the maximally ambiguous middle region of the continuum, this can result in an extinction of the initial recalibration effect with increasing exposure (far right).

5.3 Results

Figure 5, top panel shows the results of the unimodal model. While this model clearly captures the direction of the effects caused by ambiguous and unambiguous exposure, it fails to account for a significant qualitative feature of the human data: the rise and then fall of the recalibration effect (red line).

The reason for this is that the audio component of the audio-visual exposure stimuli is identical to the maximally ambiguous (audio-only) test stimulus. Under this model, the probability with which a stimulus is classified as /b/ is proportional to the likelihood assigned to that cue value by category /b/, relative to the total likelihood assigned by /b/ and /d/. In addition, under rational belief updating the likelihood assigned to the exposure stimulus' cue value will always increase with more exposure. In the unimodal model the cue dimension is only auditory (with the visual information in the exposure stimuli only being used to assign category labels), and so to the unimodal model the ambiguous exposure stimuli and the ambiguous test stimuli are exactly the same. Thus, the probability that the test stimuli will be categorized as the exposure category increases monotonically with further exposure.

6 The multimodal model

The unimodal model assumes that the cue dimensions which phonetic categories are defined over are *acoustic*, incorporating information from other modalities only indirectly. This assumption is almost certainly wrong, based on work on audio-visual speech, which shows strong and pervasive cross-modal interactions (McGurk and MacDonald, 1976; Bejjanki et al., 2011). Indeed, Bertelson et al. (2003) report strong effects of the visual cue used by Vroomen et al. (2007): subjects were at chance in discriminating acoustically ambiguous versus unambiguous bimodal tokens when the visual cue matched.

The multimodal model replaces the acoustic percept x in the unimodal model with a phonetic percept which integrates information from audio and visual cues. Under reasonably general assumptions, information from auditory and visual cues to the same phonetic dimension can be optimally combined by a simple weighted sum $x = w_a x_a + w_v x_v$, where the weights w_a and w_v sum to 1 and are proportional to the reliability of the auditory and visual cues (Ernst and Banks, 2002; Knill and Saunders, 2003; Jacobs, 2002; Toscano and McMurray, 2010).

Such optimal linear cue-combination can be incorporated into our model in an approximate way by replacing x with a weighted sum of the continuum values for the auditory and visual tokens $x = wx_a + (1 - w)x_v$. In the unambiguous conditions, there is no mismatch between these values ($x_a, x_v = 1$ for /aba/ trials and 9 for /ada/ trials), and behavior is the same. In the ambiguous trials, however, the combination of visual and auditory cues creates a McGurk illusion, and pulls the observed stimulus—now located on a phonetic /aba/-/ada/ continuum rather than an acoustic one—away

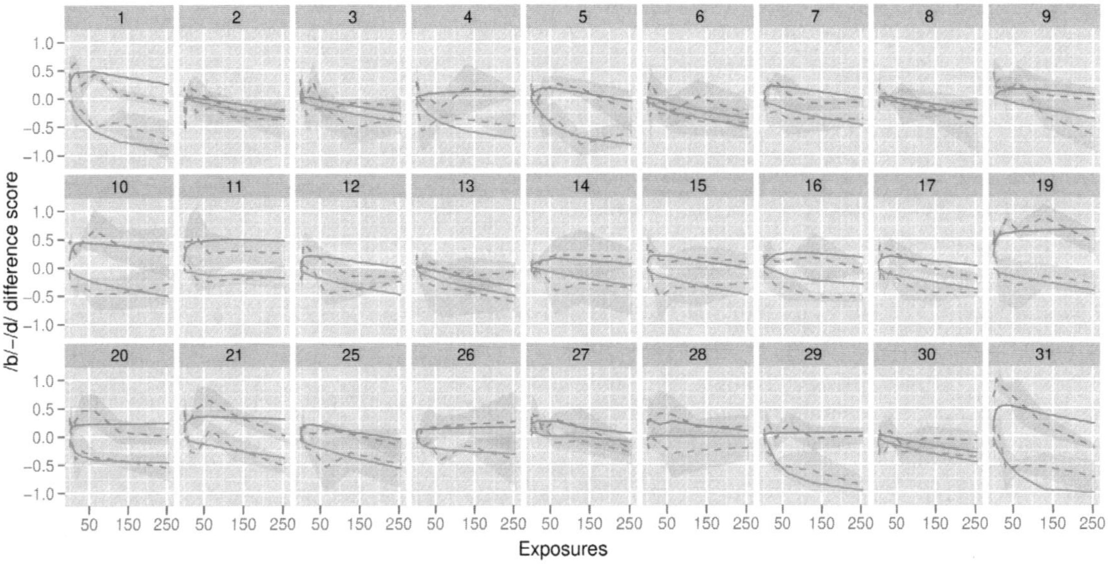

Figure 7: Best model fit for each individual subject. Dashed lines are empirical difference scores (shaded regions are 95% confidence intervals) and solid lines are the best-fitting model for that subject. Mean $R^2 = 0.57$, SE= 0.04.

from the maximally ambiguous test stimuli, which are still located at the middle of the continuum, being audio-only. This allows recalibration to dominate early, as the mean of the adapted category moves towards the adapting percept, but be reversed later, as the precision increases with further exposure percepts, all tightly clustered around the new, intermediate mean (Figure 6).

To be optimal, w must be the relative reliability (precision) of audio cues relative to visual cues, but in this preliminary model it is treated as a free parameter, between 0 and 1, and fit to each subject's test data individually, in the same way as the confidence parameters α and κ.

The best fitting models' predictions are shown averaged across subjects in Figure 5 (bottom panel). Unlike the unimodal model, the multimodal model clearly captures the initial rise and later fall of recalibration for ambiguous stimuli, and captures a fair amount of the variation between subjects (Figure 7).

7 Discussion

The Bayesian belief updating model developed in this paper, which takes into account cross-modal cue integration, provides a good qualitative fit to both the overall direction and detailed time-course of two very different types of adaptation of phonetic categories, recalibration and selective adaptation, as studied by Vroomen et al. (2007). This constitutes a first step towards a novel theoretical framework for understanding the flexibility that characterizes the mapping between phonetic categories to acoustic (and other) cues. There is a large number of models which adhere to the basic principles outlined here, and we have investigated only two of the simplest ones in order to show that, firstly, selective adaptation and recalibration can be considered the product of the same underlying inferential process, and secondly, this process likely occurs at the level of multimodal phonetic percepts.

One of the most striking findings from this work, which space precludes discussing in depth, is that all subjects' data is fit best when the strength of the prior beliefs is quite low, corresponding to a few hundred or thousand prior examples, which is many orders of magnitude less than the number of /b/s and /d/s a normal adult has encountered in their life. Why should this number be so low? The answer lies in the fact that phonetic adaptation is often extremely specific, at the level of a single speaker or situation. In the future, we plan to model these patterns of specificity and generalization (Kraljic and

Samuel, 2007; Kraljic and Samuel, 2006) via hierarchical extensions of the current model, with connected mixtures of Gaussians for phonetic categories that vary in predictable ways between groups of speakers.

Besides being a principled, mathematical framework, Bayesian belief updating and the broader framework of rational inference under uncertainty also provides a good framework for understanding how and why multiple cues are combined in phonetic categorization (Toscano and McMurray, 2010; Jacobs, 2002). Finally, this approach is similar in spirit and in its mathematical formalisms to models which treat the acquisition of phonetic categories as statistical inference, where the number of categories needs to be inferred, as well as the means and precisions of those categories (Vallabha et al., 2007; Feldman et al., 2009a). It is also similar to recent work on syntactic adaptation (Fine et al., 2010), and thus constitutes a central part of an emerging paradigm for understanding language as inference and learning under uncertain conditions.

Acknowledgements

We would like to thank Jean Vroomen for generously making the raw data from Vroomen et al. (2007) available.

This work was partially funded by NSF Grant BCS-0844472 and an Alfred P. Sloan Fellowship to TFJ.

References

Vikranth Rao Bejjanki, Meghan A Clayards, David C Knill, and Richard N Aslin. 2011. Cue Integration in Categorical Tasks : Insights from Audio-Visual Speech Perception. *PLoS ONE*, in press.

Paul Bertelson, Jean Vroomen, and Béatrice de Gelder. 2003. Visual recalibration of auditory speech identification: a McGurk aftereffect. *Psychological Science*, 14(6):592–597, November.

Ann R Bradlow and Tessa Bent. 2008. Perceptual adaptation to non-native speech. *Cognition*, 106(2):707–29, February.

Naama Brenner, William Bialek, and Rob de Ruyter Van Steveninck. 2000. Adaptive Rescaling Maximizes Information Transmission. *Neuron*, 26(3):695–702, June.

Matthew H Davis, Ingrid S Johnsrude, Alexis Hervais-Adelman, Karen Taylor, and Carolyn McGettigan. 2005. Lexical information drives perceptual learning of distorted speech: evidence from the comprehension of noise-vocoded sentences. *Journal of experimental psychology. General*, 134(2):222–41, May.

Marc O Ernst and Martin S Banks. 2002. Humans integrate visual and haptic information in a statistically optimal fashion. *Nature*, 415(6870):429–33.

Naomi H Feldman, Thomas L Griffiths, and James L Morgan. 2009a. Learning phonetic categories by learning a lexicon. *Proceedings of the 31st Annual Conference of the Cognitive Science Society*, pages 2208–2213.

Naomi H Feldman, Thomas L Griffiths, and James L Morgan. 2009b. The influence of categories on perception: explaining the perceptual magnet effect as optimal statistical inference. *Psychological review*, 116(4):752–82, October.

Alex B Fine, Ting Qian, T Florian Jaeger, and Robert A Jacobs. 2010. Is there syntactic adaptation in language comprehension? In *ACL Workshop on Cognitive Modeling and Computational Linguistics*, pages 18–26.

Stephen D Goldinger. 1998. Echoes of echoes? An episodic theory of lexical access. *Psychological review*, 105(2):251–79, April.

Khalil Iskarous, Carol A Fowler, and D H Whalen. 2010. Locus equations are an acoustic expression of articulator synergy. *The Journal of the Acoustical Society of America*, 128(4):2021–32, October.

Robert A Jacobs and John K Kruschke. 2010. Bayesian learning theory applied to human cognition. *Wiley Interdisciplinary Reviews: Cognitive Science*, pages n/a–n/a, May.

Robert A Jacobs. 2002. What determines visual cue reliability? *Trends in cognitive sciences*, 6(8):345–350, August.

David C Knill and Jeffrey A Saunders. 2003. Do humans optimally integrate stereo and texture information for judgments of surface slant? *Vision Research*, 43(24):2539–2558, November.

Tanya Kraljic and Arthur G Samuel. 2006. Generalization in perceptual learning for speech. *Psychonomic bulletin & review*, 13(2):262–8, April.

Tanya Kraljic and Arthur G Samuel. 2007. Perceptual adjustments to multiple speakers. *Journal of Memory and Language*, 56(1):1–15, January.

Tanya Kraljic, Arthur G Samuel, and Susan E Brennan. 2008. First impressions and last resorts: how listeners adjust to speaker variability. *Psychological science : a journal of the American Psychological Society / APS*, 19(4):332–8, April.

Harry McGurk and John MacDonald. 1976. Hearing lips and seeing voices. *Nature*, 264(5588):746–748.

Bob McMurray, Richard N Aslin, and Joseph C Toscano. 2009. Statistical learning of phonetic categories: insights from a computational approach. *Developmental Science*, 12(3):369–78, April.

Kevin P Murphy. 2007. Conjugate Bayesian analysis of the Gaussian distribution. *Technical report, University of British Columbia.*

Dennis Norris, James M McQueen, and Anne Cutler. 2003. Perceptual learning in speech. *Cognitive Psychology*, 47(2):204–238, September.

Joseph C Toscano and Bob McMurray. 2010. Cue integration with categories: Weighting acoustic cues in speech using unsupervised learning and distributional statistics. *Cognitive science*, 34(3):434–464, April.

Gautam K Vallabha, James L McClelland, Ferran Pons, Janet F Werker, and Shigeaki Amano. 2007. Unsupervised learning of vowel categories from infant-directed speech. *Proceedings of the National Academy of Sciences of the United States of America*, 104(33):13273–8, August.

Jean Vroomen, Sabine van Linden, Mirjam Keetels, Béatrice de Gelder, and Paul Bertelson. 2004. Selective adaptation and recalibration of auditory speech by lipread information: dissipation. *Speech Communication*, 44(1-4):55–61, October.

Jean Vroomen, Sabine van Linden, Béatrice de Gelder, and Paul Bertelson. 2007. Visual recalibration and selective adaptation in auditory-visual speech perception: Contrasting build-up courses. *Neuropsychologia*, 45(3):572–7, February.

Janet F Werker and Richard C Tees. 1984. Cross-language speech perception: Evidence for perceptual reorganization during the first year of life. *Infant Behavior and Development*, 7(1):49–63, January.

Unsupervised syntactic chunking with acoustic cues: computational models for prosodic bootstrapping

John K Pate (j.k.pate@sms.ed.ac.uk)
Sharon Goldwater (sgwater@inf.ed.ac.uk)
School of Informatics, University of Edinburgh
10 Crichton St., Edinburgh EH8 9AB, UK

Abstract

Learning to group words into phrases without supervision is a hard task for NLP systems, but infants routinely accomplish it. We hypothesize that infants use acoustic cues to prosody, which NLP systems typically ignore. To evaluate the utility of prosodic information for phrase discovery, we present an HMM-based unsupervised chunker that learns from only transcribed words and raw acoustic correlates to prosody. Unlike previous work on unsupervised parsing and chunking, we use neither gold standard part-of-speech tags nor punctuation in the input. Evaluated on the Switchboard corpus, our model outperforms several baselines that exploit either lexical or prosodic information alone, and, despite producing a flat structure, performs competitively with a state-of-the-art unsupervised lexicalized parser, with a substantial advantage in precision. Our results support the hypothesis that acoustic-prosodic cues provide useful evidence about syntactic phrases for language-learning infants.

1 Introduction

Young children routinely learn to group words into phrases, yet computational methods have so far struggled to accomplish this task without supervision. Previous work on unsupervised grammar induction has made progress by exploiting information such as gold-standard part of speech tags (e.g. Klein and Manning (2004)) or punctuation (e.g. Seginer (2007)). While this information may be available in some NLP contexts, our focus here is on the computational problem facing language-learning infants, who do not have access to either part of speech tags or punctuation. However, infants do have access to certain cues that have not been well explored by NLP researchers focused on grammar induction from text. In particular, we consider the cues to syntactic structure that might be available from prosody (roughly, the structure of speech conveyed through rhythm and intonation) and its acoustic realization.

The idea that prosody provides important initial cues for grammar acquisition is known as the *prosodic bootstrapping hypothesis*, and is well-established in the field of language acquisition (Gleitman and Wanner, 1982). Experimental work has provided strong support for this hypothesis, for example by showing that infants begin learning basic rhythmic properties of their language prenatally (Mehler et al., 1988) and that 9-month-olds use prosodic cues to distinguish verb phrases from non-constituents (Soderstrom et al., 2003). However, as far as we know, there has so far been no direct *computational* evaluation of the prosodic bootstrapping hypothesis. In this paper, we provide the first such evaluation by exploring the utility of acoustic cues for unsupervised syntactic chunking, i.e., grouping words into non-hierarchical syntactic phrases.

Nearly all previous work on unsupervised grammar induction has focused on learning hierarchical phrase structure (Lari and Young, 1990; Liang et al., 2007) or dependency structure (Klein and Manning, 2004); we are aware of only one previous paper on unsupervised syntactic chunking (Ponvert et al., 2010). Ponvert et al. describe a simple method for chunking that uses only bigram counts and punctuation; when the chunks are combined using a right-branching structure, the resulting trees achieve unlabeled bracketing precision and recall that is competitive with other unsupervised parsers. The system's dependence on punctuation renders it inappropriate for addressing the questions we are interested in here, but its good performance reccommends syntactic chunking as a profitable approach to the problem of grammar induction, especially since chunks can be learned using much simpler models than are needed for hierarchical structure.

The models used in this paper are all variants of HMMs. Our baseline models are standard HMMs that learn from either lexical or prosodic observations only; we also consider three types of models (including a coupled HMM) that incorporate both lexical and prosodic observations, but vary the degree to which syntactic and prosodic variables are tied together in the latent structure of the models. In addition, we compare the use of hand-annotated prosodic information (ToBI annotations) to the use of direct acoustic measures (specifically, duration measures) as the prosodic observations. All of our models are unsupervised, receiving no bracketing information during training.

The results of our experiments strongly support the prosodic bootstrapping hypothesis: we find that using either ToBI annotations or acoustic measures in addition to lexical observations (i.e., word sequences) vastly improves chunking performance over any source of information alone. Interestingly, our best results are achieved using a combination of words and acoustic information as input, rather than words and ToBI annotations. Our best combined model achieves an F-score of 41% when evaluated on the lowest level of syntactic structure in the Switchboard corpus[1], as compared to 25% for a words-only model and only 3% for an acoustics-only model. Although the combined model's score is still fairly low, additional results suggest that our corpus of transcribed naturalistic speech is significantly more difficult for unsupervised parsing than the written text that is typically used for training. Specifically, we find that a state-of-the-art unsupervised lexicalized parser, the Common Cover Link (CCL) parser (Seginer, 2007), achieves only 38% unlabeled bracketing F-score on our corpus, as compared to published results of 76% on WSJ10 (English) and 59% on Negra10 (German). Interestingly, we find that when evaluated against full parse trees, our best chunker achieves an F-score comparable to that of CCL despite positing only flat structure.

Before describing our models and experiments in more detail, we first present a brief review of relevant information about prosody and its relationship to syntax, including previous work combining prosody and syntax in supervised parsing systems.

2 Prosody and syntax

Prosody is a theoretical linguistic concept positing an abstract organizational structure for speech.[2] While it is often closely associated with such measurable phenomena as movement in fundamental frequency or variation in spectral tilt, these are merely observable acoustic correlates that provide evidence of varying quality about the hidden prosodic structure, which specifies such hidden variables as contrastive stress or question intonation.

Prosody has been hypothesized to be useful for learning syntax because it imposes a grouping structure on word sequences that sometimes coincides with traditional constituency analyses (Ladd, 1996; Shattuck-Hufnagel and Turk, 1996). Moreover, laboratory experiments have shown that adults use prosody both for syntactic disambiguation (Millotte et al., 2007; Price et al., 1991) and, crucially, in learning the syntax of an artificial language (Morgan et al., 1987). Accordingly, if prosodic structure is sufficiently prominent in the acoustic signal, and coincides often enough with syntactic structure, then it may provide children with useful information about how to combine words into phrases.

Although there are several theories of how to represent and annotate prosodic structure, one of the most influential is the ToBI (Tones and Break Indices) theory (Beckman et al., 2005), which we will use in some of our experiments. ToBI proposes, among other things, that the prosodic phrasing of languages can be represented in terms of sequences of break indices indicating the strength of

[1] Since our interest is in child language acquisition, we would prefer to evaluate our system on data from the CHILDES database of child-directed speech (MacWhinney, 2000). Unfortunately, there are no corpora in the database that include phrase structure annotations. We are in the process of annotating a small evaluation corpus with phrase structure trees, and hope to use this for evaluation in future work.

[2] Signed languages also exhibit prosodic phenomena, but they are not addressed here.

word boundaries. In Mainstream American English ToBI, for example, the boundary between a clitic and its base word (e.g. "do" and "n't" of "don't") is 0, representing a very weak boundary, while the boundary following a word at the end of an intonational phrase is 4, indicating a very strong boundary. Below we examine how useful these break indices are for identifying syntactic boundaries.

Finally, we note that our work is not the first computational approach to using prosody for identifying syntactic structure. However, previous work (Gregory et al., 2004; Kahn et al., 2005; Dreyer and Shafran, 2007; Nöth et al., 2000) has focused on supervised parsing rather than unsupervised chunking, and also makes different assumptions about prosody. For example, Gregory et al. (2004) assume that prosody is an acoustically-realized substitute for punctuation; our own treatment is much less constrained. Kahn et al. (2005) and Dreyer and Shafran (2007) use ToBI labels to represent prosodic information, whereas we explore both ToBI and direct acoustic measures. Finally, Nöth et al. (2000) do not use ToBI, instead developing a novel prosodic annotation system designed specifically to provide cues to syntax and for annotation efficiency. However, their system is supervised and focuses on improving parse *speed* rather than accuracy.

3 Models

Following previous work (e.g. Molina and Pla (2002) Sha and Pereira (2003)), we formulate chunking as a tagging task. We use Hidden Markov Models (HMMs) and their variants to perform the tagging, with carefully specified tags and constrained transition distributions to allow us to interpret the results as a bracketing of the input. Specifically, we use four chunk tags: **B** ("Begin") and **E** ("End") tags are interpreted as the first and last words of a chunk, respectively, with **I** ("Inside") corresponding to other words inside a chunk and **O** ("Outside") to all other words. The transition matrices are constrained to afford 0 probability to transitions that violate these definitions. Additionally, the initial probabilities are constrained to forbid the models from starting inside or at the end of a phrase.

We use this four-tag **OBIE** tagset rather than the more typical three-tag **IOB** tagset for two reasons. First, the **OBIE** set forces all chunks to be at least two words long (the shortest chunk allowed is **B E**). Imposing this requirement allows us to characterize the task in concrete terms as "learning when to group words together." Second, as we seek to incorporate acoustic correlates of prosody into chunking, we expect edge behavior to merit explicit modeling.[3]

In the following subsections, we describe the various models we use. Note that input to all models is discrete, consisting of words, ToBI annotations, and/or discretized acoustic measures (we describe these measures and their discretization in Section 3.3). See Figure 1 for examples of system input and output; different models will receive different combinations of the three kinds of input.

3.1 Baseline Models

Our baseline models are all standard HMMs, with the graphical structure shown in Figure 2(a). The first baseline uses *lexical* information only; the observation at each time step is the phonetic transcription of the current word in the sentence. To handle unseen words at test time, we use an "UNK." token to replace all words in the training and evaluation sets that appear less than twice in the training data. Our second baseline uses *prosodic* information only; the observation at each time step is the hand-annotated ToBI Break Index for the current word, which takes on one of six values: { 0, 1, 2, 3, 4, X, None }.[4] Our final baseline uses *acoustic* information only. The observations are one of six automatically determined clusters in an acoustic space, as described in Section 3.3.

We trained the HMMs using Baum-Welch, and used Viterbi for inference.[5]

[3]Indeed, when we tried using the **IOB** tag set in preliminary experiments, dev-set performance dropped substantially, supporting this latter intuition.

[4]The numerical break indices indicate breaks of increasing strength, "X" represents a break of uncertain strength, and "None" indicates that the preceding word is outside one of the fluent prosodic phrases selected for annotation. Additional distinctions marked by "-" and "p" were ignored.

[5]We actually used the junction tree algorithm from MALLET, which, in the special case of an HMM, reduces to the Forward-Backward algorithm when using Sum-Product messages, and to the Viterbi algorithm when using Max-Product messages. Our extension of MALLET to build junction trees efficiently for Dynamic Bayes Nets is available online, and is being prepared for submission to the main MALLET project.

		g.aa	dh.ae.t.s	dh.ae.t	s.aw.n.d.z	p.r.ih.t.iy	b.ae.d	t.ax	m.iy
(a)	Words	g.aa	dh.ae.t.s	dh.ae.t	s.aw.n.d.z	p.r.ih.t.iy	b.ae.d	t.ax	m.iy
	Acoustics	4	4	6	4	5	4	5	6
	ToBI	1	2	1	1	1	1	1	3
(b)		O	O	B	I	I	E	B	E
(c)				(			)	(	)
(d)		(		(			)	(	))

Figure 1: (a) Example input sequences for the three types of input (phonetic word transcriptions, acoustic clusters, and ToBI break indices). (b) Example output tags. (c) The bracketing corresponding to (b). (d) The flat tree built from (b).

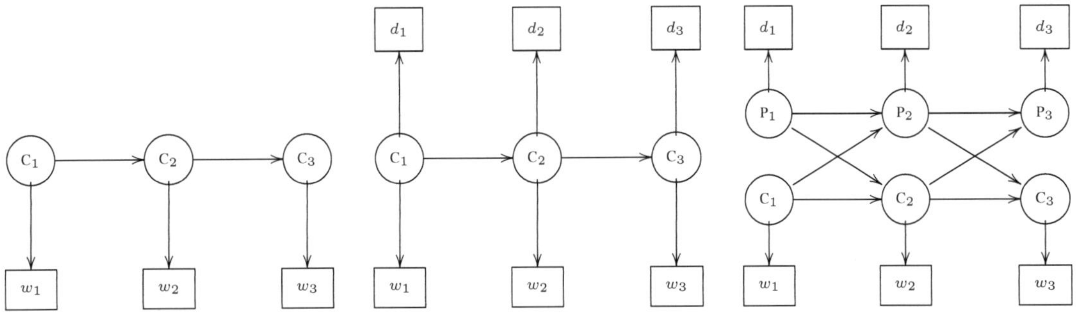

(a) Standard HMM (HMM) (b) Two Output HMM (THMM) (c) Coupled HMM (CHMM)

Figure 2: Graphical structures for our various HMMs. c_i nodes are constrained using the **OBIE** system, p_i nodes are not. w_i nodes represent lexical outputs, and d_i nodes represent acoustic or ToBI outputs. (Rectangular nodes are observed, circular nodes are hidden).

3.2 Combined Models

As discussed in Section 2, previous theoretical and experimental work suggests a combined model which models uncertainty both between prosody and acoustics, and between prosody and syntax. To measure the importance of modeling these kinds of uncertainty, we will evaluate a series of model structures that gradually divorce acoustic-prosodic cues from lexical-syntactic cues.

Our first model is the standard HMM from Figure 2(a), but generates a (word, acoustics) or (word, ToBI) pair at each time step. This model has the simplest structure, but includes a separate parameter for every unique (state, word, acoustics) triple, so may be too unconstrained to learn anything useful.

To reduce the number of parameters, we propose a second model that assumes independence between the acoustic and lexical observations, given the syntactic state. We call this a "Two-output HMM (THMM)" and present its graphical structure in Figure 2(b). It is straightforward to extend Baum-Welch to accommodate the extra outputs of the THMM.

Finally, we consider a model that explicitly represents prosodic structure distinctly from syntactic structure with a second sequence of tags. We use a Coupled HMM (CHMM) (Nefian et al., 2002), which models a set of observation sequences using a set of hidden variable sequences. Figure 2(c) presents a two-stream Coupled HMM for three time steps. The model consists of an initial state probability distribution π_s for each stream s, a transition matrix a_s for each stream s conditioning the distribution of stream s at time $t+1$ on the state of both streams at time t, and an emission matrix b_s for each stream conditioning the observation of stream s at time t on the hidden state of stream s at time t.[6]

Intuitively, the states emitting acoustic measures operationalize prosodic structure, and the states emitting words operationalize syntactic structure. Crucially, Coupled HMMs impose no *a priori* correspondence between variables of different streams, allowing our "syntactic" states to vary freely from our "prosodic" states. As two-stream CHMMs maintain two emission matrices, two transition ma-

[6]We explored a number of minor variations on this graphical structure, but preliminary experiments yielded no improvement.

trices, and two initial state distributions, they are more complex than the other combined models, but more closely embody intuitions inspired by previous work on the prosody-syntax interface.

Our Coupled HMMs were also trained using EM. Marginals for the E-step were computed using the implementation of the junction tree algorithm available in MALLET (McCallum, 2002; Sutton, 2006). During test, the Viterbi tag sequence for each model is obtained by simply replacing the sum-product messages with max-product messages.

3.3 Acoustic Cues

As explained in Section 2, prosody is an abstract hidden structure which only correlates with observable features of the acoustic signal, and we seek to select features which are both easy to measure and likely to correlate strongly with the hidden prosodic phrasal structure. While there are many possible cues, we have chosen to use duration cues. These should provide good evidence about phrases due to the phenomenon of pre-boundary lengthening (e.g. Beckman and Edwards (1990), Wightman et al. (1992)), wherein words, and their final rime, lengthen phrase-finally. This is likely especially useful for English due to the lack of confounding segmental duration contrasts (although variation in duration is unpredictably distributed (Klatt, 1976)), but should be useful in varying degrees for other languages.

We gather five duration measures:

1. Log total word duration: The annotated word end time minus the annotated word start time.
2. Log onset duration: The duration from the beginning of the word to the end of the first vowel.
3. Log offset duration: The duration from the beginning of the last vowel to the end of the word.
4. Onset proportion consonant: The duration of the non-vocalic portion of the word onset divided by the total onset duration.
5. Offset proportion consonant: The duration of the non-vocalic portion of the word offset divided by the total offset duration.

If a word contains no canonical vowels, then the first and last sonorants are counted as vocalic. If a word contains no vowels or sonorants, then the onset and offset are the entire word and the proportion consonant for both onset and offset is 1 (this occurred for 186 words in our corpus).

	Train	Dev	Test
Words	68,533	7,981	8,746
Sentences	6,420	778	802

Table 1: Data set statistics

The potential utility of this acoustic space was verified by visual inspection of the first few PCA components, which suggested that the position of a word in this acoustic space correlated with bracket count. We discretize the raw (i.e. non-PCA) space with k-means with six initially random centers for consistency with the number of ToBI break indices.

4 Experiments

4.1 Dataset

All experiments were performed on part of the Nite XML Toolkit edition of the Switchboard corpus (Calhoun et al., 2010). Specifically, we gathered all conversations which have been annotated for syntax, ToBI, and Mississippi State phonetic alignments (which lack punctuation).[7] The syntactic parses, word sequences, and ToBI break indices were hand-annotated by trained linguists, while the Mississippi State phonetic alignments were automatically produced by a forced alignment of the speech signal to a pronunciation-dictionary based phone sequence, providing an estimate of the beginning and end time of each phone. A small number of annotation errors (in which the beginning and end times of some phones had been swapped) were corrected by hand. This corpus has 74 conversations with two sides each.

We split this corpus into an 80%/10%/10% train/dev/test [8] partition by dividing the entire corpus into ten-sentence chunks, assigning the first eight to the training partition, and the ninth and tenth to the dev and test partitions, respectively. We then removed all sentences containing only one or two

[7]We threw out a small number of sentences with annotations errors, e.g. pointing to missing words.

[8]The dev set was used to explore different model structures in preliminary experiments; all reported results are on the test set.

words. Sentences this short have a trivial parse, and are usually formulaic discourse responses (Bell et al., 2009), which may influence their prosody. The final corpus statistics are presented in Table 1.

4.2 Evaluation

We use the Penn Treebank parsed version of Switchboard for evaluation. This version uses a slightly different tokenization from the Mississippi State transcriptions that were used as input to the models, so we transformed the Penn treebank tokenization to agree with the Mississippi State tokenization (primarily by concatenating clitics to their base words—i.e. "do" and "'nt" into "don't"—and splitting multi-word expressions). We also removed all gold-standard nodes spanning only `Trace` or `PUNC` (recall that the input to the models did not include punctuation) and collapsed all unary productions.[9]

In all evaluations, we convert our models' output tag sequence to a set of matched brackets by inserting a left bracket preceding each word tagged **B** tag and a right bracket following each word tagged **E**. This procedure occasionally results in a sentence with an unmatched opening bracket. If the unmatched opening bracket is one word from the end of the sentence, we delete it, otherwise we insert a closing bracket at the end of the sentence. Figure 1 shows example input sequences together with example output tags and their corresponding bracketings.

Previous work on chunking, most notably the 2000 CONLL shared task (Tjong et al., 2000), has defined gold standard chunks that are useful for finding grammatical relations but which do not correspond to any particular linguistic notion. It is not clear that such chunks should play a role in language acquisition, so instead we evaluate against traditional syntactic constituents from Penn Treebank-style parses in two different ways.

Our first evaluation method compares the output of the chunkers to what Ponvert et al. (2010) call *clumps*, which are just syntactic constituents that span only terminals. We created our clump gold-standard by taking the parse trees resulting from the preprocessing described above and deleting nodes that span a non-terminal. Figure 3 presents an ex-

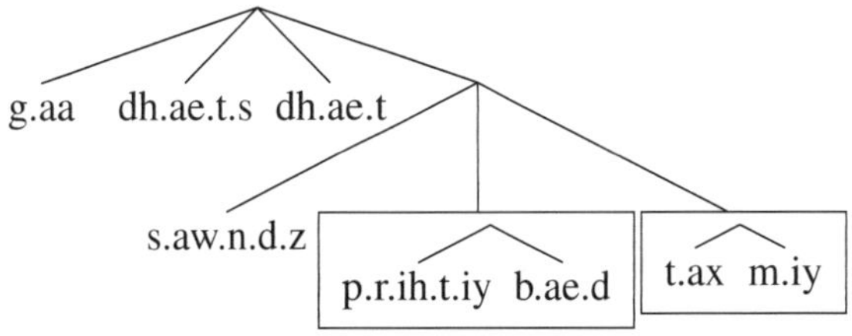

Figure 3: Example gold-standard with clumps in boxes.

ample gold-standard parse tree with the clumps in boxes. This evaluation avoids penalizing chunkers for not positing hierarchical structure, but rewards chunkers only for finding very low-level structure.

In the interest of making no *a priori* assumptions about the kinds of phrases our unsupervised method recovers, we also evaluate our completely flat, non-recursive chunks directly against the fully recursive parses in the treebank. To do so, we turn our chunked utterance into a flat tree by simply putting brackets around the entire utterance as in Figure 1(d). This evaluation penalizes chunkers for never positing hierarchical structure, but makes no assumptions about which kinds of phrases ought to be found.

4.3 Models and training

In all, nine HMM models, two versions of the CCL parser, and a uniform right-branching baseline were evaluated. Three of the HMMs were standard HMMs with chunking constraints on the four hidden states (as described in Section 3.2) that received as input either words, ToBI break indices, or word duration cluster information, intended as baselines to illuminate the utility of each information source in isolation. We also ran two each of Coupled HMM and Two-output HMM models that received words in one observed chain and either ToBI break index or duration cluster in the other observed chain. In the CHMM models, chunking constraints were enforced on the chain generating the words, while variables generating the duration or ToBI information ranged over four discrete states with no constraints.[10] All non-zero parameters were initialized approximately uniformly at random,[11] and we ran EM until the log

[9]As we evaluate unlabeled bracketing precision and recall, the label of the resulting nodes is irrelevant.

[10]We also tried imposing chunking constraints on the second chain, but dev-set performance dropped slightly.

[11]In preliminary dev-set experiments, different random initializations performed within two points of each other.

		Condition	Prec	Rec	F-sc
Baselines	HMM	Wds	23.5	39.9	26.3
		BI	7.2	4.8	5.8
		Ac	4.7	2.5	3.3
Combined Models	HMM	Wds+BI	24.4	22.2	23.2
		Wds+Ac	20.7	22.7	21.7
	THMM	Wds+BI	18.2	19.6	18.9
		Wds+Ac	36.1	47.8	**41.2**
	CHMM	Wds+BI	25.5	36.3	29.9
		Wds+Ac	33.6	**48.1**	39.5
CCL		Parser	15.4	41.5	22.4
		Clumper	**36.8**	37.9	37.3

Table 2: Scores for all models, evaluated on clumps. Input is words (Wds), break indices (BI), and/or acoustics.

		Condition	% Covered Words	% Covered Utts	$\frac{words}{chunk}$	$\frac{chunk}{utt}$
Baselines	HMM	Wds	81.9	98.4	3.16	2.82
		BI	68.2	68.1	4.95	1.50
		Ac	46.3	71.1	4.18	1.21
Combined Models	HMM	Wds+BI	79.8	98.3	4.30	2.02
		Wds+Ac	83.3	98.5	3.71	2.45
	THMM	Wds+BI	84.6	99.0	3.84	2.40
		Wds+Ac	68.0	96.1	2.52	2.94
	CHMM	Wds+BI	83.1	99.0	2.86	3.17
		Wds+Ac	76.5	97.6	2.62	3.19
CCL		Clumper	48.3	99.9	2.30	2.29

Table 3: % words in a chunk, % utterances with >0 chunks, and mean chunk length and chunks per utterance.

		Condition	Prec	Rec	F-sc
Baselines	HMM	Wds	48.8(32)	26.3(15)	34.2(20)
		BI	52.4(21)	18.5(5)	27.3(8)
		Ac	52.5(15)	16.3(3)	24.9(5)
Combined Models	HMM	Wds+BI	54.4(32)	23.2(11)	32.5(16)
		Wds+Ac	51.0(32)	24.7(13)	33.3(18)
	THMM	Wds+BI	55.9(38)	26.8(15)	36.2(21)
		Wds+Ac	55.8(41)	31.0(20)	39.9(27)
	CHMM	Wds+BI	48.4(32)	28.4(17)	35.8(22)
		Wds+Ac	54.1(40)	31.9(21)	**40.1**(**28**)
CCL		Parser	38.2(28)	**37.6**(**28**)	37.9(**28**)
		Clumper	**58.8**(**42**)	27.3(16)	37.3(23)

Table 4: Model performance, evaluated on full trees. Scores in parentheses were computed after removing the full sentence bracket, which provides a free true positive.

corpus probability changed less than 0.001%, typically for 50-150 iterations.

The CCL parser was trained on the same word sequences provided to our models. We also evaluated the CCL parser as a clumper (CCL Clumper) by removing internal nodes spanning a non-terminal. The right-branching baseline was generated by inserting one opening bracket in front of all but the last word, and closing all brackets at the end of the sentence.

4.4 Results and Discussion

Table 2 presents results for our flat chunkers evaluated against Ponvert et al. (2010)-style clumps. Several points are apparent. First, all three HMM baselines yield very poor results, especially the prosodic baselines, whose precision and recall are both below 10%. Although the best combined models still have relatively low performance, it is markedly higher than either of the individual baselines, and also higher than the clumps identified by the CCL parser. Particularly notable is the fact that lexical and prosodic information appear to be superadditive in some cases, yielding combined performance that is higher than the sum of the individual scores. Not all combined models work equally well, however: the poor performance of the HMM combined model supports our initial hypothesis that it is over parameterized. Interestingly, our acoustic clusters work better than break indices when combined with words. Finally, we see that the THMM and CHMM obtain similar performance using words + acoustics, suggesting that modeling prosodic structure separately from syntactic structure may be unnecessary (or that the CHMM does so badly).

To provide further intuition into the kinds of chunks recovered by the different models, we list some relevant statistics in Table 3. These statistics show that the models using lexical information identify at least one chunk in virtually all utterances, with the better models averaging 2-3 chunks per utterance of around 3 words each. In contrast, the unlexicalized models find longer chunks (4-5 words each) but far fewer of them, with about 30% of utterances containing none at all.

We turn now to the models' performance on full parse trees, shown in Table 4. Two different scores are given for each system: the first includes the top-level bracketing of the full sentence (which is standard in computing bracketing accuracy, but is a free true positive), while the second does not (for a more accurate picture of the system's performance on ambiguous brackets). Comparing the second set of scores to the clumping evaluation, recall is much lower for all the chunkers; the relatively small increase in precision indicates that the chunkers are most effective at finding low-level structure. For both sets of scores, the relative F-scores of the chunkers are similar to the clumping evaluation, with the words + acoustics versions of the THMM and CHMM scoring best. Not surprisingly, the CCL parser has much higher recall than the chunkers, though the best chunkers have much higher precision. The result is that, using standard Parseval scoring (first column), the best chunkers outperform CCL on F-score; even discounting the free sentence-level bracket (second column) they do about as well.

It is worth noting that, although CCL achieves state-of-the-art performance on the English WSJ and German Negra corpora (Seginer (2007) reports 75.9% F-score on WSJ10, for example), its performance on our corpus is far lower. In fact, on this corpus the CCL parser (as well as our chunkers) underperform a uniform right-branching baseline, which obtains 42.2% precision and 64.8% recall (including the top-level bracket), leading to an overall F-score of 51.1%. This suggests that our corpus is significantly more difficult than WSJ, probably due to disfluencies and/or lack of punctuation.[12] Moreover, we stress that the use of a right-branching baseline, while useful as a measure of overall performance, is not plausible as a model of language acquisition since it is highly language-specific.

5 Conclusion

Taken together, our results indicate that a purely local model that combines lexical and acoustic-prosodic information in an appropriate way can identify syntactic phrases far more effectively than a similar model using either source of information alone. Our best combined models outperformed the baseline individual models by a wide margin when evaluated against the lowest level of syntactic structure, and their performance was comparable to CCL, a state-of-the-art unsupervised lexicalized parser, when evaluated against full parse trees. It is disappointing that all of these systems scored worse than a right-branching baseline, but this result underscores the major differences between parsing spoken utterances (even using transcriptions) and parsing written text (where CCL and other unsupervised parsers were developed and tested). Since children learning language do not (at least initially) know the head direction of their language, the right-branching baseline for English is not available to them. Thus, combining lexical and acoustic cues may provide them with initial useful information about the location of syntactic phrases, as suggested by the prosodic bootstrapping hypothesis.

Nevertheless, we caution against assuming that the usefulness of acoustic information must result from its relation to prosody (especially because we found that direct acoustic information was more useful than hand-annotated prosodic labels). The "Smooth Signal Hypothesis" (Aylett and Turk, 2004) posits that talkers modulate their communicative effort according to the predictability of their message in order to achieve efficient communication, pronouncing more predictable parts of messages more quickly or less distinctly. If talkers consider syntactic predictability in this process, then it is possible that acoustic cues help initial grammar learning not by serving as cues to prosody but by serving as cues to the talker's syntax-dependent view of predictability. In this case, it may make more sense to discuss "predictability bootstrapping" rather than "prosodic bootstrapping."

Regardless of the underlying reason, we have shown that acoustic cues can be useful for identifying syntactic structure when used in combination with lexical information. In order to further substantiate these results, we plan to replicate our experiments on a corpus of child-directed speech, which we are currently annotating for evaluation purposes. We also hope to extend our findings to a model that can identify hierarchical structure, and to analyze more carefully the reasons for CCL's poor performance on the Switchboard corpus, in hopes of developing a model that can reach levels of performance closer to those typical of unsupervised parsers for written text.

[12] Including punctuation improves CCL little, possibly because the punctuation in this corpus is nearly all sentence-final.

References

Matthew Aylett and Alice Turk. 2004. The smooth signal redundancy hypothesis: A functional explanation for relationships between redundancy, prosodic prominence, and duration in spontaneous speech. *Language and Speech*, 47(1):31 – 56.

Mary E. Beckman and Jan Edwards. 1990. Lengthenings and shortenings and the nature of prosodic constituency. In J. Kingston and Mary E. Beckman, editors, *Between the grammar and physics of speech: Papers in laboratory phonology I*, pages 152–178. Cambridge: Cambridge University Press.

M Beckman, J Hirschberg, and S Shattuck-Hufnagel. 2005. The original tobi system and the evolution of the tobi framework. In S.-A. Jun, editor, *Prosodic Typology – The Phonology of Intonation and Phrasing*. Oxford University Press.

Alan Bell, Jason M. Brenier, Michelle Gregory, Cynthia Girand, and Dan Jurafsky. 2009. Predictability effects on durations of content and function words in conversational english. *Journal of Memory and Language*, 60:92 – 111.

S Calhoun, J Carletta, J Brenier, N Mayo, D Jurafsky, M Steedman, and D Beaver. 2010. The nxt-format switchboard corpus: A rich resource for investigating the syntax, semantics, pragmatics and prosody of dialogue. *Language Resources and Evaluation*, 44(4):387 – 419.

Markus Dreyer and Izhak Shafran. 2007. Exploiting prosody for pcfgs with latent annotations. In *Proc. of Interspeech*, Antwerp, Belgium, August.

L. Gleitman and E. Wanner. 1982. Language acquisition: The state of the art. In E. Wanner and L. Gleitman, editors, *Language acquisition: The state of the art*, pages 3–48. Cambridge University Press, Cambridge, UK.

Michelle L. Gregory, Mark Johnson, and Eugene Charniak. 2004. Sentence-internal prosody does not help parsing the way punctuation does. In *Proceedings of the North American Association for Computational Linguistics (NAACL)*, pages 81–88.

J. G. Kahn, M. Lease, E. Charniak, M. Johnson, and M. Ostendorf. 2005. Effective use of prosody in parsing conversational speech. In *Proc. of HLT/EMNLP-05*.

D H Klatt. 1976. Linguistic uses of segmental durations in english: Acoustic and perceptual evidence. *JASA*, 59:1208 – 1221.

Dan Klein and Christopher D. Manning. 2004. Corpus-based induction of syntactic structure: Models of dependency and constituency. In *Proceedings of the 42nd Annual Meeting of the Association for Computational Linguistics (ACL 2004)*, pages 479–486.

Bob Ladd. 1996. *Intonational Phonology*. Cambridge University Press.

K Lari and S J Young. 1990. The estimation of stochastic context-free grammars using the inside-outside algorithm. *Computer Speech and Language*, 5:237 – 257.

P. Liang, S. Petrov, M. I. Jordan, and D. Klein. 2007. The infinite PCFG using hierarchical Dirichlet processes. In *Empirical Methods in Natural Language Processing and Computational Natural Language Learning (EMNLP/CoNLL)*.

Brian MacWhinney. 2000. *The CHILDES project: Tools for analyzing talk*. Lawrence Erlbaum Associates, Mahwah, NJ, third edition.

Andrew Kachites McCallum. 2002. Mallet: A machine learning for language toolkit. http://mallet.cs.umass.edu.

Jacques Mehler, Peter Juszcyk, Ghislaine Lambertz, Nilofar Halsted, Josiane Bertoncini, and Claudine Amiele-Tison. 1988. A precursor to language acquisition in young infants. *Cognition*, 29:143 – 178.

Séverine Millotte, Roger Wales, and Anne Christophe. 2007. Phrasal prosody disambiguates syntax. *Language and Cognitive Processes*, 22(6):898 – 909.

Antonio Molina and Feran Pla. 2002. Shallow parsing using specialized HMMs. *Journal of Machine Learning Research*, 2:595 – 613.

James L. Morgan, Richard P. Meier, and Elissa L. Newport. 1987. Structural packaging in the input to language learning: contributions of prosodic and morphological marking of phrases to the acquisition of language. *Cognitive Psychology*, 19:498 – 550.

Ara V. Nefian, Luhong Liang, Xiaobao Pi, Liu Xiaoxiang, Crusoe Moe, and Kevin Murphy. 2002. A coupled hmm for audiovisual speech recognition. In *International Conference on Acoustics, Speech and Signal Processing*.

Elmer Nöth, Anton Batliner, Andreas Kieling, and Ralfe Kompe. 2000. Verbmobil: The use of prosody in the linguistic components of a speech understanding system. *IEEE Transactions on Speech and Audio Processing*, 8(5).

Elias Ponvert, Jason Baldridge, and Katrin Erk. 2010. Simple unsupervised identification of low-level constituents. In *ICSC*.

P J Price, M Ostendorf, S Shattuck-Hufnagel, and C Fong. 1991. The use of prosody in syntactic disambiguation. *JASA*, pages 2956 – 2970.

Yoav Seginer. 2007. Fast unsupervised incremental parsing. In *Proceedings of the Association of Computational Linguistics*.

Fei Sha and Fernando Pereira. 2003. Shallow parsing with conditional random fields. In *Proceedings of HLT-NAACL 03*, pages 213–220.

Stefanie Shattuck-Hufnagel and Alice E Turk. 1996. A prosody tutorial for investigators of auditory sentence processing. *Journal of Psycholinguistic Research*, 25(2):193 – 247.

M. Soderstrom, A. Seidl, D. G. K. Nelson, and P. W. Jusczyk. 2003. The prosodic bootstrapping of phrases: Evidence from prelinguistic infants. *Journal of Memory and Language*, 49:249–267.

Charles Sutton. 2006. Grmm: Graphical models in mallet. http://mallet.cs.umass.edu/grmm/.

Erik F. Tjong, Kim Sang, and Sabine Buchholz. 2000. Introduction to the conll-2000 shared task: Chunking. In *Proceedings of CoNLL-2000 and LLL-2000*, Lisbon, Portugal.

C W Wightman, S Shattuck-Hufnagel, M. Ostendorf, and P J Price. 1992. Segmental durations in the vicinity of prosodic phrase boundaries. *Journal of the Acoustical Society of America*, 91(3):1707 – 1717.

A Statistical Test for Grammar

Charles Yang
Department of Linguistics & Computer Science
Institute for Research in Cognitive Science
University of Pennsylvania
charles.yang@ling.upenn.edu

Abstract

We propose a statistical test for measuring grammatical productivity. We show that very young children's knowledge is consistent with a systematic grammar that independently combines linguistic units. To a testable extent, the usage-based approach to language and language learning, which emphasizes the role of lexically specific memorization, is inconsistent with the child language data. We also discuss the connection of this research with developments in computational and theoretical linguistics.

1 Introduction

Eistein was a famously late talker. The great physicist's first words, at the ripe age of three, were to proclaim "The soup is too hot." Apparently he hadn't had anything interesting to say.

The moral of the story is that one's linguistic behavior may not be sufficiently revealing of one's linguistic knowledge. The problem is especially acute in the study of child language since children's linguistic production is often the only, and certainly the most accessible, data on hand. Much of the traditional research in language acquisition recognizes this challenge (Shipley et al. 1969, Slobin 1971, Bowerman 1973, Brown 1973) and has in general advocated the position that child language be interpreted in terms of adult-like grammatical devices.

This tradition has been challenged by the usage-based approach to language (Tomasello 1992, 2000a) which, while reviving some earlier theories of child grammar (Braine 1964), also reflects a current trend in linguistic theorizing that emphasizes the storage of specific linguistic forms and constructions at the expense of general combinatorial linguistic principles and overarching points of language variation (Goldberg 2003, Sag 2010, etc.). Child language, especially in the early stages, is claimed to consist of specific usage-based schemas, rather than productive linguistic system as previously conceived. The main evidence for this approach comes from the lack of combinatorial diversity–the hallmark of a productive grammar–in child language data (Tomasello 2000a). For instance, verbs in young children's language tend to appear in very few frames rather than across many; this "uneveness" has been attributed to the verb-specific predicate structures rather than general/categorical rules. Similar observations have been made in the acquisition of inflectional morphology, where many stems are used only in relatively few morphosyntactic contexts (e.g., person, number). Another concrete example comes from the syntactic use of the determiners "a" and "the", which can be interchangeably used with singular nouns.[1] An *overlap* metric has been defined as the ratio of nouns appearing with both "a" and "the" out of those appearing with either. Pine & Lieven (1997) find that overlap values are generally low in child language, in fact considerably below chance level. This finding is taken to support the view that the child's determiner use is bound with specific nouns rather than reflecting a productive grammar defined over the abstract categories of determiners and nouns (Valian 1986).

[1] Although "a" is typically described as combining with countable nouns, instances such as "a water", "a sun" and "a floor" are frequently attested in both child and adult speech from CHILDES.

The computational linguistics literature has seen the influence of usage-based approach: computational models have been proposed to proceed from an initial stage of lexicalized constructions toward a more general grammatical system (Felman 2004, Steels 2004, cf. Wintner 2009). However, as far as we can tell, the evidence for an unproductive stage of grammar as discussed above was established on the basis of intuition rather than rigorous assessments. We are not aware of a statistical test against which the predictions of usage-based learning can be verified. Nor are we of any demonstration that the child language data described above is *inconsistent* with the expectation of a fully productive grammar, the position rejected in usage-based learning. It is also worth noting that while the proponents of the grammar based approach have often produced tests for the *quality* of the grammar–e.g., the errors in child language are statistically significantly low–they have likewise failed to provide tests for the *existence* of the grammar. As has been pointed out in the usage-based learning literature, low error rates could be the result of rote memorization of adult linguistic forms.

In this paper, we provide statistical analysis of grammar to fill these gaps. The test is designed to show whether a corpus of linguistic expressions can be accounted for as the output of a productive grammar that freely combines linguistic units. We demonstrate through case studies based on CHILDES (MacWhinney 2000) that children's language shows the opposite of the usage-based view, and it is the productivity hypothesis that is confirmed. We also aim to show that the child data is inconsistent with the memory-and-retrieval approach in usage-based learning (Tomasello 2000b). Furthermore, through empirical data and numerical simulations, we show that our statistical test (correctly) over-predicts productivity for linguistic combinations that are subject to lexical exceptions (e.g., irregular tense inflection). We conclude by drawing connections between this work and developments in computational and theoretical linguistics.

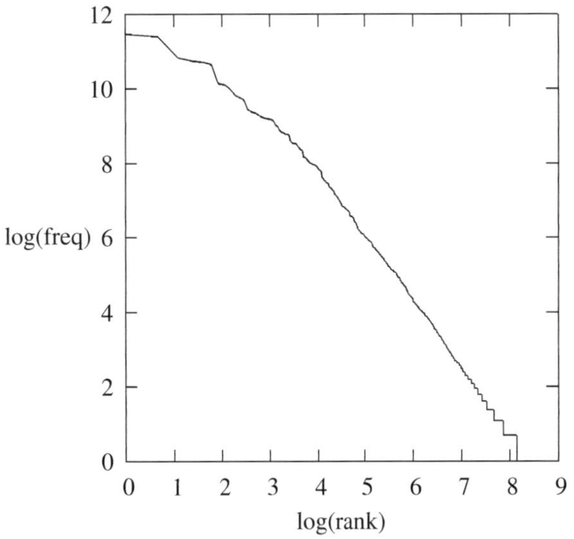

Figure 1: The power law frequency distribution of Treebank rules.

2 Quantifying Productivity

2.1 Zipfian Combinatorics

Zipf's law has long been known to be an omnipresent feature of natural language (Zipf 1949, Mendelbrot 1954). Specifically, the probability p_r of the word n_r with the rank r among N word types in a corpus can be expressed as follows:

$$p_r = \left(\frac{C}{r}\right) \Big/ \left(\sum_{i=1}^{N} \frac{C}{i}\right) = \frac{1}{rH_N}, \quad H_N = \sum_{i=1}^{N} \frac{1}{i} \tag{1}$$

Empirical tests show that Zipf's law provides an excellent fit of word frequency distributions across languages and genres (Baroni 2008).

It has been noted that the linguistic combinations such as n-grams show Zipf-like power law distributions as well (Teahna 1997, Ha et al. 2002), which contributes to the familiar sparse data problem in computational linguistics. These observations generalize the combination of morphemes (Chan 2008) and grammatical rules. Figure 1 plots the ranks and frequencies syntactic rules (on log-log scale) from the Penn Treebank (Marcus et al. 1993); certain rules headed by specific functional words have been merged.

Claims of usage-based learning build on the

premise that linguistic productivity entails diversity of usage: the "unevenness" in usage distribution such as the low overlap in D(eterminer)-N(oun) combinations is taken to be evidence against a systematic grammar. Paradoxically, however, Valian et al. (2008) find that the D-N overlap values in mothers' speech to children do not differ significantly from those in children's speech. In fact, when applied to the Brown corpus, we find that "a/the" overlap for singular nouns is only 25.2%: almost three quarters that could have appeared with both determiners only appeared with one exclusively. The overlap value of 25.2% is actually lower than those of some children reported in Pine & Lieven (1997): the language of the Brown corpus, which draws from various genres of professional print materials, must be regarded as less productive and more usage-based than that of a toddler—which seems absurd.

Consider the alternative to the usage based view, a fully productive rule that combines a determiner and a singular noun, or "DP$\rightarrow$ D N", where "D$\rightarrow$ a|the" and "N$\rightarrow$ cat|book|desk|...". Other rules can be similarly formulated: e.g., "VP$\rightarrow$ V DP", "$V_{\text{inflection}} \rightarrow V_{\text{stem}}$ + Person + Number + Tense". Suppose a linguistic sample contains S determiner-noun pairs, which consist of D and N unique determiners and nouns. (In the present case $D = 2$ for "a" and "the".) The full productivity of the DP rule, by definition, means that the two categories combine independently. Two observations, one obvious and the other novel, can be made in the study of D-N usage diversity. First, nouns will follow zipf's law. For instance, the singular nouns that appear in the form of "DP$\rightarrow$ D N" in the Brown corpus show a log-log slope of -0.97. In the CHILDES speech transcripts of six children (see section 3.1 for details for data analysis), the average value of log-log slope is -0.98. Thus, relatively few nouns occur often but many will occur only once—which of course cannot overlap with more than one determiners.

Second, while the combination of D and N in the DP rule is syntactically interchangeable, N's may favor one of the two determiners, a consequence of pragmatics and indeed non-linguistic factors. For instance, we say "the bathroom" more often than "a bathroom" but "a bath" more often than "the bath", even though all four DPs are perfectly grammatical. As noted earlier, about 75% of distinct nouns in the Brown corpus occur with exclusively "the" or "a" but not both. Even the remaining 25% which do occur with both tend to have favorites: only a further 25% (i.e. 12.5% of all nouns) are used with "a" and "the" equally frequently, and the remaining 75% are unbalanced. Overall, for nouns that appear with both determiners as least once (i.e. 25% of all nouns), the frequency ratio between the more over the less favored determiner is 2.86:1. These general patterns hold for child and adult speech data as well. In the six children's transcripts (section 3), the average percentage of balanced nouns among those that appear with both "the" and "a" is 22.8%, and the more favored vs. less favored determiner has an average frequency ratio of 2.54:1. As a result, even when a noun appears multiple times in a sample, there is still a significant chance that it has been paired with a single determiner in all instances.

We now formalize the overlap measure under the assumption of a rule and Zipfian frequencies of grammatical combinations.

2.2 Theoretical analysis

Consider a sample (N, D, S), which consists of N unique nouns, D unique determiners, and S determiner-noun pairs. The nouns that have appeared with more than one (i.e. two, in the case of "a" and "the") determiners will have an overlap value of 1; otherwise, they have the overlap value of 0. The overlap value for the entire sample will be the number of 1's divided by N.

Our analysis calculates the expected value of the overlap value for the sample (N, D, S) under the productive rule "DP$\rightarrow$D N"; let it be $O(N, D, S)$. This requires the calculation of the expected overlap value for each of the N nouns over all possible compositions of the sample. Consider the noun n_r with the rank r out of N. Following equation (1), it has the probability $p_r = 1/(rH_N)$ of being drawn at any single trial in S. Let the expected overlap value of n_r be $O(r, N, D, S)$. The overlap for the sample can be stated as:

$$O(D, N, S) = \frac{1}{N} \sum_{r=1}^{N} O(r, N, D, S) \qquad (2)$$

Consider now the calculation $O(r, N, D, S)$. Since n_r has the overlap value of 1 if and only if it has been used with more than one determiner in the sample, we have:

$$O(r,N,D,S) = 1 - \Pr\{n_r \text{ not sampled during } S \text{ trials}\} - \sum_{i=1}^{D} \Pr\{n_r \text{ sampled } i\text{th exclusively}\} = 1-(1-p_r)^S - \sum_{i=1}^{D}\left[(d_i p_r + 1 - p_r)^S - (1-p_r)^S\right] \quad (3)$$

The last term above requires a brief comment. Under the hypothesis that the language learner has a productive rule "DP→D N", the combination of determiner and noun is independent. Therefore, the probability of noun n_r combining with the ith determiner is the product of their probabilities, or $d_i p_r$. The multinomial expression

$$(p_1 + p_2 + \ldots + p_{r-1} + d_i p_r + p_{r+1} + \ldots + p_N)^S \quad (4)$$

gives the probabilities of all the compositions of the sample, with n_r combining with the ith determiner 0, 1, 2, ... S times, which is simply $(d_i p_r + 1 - p_r)^S$ since $(p_1 + p_2 + p_{r-1} + p_r + p_{r+1} + \ldots + p_N) = 1$. However, this value includes the probability of n_r combining with the ith determiner zero times—again $(1-p_r)^S$—which must be subtracted. Thus, the probability with which n_r combines with the ith determiner exclusively in the sample S is $[(d_i p_r + 1 - p_r)^S - (1-p_r)^S]$. Summing these values over all determiners and collecting terms, we have:

$$O(r,N,D,S) = 1 + (D-1)(1-p_r)^S - \sum_{i=1}^{D}\left[(d_i p_r + 1 - p_r)^S\right] \quad (5)$$

The formulations in (2)—(5) allow us to calculate the expected value of overlap using only the sample size S, the number of unique noun N and the number of unique determiners D.[2] We now turn to the empirical evaluations of the overlap test (2).

[2]For the present case involving only two determiners "the" and "a", $d_1 = 2/3$ and $d_2 = 1/3$. As noted in section 2.1, the empirical probabilities of the more vs. less frequent determiners deviate somewhat from the strict Zipfian ratio of 2:1, numerical results show that the 2:1 ratio is a very accurate surrogate for a wide range of actual rations in the calculation of (2)—(5). This is because most of average overlap value comes from the relatively few and high frequent nouns.

3 Testing Grammar Productivity

3.1 Testing grammar in child language

To study the determiner system in child language, we consider the data from six children Adam, Eve, Sarah, Naomi, Nina, and Peter. These are the all and only children in the CHILDES database with substantial longitudinal data that starts at the very beginning of syntactic development (i.e, one or two word stage) so that the usage-based stage, if exists, could be observed. For comparison, we also consider the overlap measure of the Brown corpus (Kucera & Francis 1967), for which the writers' productivity is not in doubt.

We applied a variant of the Brill tagger (1995) (http://gposttl.sourceforge.net/) to prepare the child data before extracting adjacent pairs of determiners followed by singular nouns. While no tagger works perfectly, the determiners "a" and "the" are not ambiguous which reliably contribute the tagging of the following word. The Brown Corpus is already manually tagged and the D-N pairs are extracted directly. In an additional test, we pooled together the first 100, 300, and 500 D-N pairs from the six children and created three hypothetical children in the very earliest, and presumably least productive, stage of learning.

For each child, the theoretical expectation of overlap is calculated based on equations in (2)—(5), that is, only with the sample size S and the number of unique nouns N in determiner-noun pairs while $D = 2$. These expectations are then compared against the empirical overlap values computed from the determiner-noun samples extracted with the methods above; i.e., the percentage of nouns appearing with both "a" and "the". The results are summarized in Table 1.

The theoretical expectations and the empirical measures of overlap agree extremely well (column 5 and 6 in Table 1). Neither paired t- nor paired Wilcoxon test reveal significant difference between the two sets of values. A linear regression produces empirical $= 1.08 \times$ theoretical, $R^2 = 0.9716$: a perfect fit between theory and data would have the slope of 1.0. Thus we may conclude that the determiner usage data from child language is consistent

Subject	Sample Size (S)	*a* or *the* Noun types (N)	Overlap% (expected)	Overlap% (empirical)	$\frac{S}{N}$
Naomi (1;1-5;1)	884	349	21.8	19.8	2.53
Eve (1;6-2;3)	831	283	25.4	21.6	2.94
Sarah (2;3-5;1)	2453	640	28.8	29.2	3.83
Adam (2;3-4;10)	3729	780	33.7	32.3	4.78
Peter (1;4-2;10)	2873	480	42.2	40.4	5.99
Nina (1;11-3;11)	4542	660	45.1	46.7	6.88
First 100	600	243	22.4	21.8	2.47
First 300	1800	483	29.1	29.1	3.73
First 500	3000	640	33.9	34.2	4.68
Brown corpus	20650	4664	26.5	25.2	4.43

Table 1: Empirical and expected determiner-noun overlaps in child speech and the Brown corpus (last row).

with the productive rule "DP→ D N".

The results in Table 1 also reveal considerable individual variation in the overlap values, and it is instructive to understand why. As the Brown corpus result shows (Table 1 last row), sample size S, the number of nouns N, or the language user's age alone is not predictive of the overlap value. The variation can be roughly analyzed as follows. Given N unique nouns in a sample of S, greater overlap value can be obtained if more nouns occur more than once. Zipf's law (1) allows us to express this cutoff line in terms with ranks, as the probability of the noun n_r with rank r has the probability of $1/(rH_N)$. The derivation below uses the fact that the $H_N = \sum_{i=1}^{N} 1/i$ can be approximated by $\ln N$.

$$S\frac{1}{rH_N} = 1$$

$$r = \frac{S}{H_N} \approx \frac{S}{\ln N} \qquad (6)$$

That is, only nouns whose ranks are lower than $S/(\ln N)$ can be expected to be non-zero overlaps. The total overlap is thus a monotonically increasing function of $S/(N \ln N)$ which, given the slow growth of $\ln N$, is approximately S/N, a term that must be positively correlated with overlap measures. This result is strongly confirmed: S/N is a near perfect predictor for the empirical values of overlap (last two columns of Table 1): $r = 0.986$, $p < 0.00001$.

3.2 Testing usage-based learning

We turn to the question whether children's determiner usage data can be accounted for equally well by the usage based approach. In the limiting case, the usage-based child learner could store the input data in its entirety and simply retrieve these memorized determiner-noun pairs in production.

Our effort is hampered by the lack of concrete predictions about child language from the usage-based literature. Explicit models in usage-based learning and similar approaches (e.g., Chang et al. 2005, Freudenthal et al. 2007, etc.) generally involve programming efforts for which no analytical results such as (2)–(5) are possible. Nevertheless, a plausible approach can be construed based on a central tenet of usage-based learning, that the child does not form grammatical generalizations but rather memorizes and retrieves specific and item-based combinations. For instance, Tomasello (2000b) suggests "(w)hen young children have something they want to say, they sometimes have a set expression readily available and so they simply retrieve that expression from their stored linguistic experience." Following this line of reasoning, we consider a learning model that memorizes *jointly* formed, as opposed to productively composed, determiner-noun pairs from the input. These pairs will then be sampled; for each sample, the overlap values can be calculated and compared against the empirical values in Table 1.

We consider two variants of the memory model. The first can be called a *global memory* learner in which the learner memorizes all past linguistic ex-

Child	sample	% (global)	% (local)	% (emp.)
Eve	831	16.0	17.8	21.6
Naomi	884	16.6	18.9	19.8
Sarah	2453	24.5	27.0	29.2
Peter	2873	25.6	28.8	40.4
Adam	3729	27.5	28.5	32.3
Nina	4542	28.6	41.1	46.7
First 100	600	13.7	17.2	21.8
First 300	1800	22.1	25.6	29.1
First 500	3000	25.9	30.2	34.2

Table 2: The comparison of determiner-noun overlap between two variants of usage-based learning and empirical results.

perience. To implement this, we extracted all D-N pairs from about 1.1 million child directed English utterances in CHILDES. The second model is a *local memory* learner, which is construed to capture the linguistic experience of a particular child. The local memory learner only memorizes the determiner-noun pairs from the adult utterances in that particular child's CHILDES transcripts. In both models, the memory consists of a list of jointly memorized D-N pairs, which are augmented with their frequencies in the input.

For each child with a sample size of S (see Table 1, column 2), and for each variant of the memory model, we use Monte Carlo simulation to randomly draw S pairs from the memorized lists. The probability with which a pair is drawn is proportional to its frequency. We then calculate the D-N overlap value, i.e, the the percentage of nouns that appear with both "a" and "the", for each sample. The results are averaged over 1000 draws and presented in Table 2.

Both sets of overlap values from the two variants of usage-based learning (column 3 and 4) differ significantly from the empirical measures (column 5): $p < 0.005$ for both paired t-test and paired Wilcoxon test. This suggests that children's use of determiners does not follow the predictions of the usage-based learning approach. This conclusion is tentative, of course, as we reiterate the need for the usage-based approach to provide testable quantitative predictions about child language. At the minimum, child language does not appear to stem from frequency sensitive retrieval of jointly stored determiner-noun constructions (Tomasello 2000b).

Similar considerations apply to other linguistic examples. For instance, it is often noted (Lieven, Pine & Baldwin 1997) that child language is dominated by a small number of high frequency frozen frames (e.g, "give me (a) X").[3] True, but that appears no more than the reflection of the power law distribution of linguistic units. In the Harvard corpus of child English (Brown 1973), the frequencies of "give me", "give him" and "give her" are 93:15:12, or 7.75:1.23:1, and the frequencies of "me", "him" and "her" are 2870:466:364, or the virtually identical 7.88:1.28:1.

3.3 Testing for Unproductivity

Any statistical test worth its salt should be able to distinguish occurrences from non-occurrences of the pattern which it is designed to detect. If the productivity test predicts *higher* overlap values than empirically attested–assuming that these classes and their combinations follow Zipfian distribution–then there would be reason to suspect that the linguistic types in question do not combine completely independently, and that some kind of lexically specific processes are at work.

We test the utility of the productivity test on inflectional morphology. In English, the -ing suffix can attach to all verb stems, only some of which can take the -ed suffix–the rest are irregulars. Chan (2008) shows that in morphological systems across languages, stems, affixes, and their combinations tend to show Zipf-like distributions. Therefore, if we apply the productivity test to -ing and -ed inflected forms (i.e, assuming that -ing and -ed were fully interchangeable), then the predicted overlap value should be higher than the empirical value. Table 3 gives the results based on the verbal morphology data from the Brown corpus and the six children studied in section 3.1. Clearly there are very significant discrepancies between the empirical and predicted overlap values.

It can be reasonably objected that English irregular paste tense forms are highly frequent, which may contribute to the large discrepancies observed in Table 3. To address this concern, we created an artificial morphological system in which 100 stems

[3]Thanks to an anonymous reviewer for bringing up this example.

Subject	sample	# stems	% emp.	% pred.
Adam	6774	263	31.3	75.6
Eve	1028	120	20.0	61.7
Sarah	3442	230	28.7	76.8
Naomi	1797	192	32.3	61.9
Peter	2112	139	25.9	78.8
Nina	2830	191	34.0	77.2
Brown	62807	3044	45.5	75.6

Table 3: Empirical vs. predicted overlap values for -ing and -ed inflections.

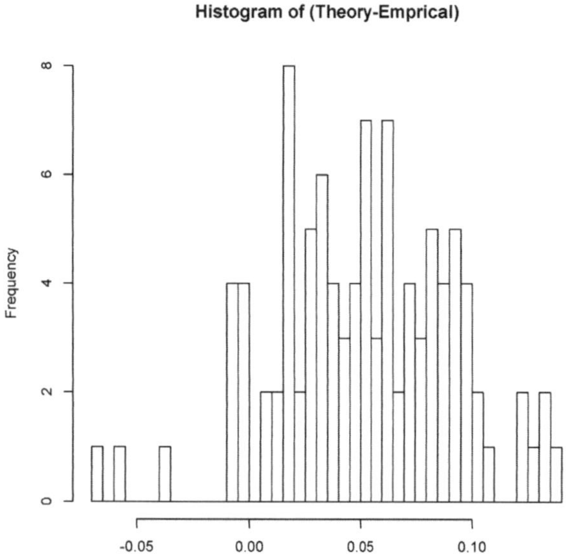

Figure 2: Overlap test applied to linguistic combinations with lexical exceptions.

may take two affixes A and B: A can attach to all stems but B can only attach to 90 while the other 10, randomly chosen from the 100, are exceptions. Again, we assume that frequencies of the stems and their combinations with affixes follow Zipfian distribution. We random combine stems with affixes 1000 times obtaining a sample size of 1000, and count the percentage of stems that are combined with both A and B. We then compare this value against the calculation from (2) which assumes A and B are fully interchangeable (where in this case they are not). The histogram of the difference between the theoretical and empirical values from 100 such simulations are given in Figure 3. The overlap test correctly overpredicts ($p < 10^{-15}$).

4 Discussion

For the study of child language acquisition, our results show that the usage-based approach to language learning is not supported by the child data once the statistical properties of linguistic units and their combinations are taken into account. A grammar based approach is supported (section 3.1) These results do not resolve the innateness debate in language acquisition: they only point to the very early availability of an abstract and productive grammar.

The simulation results on the inadequacy of the memory-and-retrieval approach to child language (section 3.2) show the limitations of lexically specific approach to language learning. These results are congruent with the work in statistical parsing that also demonstrates the diminishing returns of lexicalization (Gildea 2001, Klein & Manning 2003, Bikel 2004). They are also consistent with previous statistical studies (Buttery & Korhonen 2005) that child directed language data appear to be even more limited in syntactic usage diversity. The "uneveness" in verb islands (Tomasello 1992) is to be expected especially when the language sample is small as in the case of most child language acquisition studies. It thus seems necessary for the child learner to derive syntactic rules with overarching generality in a relatively short period of time (and with a few million utterances).

Finally, we envision the overlap test to be one of many tests for the statistical properties of grammar. Similar tests may be constructed to include a wider linguistic context (e.g., three or more words instead of two, but the sparse data problem becomes far more severe). The ability to detect lexicalized processes (section 3.3) may prove useful in the automatic induction of grammars. Such tests would be a welcome addition to the quantitative analysis tools in the behavioral study of language, which tend to establish mismatches between observations and null hypotheses; the favored hypotheses are those that cannot be rejected (though cannot be confirmed either). The present work shows that it is possible to test for statistical matches between observations and well formulated hypotheses.

References

Baroni, M. (2008). Distributions in text. In Lüdelign, A. & Kytö, M. (Eds.) *Corpus linguistics: An international hanbook*. Berlin: Mouton de Gruyter.

Bikel, D. (2004) Intricacies of Collins' parsing model. *Computational Linguistics*, 30, 479–511.

Bowerman, M. (1973). *Early syntactic development: A cross-linguistic study with special reference to Finnish*. Cambridge: Cambridge University Press.

Braine, M. (1963). The ontogeny of English phrase structure: The first phase. *Language*, 39, 3-13.

Brill, E. (1995). Transformation-based error-driven learning and natural language processing: A case study in part-of-speech tagging. *Computational Linguistics*, 21 (4), 543–565.

Brown, R. (1973). *A first language*. Cambridge, MA: Harvard University Press.

Buttery, P. & Korhonen, A. (2005). Large-scale analysis of verb subcategorization differences between child directed speech and adult speech. Interdisciplinary Workshop on the Identification and Representation of Verb Features and Verb Classes, Saarland University.

Chan, E. (2008). Structures and distributions in morphology learning. Ph.D. Dissertation. Department of Computer and Information Science. University of Pennsylvania. Philadelphia, PA.

Chang, F., Lieven, E., & Tomasello, M. (2006). Using child utterances to evaluate syntax acquisition algorithms. In *Proceedings of the 28th Annual Conference of the Cognitive Science Society*. Vancouver, Canada

Feldman, J. (2004). Computational cognitive linguistics. In COLING 2004.

Freudenthal, D., Pine, J. M., Aguado-Orea, J. & Gobet, F. (2007). Modelling the developmental patterning of finiteness marking in English, Dutch, German and Spanish using MOSAIC. *Cognitive Science*, 31, 311-341.

Gildea, D. (2001) Corpus variation and parser performance. In 2001 Conference on Empirical Methods in Natural Lan- guage Processing (EMNLP).

Goldberg, A. (2003). Constructions. *Trends in Cognitive Science*, 219–224.

Ha, Le Quan, Sicilia-Garcia, E. I., Ming, Ji. & Smith, F. J. (2002). Extension of Zipf's law to words and phrases. *Proceedings of the 19th International Conference on Computational Linguistics*. 315-320.

Klein, D. & Manning, C. (2003). Accurate unlexicalized parsing. In ACL 2003. 423-430.

Kučera, H & Francis, N. (1967). *Computational analysis of present-day English*. Providence, RI: Brown University Press.

Lieven, E., Pine, J. & Baldwin, G. (1997). Lexically-based learning and early grammatical development. *Journal of Child Language*, 24, 187-219.

MacWhinney, B. (2000). *The CHILDES Project*. Lawrence Erlbaum.

Mandelbrot, B. (1954). Structure formelle des textes et communication: Deux études. *Words*, 10, 1–27.

Marcus, M., Marcinkiewicz, M. & Santorini, B. (1993). Building a large annotated corpus of English: the Penn Treebank. *Computational Linguistics*, 19, 313-330.

Pine, J. & Lieven, E. (1997). Slot and frame patterns in the development of the determiner category. *Applied Psycholinguistics*, 18, 123-138.

Sag, I. (2010). English filler-gap constructions. *Language*, 486–545.

Shipley, E., Smith, C. & Gleitman, L. (1969). A study in the acquisition of language: Free reponses to commands. *Language*, 45, 2: 322-342.

Slobin, Dan. (1971). Data for the symposium. In Slobin, Dan (Ed.) *The Ontogenesis of grammar*. New York: Academic Press. 3-14.

Steels, L. (2004). Constructivist development of grounded construction grammars. In ACL 2004.

Teahan, W. J. (1997). Modeling English text. DPhil thesis. University of Waikato, New Zealand.

Tomasello, M. (1992). *First verbs: A case study of early grammatical development*. Cambridge, MA: Harvard University Press.

Tomasello, M. (2000a). Do young children have adult syntactic competence. *Cognition*, 74, 209-253.

Tomasello, M. (2000b). First steps toward a usage-based theory of language acquisition. *Cognitive Linguistics*, 11, 61-82.

Valian, V. (1986). Syntactic categories in the speech of young children. *Developmental Psychology*, 22, 562-579.

Valian, V., Solt, S. & Stewart, J. (2008). Abstract categories or limited-scope formulae? The case of children's determiners. *Journal of Child Language*, 35, 1-36.

Wintner, S. (2009). What science underlies natural language engineering. *Computational Linguistics*, 641–644.

Zipf, G. K. (1949). *Human behavior and the principle of least effort: An introduction to human ecology*. Addison-Wesley.

Top-down recognizers for MCFGs and MGs

Edward P. Stabler
stabler@ucla.edu

Abstract

This paper defines a normal form for MCFGs that includes strongly equivalent representations of many MG variants, and presents an incremental priority-queue-based TD recognizer for these MCFGs. After introducing MGs with overt phrasal movement, head movement and simple adjunction are added without change in the recognizer. The MG representation can be used directly, so that even rather sophisticated analyses of properly non-CF languages can be defined very succinctly. As with the similar stack-based CF-methods, finite memory suffices for the recognition of infinite languages, and a fully connected left context for probabilistic analysis is available at every point.

1 Introduction

In the years after Joshi (1985) proposed that human languages are weakly and strongly "mildly context sensitive" (MCS), it was discovered that many independently proposed grammar formalisms define exactly the same MCS languages. The languages defined by Joshi's tree adjoining grammars (TAGs) are exactly the same as those defined by a version of Steedman's combinatory categorial grammars, and the same as those defined by head wrapping grammars (Vijay-Shanker and Weir, 1994). A slightly larger class of languages is defined by another variant of TAGs (set-local multicomponent), by a version of Pollard's generalized phrase structure grammars called multiple context free grammars (MCFGs), and by a wide range of minimalist grammar (MG) formalizations of Chomskian syntax (Seki et al., 1991; Michaelis, 1998; Michaelis, 2001b; Harkema, 2001a; Stabler, 2011). These remarkable convergences provide evidence from across grammatical traditions that something like these MCS proposals may be approximately right, and so it is natural to consider psychological models that fit with these proposals. With a range of performance models for a range of MCS grammars, it becomes possible to explore how grammatical dependencies interact with other factors in the conditioning of human linguistic performance.

For context free grammars (CFGs), perhaps the simplest parsing model is top-down: beginning with the prediction of a sentence, rules are applied to the leftmost predicted category until a terminal element is reached, which is then checked against the input. This parsing method is of interest in psychological modeling not only because it uses the grammar in a very transparent way, but also it is because it is predictive in a way that may be similar to human parsing. At every point in analyzing a sentence from left to right, the structure that has been constructed is fully connected: grammatical relationships among the elements that have been heard have been guessed, and there are no pieces of structure which have not been integrated. Consequently, this structure can be interpreted by a standard compositional semantics and may be appropriate for "incremental" models of sentence interpretation (cf. Haddock, 1989; Chambers et al., 2004; Shen and Joshi, 2005; Altmann and Mirković, 2009; Demberg and Keller, 2009, Kato and Matsubara, 2009; Schuler, 2010). And like human parsing, when used with backtracking or a beam search, TD memory demands need not continually increase with sentence length: a fixed bound on stack depth and on backtrack or beam depth suffices for infinitely many sentences. Furthermore, TD parsing provides explicit, relevant "left contexts" for probabilistic conditioning (Roark and Johnson, 1999; Roark, 2001; Roark, 2004). But it has not been clear until recently how to apply this method to Chomskian syntax or any of the other MCS grammar formalisms. There have been some proposals along these lines, but they have either been unnecessarily complex or applicable to only a restricted to range of grammatical proposals (Chesi, 2007; Mainguy, 2010).

This paper extends TD parsing to minimalist context free grammars (MCFGs) in a certain normal form and presents minimalist grammars (MGs) as a succinct representation for some of those MCFGs. With this extension, the TD parsing method handles an infinite range of MCFGs that encompasses, strongly and weakly, an infinite range of (many variants of) MGs in a very transparent and direct way. The parsing method can be defined in complete detail very easily, and, abstracting away from limitations of time and memory, it is provably sound and complete for all those grammars.

The TD recognizer for MCFGs is presented in §4, generalizing and adapting ideas from earlier work (Mainguy, 2010; Villemonte de la Clergerie, 2002). Instead of using a stack memory, this recognizer uses a "priority queue," which just means that we can access all the elements in memory, sorting them into left-to-right order. Then it is easy to observe: (§3.2) while the reference to MCFG is useful for understanding the recognizer, an MG representation can be used directly without explicitly computing out its MCFG equivalent; (§5.1) the extensions for head movement and simple adjunction allow the recognizer of §4 to apply without change; (§5.2) like its stack-based CF counterpart, the MG recognizer requires only finite memory to recognize certain infinite subsets of languages – that is, memory demands do not always strictly increase with sentence length; and (§5.3) the TD recognizer provides, at every point in processing the input, a fully connected left context for interpretation and probabilistic conditioning, unlike LC and other familiar methods. Since a very wide range of grammatical proposals can be expressed in this formalism and parsed transparently by this method, it is straightforward to compute fully explicit and syntactically sophisticated parses of the sorts of sentences used in psycholinguistic studies.

2 MCFGs

MCFGs are first defined by Seki et al. (1991), but here it will be convenient to represent MCFGs in a Prolog-like Horn clause notation, as in Kanazawa (2009). In this notation, the familiar context free rule for sentences would be written

$$S(x_{0_1}x_{1_1}) \text{ :- } NP(x_{0_1}),\\ VP(x_{1_1}).$$

Reading :- as "if", this formula says that a string formed by concatenating any string x_{0_1} with string x_{1_1} is an S, if x_{0_1} is an NP, and x_{1_1} is a VP. We number the variables on the right side in such a way as to indicate that each variable that appears on the right side of any rule appears exactly once on the right and once on the left. Lexical rules like

$$NP(\text{Mary})\\ VP(\text{sings}),$$

have empty "right sides" and no variables in this notation.

MCFGs allow categories to have multiple string arguments, so that, for example, a VP with a wh-phrase that is moving to another position could be represented with two string arguments, one of which holds the moving element. In general, each MCFG rule for building an instance of category A from categories $B_0 \ldots B_n$ ($n \geq 0$) has the form,

$$A(t_1, \ldots, t_{d(A)}) \text{ :- } B_0(x_{0_1}, \ldots, x_{0_{d(B0)}}),\\ \ldots,\\ B_n(x_{n_1}, \ldots, x_{n_{d(Bn)}}),$$

where each t_i is an term (i.e. a sequence) over the (finite nonempty) vocabulary Σ and the variables that appear on the right; no variable on the right occurs more than once on the left (no copying); and the designated 'start' category S has 'arity' or 'dimension' $d(S) = 1$. For any such grammar, the language $L(G)$ is the set of strings $s \in \Sigma^*$ such that we can derive $S(s)$.

Here, we restrict attention to a normal form in which (i) each MCFG rule is *nondeleting* in the sense that every variable x_{i_j} on the right occurs exactly once on the left, and (ii) each rule is either lexical or nonlexical, where a *lexical rule* is one in which $n = 0$ and $d(A) = 1$ and $t_1 \in \Sigma \cup \{\epsilon\}$, and a *nonlexical rule* is one in which $n > 0$ and each $t_i \in Var^*$. Clearly these additional restrictions do not affect the expressive power of the grammars.

2.1 Example 1

Consider this MCFG for $\{a^i b^j c^i d^j \mid i, j > 0\}$, with 5 non-lexical rules, 4 lexical rules, and start category S. We letter the rules for later reference:

$a.$ $S(x_0x_1x_2x_3)$:- $AC(x_0, x_2), BD(x_1, x_3)$
$b.$ $AC(x_0x_2, x_1x_3)$:- $A(x_0), C(x_1), AC(x_2, x_3)$
$c.$ $AC(x_0, x_1)$:- $A(x_0), C(x_1)$
$d.$ $BD(x_0x_2, x_1x_3)$:- $B(x_0), D(x_1), BD(x_2, x_3)$
$e.$ $BD(x_0, x_1)$:- $B(x_0), D(x_1)$
$f.$ $A(a)$
$g.$ $B(b)$
$h.$ $C(c)$
$i.$ $D(d)$

With this grammar we can show that *abbcdd* has category S with a derivation tree like this:

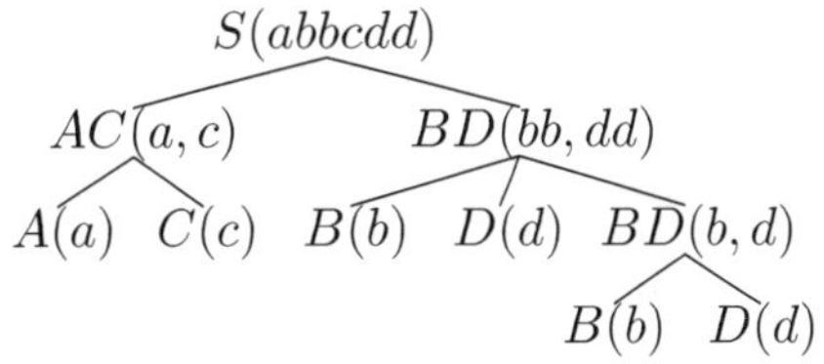

See, for example, Kanazawa (2009) for a more detailed discussion of MCFGs in this format.

3 MGs as MCFGs

Michaelis (1998; 2001a) shows that every MG has a 'strongly equivalent' MCFG, in the sense that the MG derivation trees are a relabeling of the MCFG derivation trees. Here we present MGs as finite sets of lexical rules that define MCFGs. MG categories contain finite tuples of feature sequences, where the features include *categories* like N,V,A,P,..., *selectors* for those categories =N,=V,=A,=P,..., *licensors* +case,+wh,..., and *licensees* −case,−wh,.... In our MCFG representation, a category is a tuple

$$\langle\, x, \delta_0, \delta_1, \ldots, \delta_j \,\rangle$$

where (i) $j \geq 0$, (ii) $x = 1$ if the element is lexical and 0 otherwise, (iii) each δ_i is a nonempty feature sequence, and (iv) the category has dimension $j + 1$. An MG is then given by a specified start category and a finite set of lexical rules

$$\langle\, 1, \delta_0 \,\rangle(a).$$

for some $a \in \Sigma$. The MG defines the language generated by its lexicon together with MCFG rules determined by the lexicon, as follows. Let $\pi_2(Lex)$ be the set of feature sequences δ_0 contained in the lexical rules, and let k be the number of different types of licensees f that occur in the lexical rules. For all $0 \leq i, j \leq k$, all $x, y \in \{0, 1\}$, all $\alpha, \beta, \delta_i, \gamma_i \in \text{suffix}(\pi_2(\text{Lex}))$, and $\beta \neq \epsilon$, we have these 'merge' rules, broken as usual into the cases where (i) we are merging into complement position on the right, (ii) merging into specifier position on the left, or (iii) merging with something that is moving:

$$\begin{array}{l}\langle\, 0, \alpha, \delta_1, \ldots, \delta_j \,\rangle(s_0t_0, t_1, \ldots, t_j) \text{ :-} \\ \quad \langle\, 1, {=}f\alpha \,\rangle(s_0), \\ \quad \langle\, x, f, \delta_1, \ldots, \delta_j \,\rangle(t_0, \ldots, t_j)\end{array}$$

$$\begin{array}{l}\langle\, 0, \alpha, \delta_1, \ldots, \delta_i, \gamma_1, \ldots, \gamma_j \,\rangle(t_0s_0, s_1, \ldots, s_i, t_1, \ldots, t_j) \text{ :-} \\ \quad \langle\, 0, {=}f\alpha, \delta_1, \ldots, \delta_i, \rangle(s_0, \ldots, s_i), \\ \quad \langle\, x, f, \gamma_1, \ldots, \gamma_j \,\rangle(t_0, \ldots, t_j)\end{array}$$

$$\begin{array}{l}\langle\, 0, \alpha, \delta_1, \ldots, \delta_i, \beta, \gamma_1, \ldots, \gamma_j \,\rangle(s_0, \ldots, s_i, t_0, \ldots, t_j) \text{ :-} \\ \quad \langle\, x, {=}f\alpha, \delta_1, \ldots, \delta_i, \rangle(s_0, \ldots, s_i), \\ \quad \langle\, y, f\beta, \gamma_1, \ldots, \gamma_j \,\rangle(t_0, \ldots, t_j)\end{array}$$

And we have these 'move' rules, broken as usual into the cases where the moving element is landing, when $\delta_i = \text{-}f$,

$$\begin{array}{l}\langle\, 0, \alpha, \delta_1, \ldots, \delta_{i-1}, \delta_{i+1}, \ldots, \delta_j \,\rangle \\ \qquad\qquad (s_is_0, s_1, \ldots, s_{i-1}, s_{i+1}, \ldots, s_j) \text{ :-} \\ \quad \langle\, 0, {+}f\alpha, \delta_1, \ldots, \delta_j \,\rangle(s_0, \ldots, s_j),\end{array}$$

and cases where the moving element must move again, when $\delta_i = \text{-}f\beta$,

$$\begin{array}{l}\langle\, 0, \alpha, \delta_1, \ldots, \delta_{i-1}, \beta, \delta_{i+1}, \ldots, \delta_j \,\rangle(s_0, \ldots, s_i) \text{ :-} \\ \quad \langle\, 0, {+}f\alpha, \delta_1, \ldots, \delta_j \,\rangle(s_0, \ldots, s_i),\end{array}$$

where none of $\delta_1, \ldots, \delta_{i-1}, \delta_{i+1}, \ldots, \delta_j$ begin with $\text{-}f$. The language of the MG is the MCFL defined by the lexicon and all instances of these 5 rule schemes (always a finite set).

By varying the lexicon, MGs can define all the MCFLs (Michaelis, 2001b; Harkema, 2001b), i.e., the set-local multi-component tree adjoining languages (MCTALs) (Weir, 1988; Seki et al., 1991). TALs are a proper subset, defined by 'well-nested 2-MCFGs' (Seki et al., 1991; Kanazawa, 2009).

3.1 Example 2

Consider the following lexicon containing 7 items, with the 'complementizer' start category C,

$\langle 1, =\text{D} =\text{D V}\rangle$(likes)	$\langle 1, \text{D}\rangle$(Mary)
$\langle 1, =\text{C} =\text{D V}\rangle$(knows)	$\langle 1, \text{D}\rangle$(John)
$\langle 1, =\text{V C}\rangle(\epsilon)$	$\langle 1, \text{D -wh}\rangle$(who)
$\langle 1, =\text{V +wh C}\rangle(\epsilon)$	

Using the definition given just above, this determines an MG. This is a derivation tree for one of the infinitely many expressions of category C:

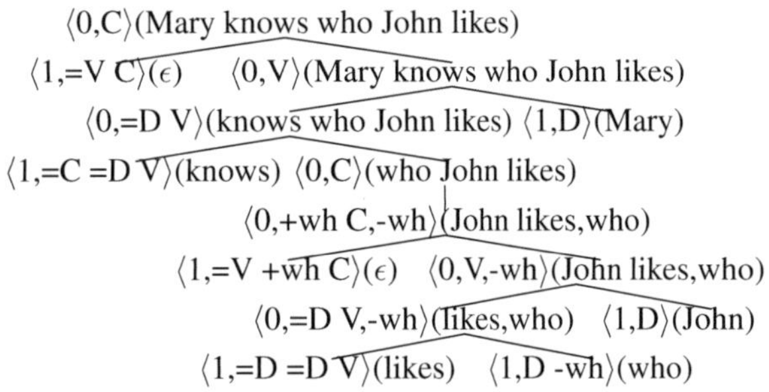

If we relabel this tree so that each instance of merge is labeled Merge or •, and each instance of move is labeled Move or ∘, the result is the corresponding MG derivation tree, usually depicted like this:

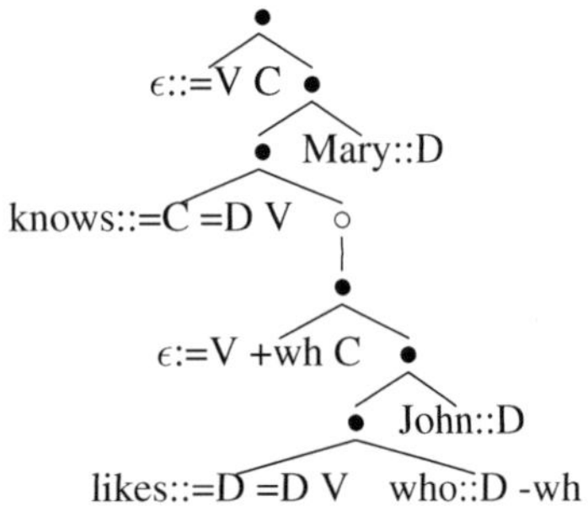

In fact, the latter tree fully specifies the MCFG derivation above, because, in every MG derivation, for *every* internal node, the categories of the children determine which rule applies. This is easily verified by checking the 5 schemes for non-lexical rules on the previous page; the left side of each rule is a function of the right. Consequently the MCFG categories at the internal nodes can be regarded as specifying the states of a deterministic finite state bottom-up tree recognizer for the MG derivation trees (Kobele et al., 2007; Graf, 2011; Kobele, 2011).

3.2 MCFGs need not be computed

We did not explicitly present the nonlexical MCFG rules used in the previous section §3.1, since they are determined by the lexical rules. The first rule used at the root of the derivation tree is, for example, an instance of the first rule scheme in §3, namely:

$$\langle 0, C\rangle(s_0 t_0) \text{ :- } \langle 1, {=}VC\rangle(s_0), \langle 0, V\rangle(t_0).$$

Generating these non-lexical MCFG rules from the MG lexicon is straightforward, and has been implemented in (freely available) software by Guillaumin (2004). But the definition given in §3 requires that all feature sequences in all rules be suffixes of lexical feature sequences, and notice that in any derivation tree, like the one shown in §3.1, for example, feature sequences increase along the left branch from any node to the leaf which is its 'head.' Along any such path, the feature sequences increase one feature at a time until they reach the lexical leaf. So in effect, if we are building the derivation top-down, each step adds or 'unchecks' features in lexical sequences one at a time, and obviously the options for doing this can be seen without compiling out all the MCFG nonlexical rules.

4 The top-down recognizer

For any sequence s of elements of S, let $|s|$=the length of s and $nth(i, s) = a$ iff $a \in S$, and for some $u, v \in S^*$, $s = uav$ and $|u| = i$. Adapting basic ideas from earlier work (Mainguy, 2010; Villemonte de la Clergerie, 2002) for TD recognition, we will instantiate variables not with strings but with indices $i \in \mathbb{N}^*$ to represent linear order of constituents, to obtain *indexed atoms* $A(i_1, \ldots, i_{d(A)})$.

Consider any nonlexical rule α :- γ and any indexed atom β where

$$\alpha{=}A(t_1, \ldots, t_{d(A)})$$
$$\beta{=}A(i_1, \ldots, i_{d(A)})$$
$$\gamma{=}B_0(x_{0_1}, \ldots, x_{0_{d(B0)}}), \ldots, B_n(x_{n_1}, \ldots, x_{n_{d(Bn)}}).$$

For each variable x_{i_j} in γ, define

$$\text{index}_{\alpha,\beta}(x_{i_j}) = \begin{cases} i_k & \text{if } t_k = x_{i_j} \\ i_k p & \text{if } |t_k| > 1, x_{i_j} = nth(p, t_k). \end{cases}$$

Let $\text{index}_{\alpha,\beta}(\gamma)$ be the result of replacing each variable x_{i_j} in γ by $\text{index}_{\alpha,\beta}(x_{i_j})$. Finally, let $\text{trim}(\gamma)$ map γ to itself except in the case when when every index in γ begins with the same integer n, in which case that initial n is deleted from every index.

Define a total order on the indices $\mathbb{N}^*$ as follows. For any $\alpha, \beta \in \mathbb{N}^*$,

$$\alpha < \beta \text{ iff } \begin{cases} \alpha = \epsilon \neq \beta, \text{ or} \\ \alpha = i\alpha', \beta = j\beta', i < j, \text{ or} \\ \alpha = i\alpha', \beta = i\beta', \alpha' < \beta'. \end{cases}$$

For any atom α, let $\mu(\alpha)$ be the least index in α. So, for example, $\mu(AB(31, 240)) = 240$. And for any indexed atoms α, β, let $\alpha < \beta$ iff $\mu(\alpha) < \mu(\beta)$. We use this order it to sort categories into left-to-right order in the 'expand' rule below.

We now define TD recognition in a deductive format. The state of the recognition sequence is given by a (remaining input,priority queue) pair, where the queue represents the memory of predicted elements, sorted according to $<$ so that they can be processed from left to right. We have 1 *initial axiom*, which predicts that input s will have start category S, where S initially has index ϵ:

$$\frac{}{(s, S(\epsilon))}$$

The main work is done by the *expand rule*, which pops atom α off the queue, leaving sequence Θ underneath. Then, for any rule β :- γ with β of the same category as α, we compute $\text{index}_{\alpha,\beta}(\gamma)$, append the result and Θ, then sort and trim:

$$\frac{(s, \alpha\Theta)}{(s, \text{sort}(\text{trim}(\text{index}_{\alpha,\beta}(\gamma)\Theta)))} \beta \text{ :- } \gamma$$

(We could use ordered insertion instead of sorting, and we could trim the indices much more aggressively, but we stick to simple formulations here.) Finally, we have a *scan rule*, which scans input a if we have predicted an A and our grammar tells us that $A(a)$. For all $a \in (\Sigma \cup \epsilon), s \in \Sigma^*, n \in \mathbb{N}^*$:

$$\frac{(as,\ A(n)\ \Theta)}{(s, \Theta)} \text{A(a)}$$

A string s is accepted if we can use these rules to get from the start axiom to (ϵ,ϵ). This represents the fact that we have consumed the whole input and there are no outstanding predictions in memory.

4.1 Example 1, continued.

Here is the sequence of recognizer states that accepts *abbcdd*, using the grammar presented in §2.1:

initial axiom:		
init.	(abbcdd,	S(ϵ))
expand with rule a:		
1.	(abbcdd,	AC(0,2),BD(1,3))
expand with rule c (note sort):		
2.	(abbcdd,	A(0),BD(1,3),C(2))
scan with rule f:		
3.	(bbcdd,	BD(1,3),C(2))
expand with rule d:		
4.	(bbcdd,	B(10),BD(11,31),C(2),D(30))
scan with rule g:		
5.	(bcdd,	BD(11,31),C(2),D(30))
expand with rule e:		
6.	(bcdd,	B(11),C(2),D(30),D(31))
scan with rule g:		
7.	(cdd,	C(2),D(30),D(31))
scan with rule h (note trim removes 3):		
8.	(dd,	D(0),D(1))
scan with rule i:		
9.	(d,	D(1))
scan with rule i:		
10.	(ϵ,	ϵ)

The number of recognizer steps is always exactly the number of nodes in the corresponding derivation tree; compare this accepting sequence to the derivation tree shown in §2.1, for example.

5 Properties and extensions

5.1 Adding adjunction, head movement

Frey and Gärtner (2002) propose that adjunction be added to MGs by (i) allowing another kind of selecting feature $\approx f$, which selects but does not 'check and delete' the feature f of a phrase that it modifies, where (ii) the head of the result is the selected, 'modified' phrase that it combines with, and (iii) the selecting 'modifier' cannot have any constituents moving out of it. We can implement these ideas by adding a rule scheme like the following (compare the first rule scheme in §3):

$$\begin{aligned} &\langle 0, f\alpha, \delta_1, \ldots, \delta_j \rangle (t_0 s_0, t_1, \ldots, t_j) \text{ :-} \\ &\quad \langle y, f\alpha, \delta_1, \ldots, \delta_j \rangle (t_0, \ldots, t_j), \\ &\quad \langle x, \approx f \rangle (s_0). \end{aligned}$$

Note this rule 'attaches' the modifier on the right. We could also allow left modifiers, but in the examples below will only use this one.

Some analyses of simple tensed sentences say that tense affixes 'hop' onto the verb after the verb has combined with its object. Affix hopping and head movement are more challenging that adjunction, but previous approaches can be adapted to the present perspective by making two changes: (i) we keep the head separate from other material in its phrase until that phrase is merged with another phrase, so now every non-lexical category A has $d(A) \geq 3$ and (ii) we add diacritics to the selection features to indicate whether hopping or head movement should apply in the merge step. To indicate that a head A selects category f we give A the feature $=f$, but to indicate the the head of A should hop onto the head of the selected constituent, we give A the feature $f{=}{>}$. Essentially this representation of MGs with head movement and affix hopping as MCFGs is immediate from the formalization in Stabler (2001) and the automated translation by Guillaumin (2004). The examples in this paper below will use only affix hopping which is defined by the following modified version of the first rule in §3:

$$\begin{array}{l}\langle 0, \alpha, \delta_1, \ldots, \delta_j \rangle(\epsilon, \epsilon, t_s t_h s_h t_c, t_1, \ldots, t_j) \text{ :-}\\ \quad \langle 1, f{=}{>}\alpha \rangle(s_h),\\ \quad \langle x, f, \delta_1, \ldots, \delta_j \rangle(t_s, t_h, t_c, t_1, \ldots, t_j)\end{array}$$

The first atom on the right side of this rule, the 'selector', is a lexical head with string s_h. The second atom on the right of the rule has string components t_s, t_h, t_c (these are the specifier, head, and complement strings) together with $j \geq 0$ moving elements $t_1, \ldots, t_j$. In the result on the left, we see that the lexical selector s_h is 'hopped' to the right of the selected head t_h, where it is sandwiched between the other concatenated parts of the selected phrase, leaving ϵ in the head position. Since the usual start category C now has 3 components, like every other head, we begin with a special category S that serves only to concatenate the 3 components of the matrix complementizer phrase, by providing the recognizer with this additional initializing rule:

$$S(s_s s_h s_c) \text{ :- } \langle x, C \rangle(s_s, s_h, s_c).$$

The nature of adjunction is not quite clear, and there is even less consensus about whether head movement or affix hopping or both are needed in grammars of human languages, but these illustrate how easily the MCFG approach to MGs can be extended. Like many of the other MG variants, these extensions do not change the class of languages that can be defined (Stabler, 2011), and the recognizer defined in §4 can handle them without change.

With head movement and adjunction we can, for example, provide a roughly traditional analysis of the famous example sentence from King and Just (1991) shown in Figure 1. Note again that the derivation tree in that figure has lexical items at the leaves, and these completely determine the non-lexical rules and the structure of the derivation. Various representations of the 'derived trees', like the X-bar tree shown in this figure, are easily computed from the derivation tree (Kobele et al., 2007). And Figure 2 shows the recognizer steps accepting that sentence. Plotting queue size versus recognizer step, and simply overlaying the King and Just self-paced reading times to see if they are roughly similar, we see that, at least in sentences like these, readers go more slowly when the queue gets large:

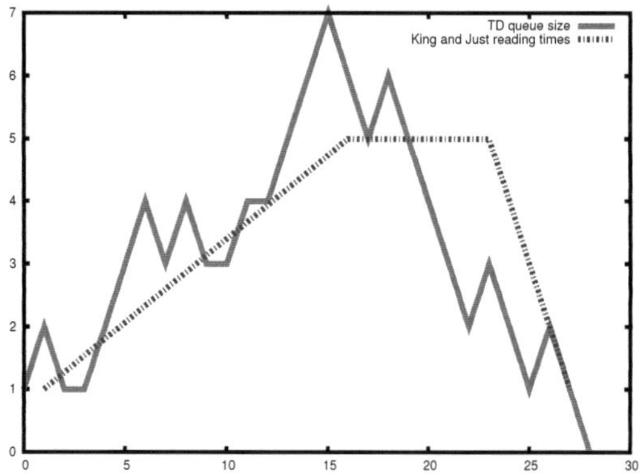

Recent work has challenged the claim that reading times are a function of the number of predictions in memory, (e.g., Nakatani and Gibson, 2008, p.81) but preliminary studies suggest that other performance measures may correlate (Bachrach, 2008; Brennan et al., 2010; VanWagenen et al., 2011). Exploring these possibilities is beyond the scope this paper. The present point is that any analysis expressible in the MG formalism can be parsed transparently with this approach, assessing its memory demands; partially parallel beam search models for ambiguity, used in natural language engineering, can also be straightforwardly assessed.

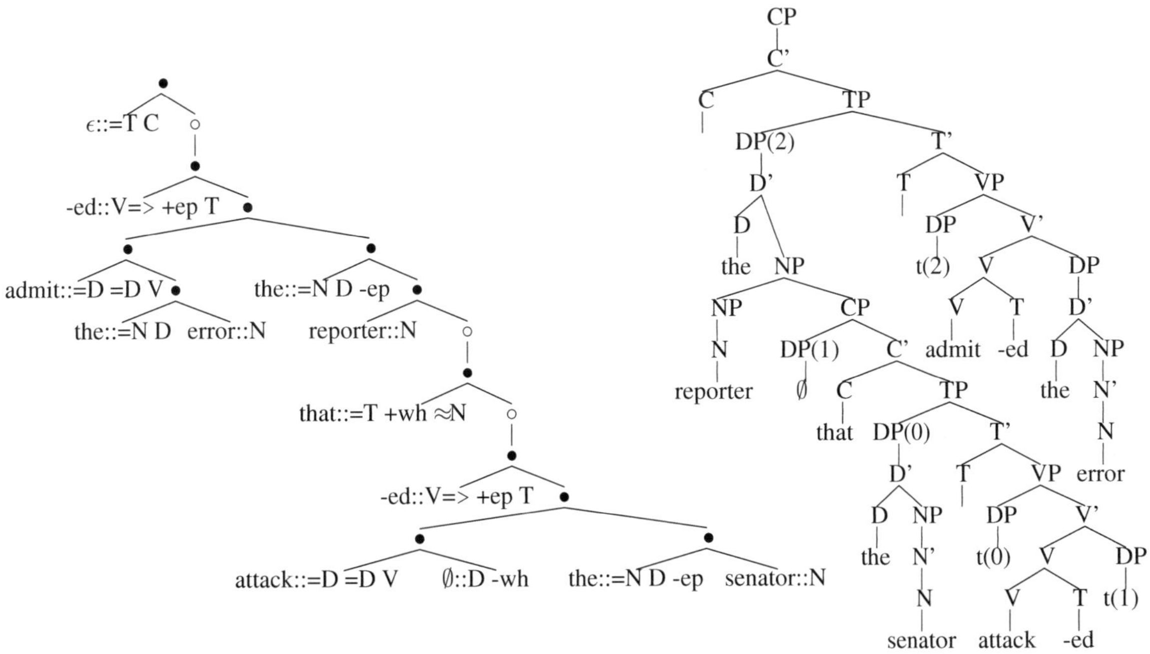

Figure 1: 28 node derivation tree and corresponding X-bar tree for King and Just (1991) example

5.2 Infinite languages with finite memory

Although memory use is not the main concern of this paper, it is worth noting that, as in stack-based CF models, memory demands do not necessarily increase without bound as sentence length increases. So for example, we can extend the naive grammar of Figure 2 to accept *this is the man that kiss -ed the maid that milk -ed the cow that toss -ed the dog that worry -ed the cat that chase -ed the rat*, a sentence with 6 clauses, and use no more memory at any time than is needed for the 2 clause King and Just example. Dynamic, chart-based parsing methods usually require more memory without bound as sentence length grows, even when there is little or no indeterminacy.

5.3 Connectedness

More directly relevant to incremental models is the fact that the portions of the derivation traversed at any point in TD recognition are all connected to each other, their syntactic relations are established. As we see in all our examples, the TD recognizer is always traversing the derivation tree on paths connected to the root; while the indexing and sorting ensures that the leaves are scanned in the order of their appearance in the derived X-bar tree. Left corner traversals do not have this property. Consider a sentence like *the reporter poured the egg in the bowl over the flour*. In a syntax in the spirit of the one we see in Figure 1, for example, *in the bowl* could be right adjoined to the direct object, and *over the flour* right adjoined to VP. Let VP1 be the parent of *over the flour*, and VP2 its sister. With LC, VP1 will be predicted right after the subject is completed. But the verb is the left corner of VP2, and VP2 will not be attached to VP1 – and so the subject and verb will not be connected – until VP1 is completed. This delay in the LC attachment of the subject to the verb can be extended by adding additional right modifiers to the direct object or the verb phrase, but the evidence suggests that listeners make such connections immediately upon hearing the words, as the TD recognizer does.

6 Future work

Standard methods for handling indeterminacy in top-down CF parsers, when there are multiple ways to expand a derivation top down, are easily adapted to the MCFG and MG parsers proposed here. With backtracking search, left recursion can cause nontermination, but a probabilistic beam search can do better. For $\alpha = (i, \Theta)$ any recognizer state, let $\text{step}(\alpha)$ be the (possibly empty) sequence of all the next states that are licensed by the rules in §3 (always finitely many). A probabilistic beam search uses the rules,

$$\frac{}{\langle(s, S(\epsilon))\rangle}\text{init} \qquad \frac{\alpha\Theta}{\text{prune}(\text{sort}_C(\text{step}(\alpha)\Theta))}\text{search},$$

popping a recognizer state α off the top of the queue $\alpha\Theta$, appending $\text{step}(\alpha)$ and Θ, then sorting and pruning the result. The sort in the search steps is done according to the probability of each parser state in context C, where the context may include a history of previous recognizer steps – i.e. of each derivation up to this point – but also possibly extrasentential information of any sort. The pruning rule acts to remove highly improbable analyses, and success is achieved if a step puts (ϵ, ϵ) on top of the queue. Roark shows that this ability to condition on material not in parser memory – indeed on anything in the left context – can allow better estimates of parse probability. On small experimental grammars, we are finding that TD beam search performance can be better than our chart parsers using the same grammar. Further feasibility studies are in

1	init.	(trttsa-a-te,	S(ϵ))
1	init.	(trttsa-a-te,	⟨0,C⟩(0,1,2))
2	1.	(trttsa-a-te,	⟨1,=TC⟩(1),⟨0,T⟩(20,21,22))
1	2.	(trttsa-a-te,	⟨0,T⟩(0,1,2))
1	3.	(trttsa-a-te,	⟨0,+epT,-ep⟩(01,1,2,00))
2	4.	(trttsa-a-te,	⟨0,V,-ep⟩(20,21,23,00),⟨1,V=>+epT⟩(22))
3	5.	(trttsa-a-te,	⟨0,D-ep⟩(000,001,002),⟨0,=DV⟩(20,21,23),⟨1,V=>+epT⟩(22))
4	6.	(trttsa-a-te,	⟨1,=ND-ep⟩(001),⟨0,N⟩(0020,0021,0022),⟨0,=DV⟩(20,21,23),⟨1,V=>+epT⟩(22))
3	7.	(rttsa-a-te,	⟨0,N⟩(0020,0021,0022),⟨0,=DV⟩(20,21,23),⟨1,V=>+epT⟩(22))
4	8.	(rttsa-a-te,	⟨1,N⟩(0021),⟨0,≈*N*⟩(00220,00221,00222),⟨0,=DV⟩(20,21,23),⟨1,V=>+epT⟩(22))
3	9.	(ttsa-a-te,	⟨0,≈*N*⟩(00220,00221,00222),⟨0,=DV⟩(20,21,23),⟨1,V=>+epT⟩(22))
3	10.	(ttsa-a-te,	⟨0,+wh≈*N*,-wh⟩(002201,00221,00222,002200),⟨0,=DV⟩(20,21,23),⟨1,V=>+epT⟩(22))
4	11.	(ttsa-a-te,	⟨0,T,-wh⟩(002220,002221,002222,002200),⟨1,=T+wh≈*N*⟩(00221),⟨0,=DV⟩(20,21,23),⟨1,V=>+epT⟩(22))
4	12.	(ttsa-a-te,	⟨0,+epT,-ep,-wh⟩(0022201,002221,002222,0022200,002200),⟨1,=T+wh≈*N*⟩(00221),⟨0,=DV⟩(20,21,23), ⟨1,V=>+epT⟩(22))
5	13.	(ttsa-a-te,	⟨0,V,-ep,-wh⟩(0022220,0022221,0022223,0022200,002200),⟨1,=T+wh≈*N*⟩(00221),⟨1,V=>+epT⟩(0022222), ⟨0,=DV⟩(20,21,23),⟨1,V=>+epT⟩(22))
6	14.	(ttsa-a-te,	⟨0,=DV,-wh⟩(0022220,0022221,0022223,002200),⟨1,=T+wh≈*N*⟩(00221), ⟨0,D-ep⟩(00222000,00222001,00222002),⟨1,V=>+epT⟩(0022222),⟨0,=DV⟩(20,21,23),⟨1,V=>+epT⟩(22))
7	15.	(ttsa-a-te,	⟨1,D-wh⟩(002200),⟨1,=T+wh≈*N*⟩(00221),⟨0,D-ep⟩(00222000,00222001,00222002),⟨1,=D=DV⟩(0022221), ⟨1,V=>+epT⟩(0022222),⟨0,=DV⟩(20,21,23),⟨1,V=>+epT⟩(22))
6	16.	(ttsa-a-te,	⟨1,=T+wh≈*N*⟩(00221),⟨0,D-ep⟩(00222000,00222001,00222002),⟨1,=D=DV⟩(0022221), ⟨1,V=>+epT⟩(0022222),⟨0,=DV⟩(20,21,23),⟨1,V=>+epT⟩(22))
5	17.	(tsa-a-te,	⟨0,D-ep⟩(00222000,00222001,00222002),⟨1,=D=DV⟩(0022221),⟨1,V=>+epT⟩(0022222), ⟨0,=DV⟩(20,21,23),⟨1,V=>+epT⟩(22))
6	18.	(tsa-a-te,	⟨1,=ND-ep⟩(00222001),⟨1,N⟩(00222002),⟨1,=D=DV⟩(0022221),⟨1,V=>+epT⟩(0022222),⟨0,=DV⟩(20,21,23), ⟨1,V=>+epT⟩(22))
5	19.	(sa-a-te,	⟨1,N⟩(00222002),⟨1,=D=DV⟩(0022221),⟨1,V=>+epT⟩(0022222),⟨0,=DV⟩(20,21,23),⟨1,V=>+epT⟩(22))
4	20.	(a-a-te,	⟨1,=D=DV⟩(0022221),⟨1,V=>+epT⟩(0022222),⟨0,=DV⟩(20,21,23),⟨1,V=>+epT⟩(22))
3	21.	(-a-te,	⟨1,V=>+epT⟩(0022222),⟨0,=DV⟩(20,21,23),⟨1,V=>+epT⟩(22))
2	22.	(a-te,	⟨0,=DV⟩(20,21,23),⟨1,V=>+epT⟩(22))
3	23.	(a-te,	⟨1,=D=DV⟩(1),⟨1,V=>+epT⟩(2),⟨0,D⟩(30,31,32))
2	24.	(-te,	⟨1,V=>+epT⟩(2),⟨0,D⟩(30,31,32))
1	25.	(te,	⟨0,D⟩(30,31,32))
2	26.	(te,	⟨1,=ND⟩(1),⟨1,N⟩(2))
1	27.	(e,	⟨1,N⟩(2))
0	28.	(ϵ,	ϵ)

Figure 2: 28 step TD recognition of derivation in Figure 1, abbreviating input words by their initial characters. The left column indicates queue size, plotted in §5.1.

progress.

The recognizer presented here simplifies Mainguy's (2010) top-down MG recognizer by generalizing it handle an MCFG normal form, so that a wide range of MG extensions are immediately accommodated. This is made easy when we adopt Kanazawa's Horn clause formulation of MCFGs where the order of variables on the left side of the rules so visibly indicates the surface order of string components. With the Horn clause notation, the indexing can be string-based and general rather than tree-based and tied to particular assumptions about how the MGs work. Transparently generalizing the operations of CF TD recognizers, the indexing and operations here are also slightly simpler than 'thread automata' (Villemonte de la Clergerie, 2002). Compare also the indexing, sometimes more or less similar, in chart-based recognizers of MCF and closely related systems (Burden and Ljunglöf, 2005; Harkema, 2001c; Boullier, 1998; Kallmeyer, 2010).

Mainguy shows that when the probability of a derivation is the product of the rule probabilities, as usual, and when those rule probabilities are given by a consistent probability assignment, a beam search without pruning will always find a derivation if there is one. When there is no derivation, though, an unpruned search can fail to terminate; a pruning rule can guarantee termination in such cases. Those results extend to the MCFG recognizers proposed here. Various applications have found it better to use a beam search with top-down recognition of left- or right-corner transforms of CF grammars (Roark, 2001; Roark, 2004; Schuler, 2010; Wu et al., 2010); those transforms can (but need not always) disrupt grammatical connectedness as noted in §5.3. Work in progress explores the possibilities for such strategies in incremental MCFG parsing. It would also be interesting to generalize Hale's (2011) "rational parser" to these grammars.

Acknowledgments

Thanks to Thomas Mainguy, Sarah VanWagenen and Éric Villemonte de la Clergerie for helpful discussions of this material.

References

Gerry T. M. Altmann and Jelena Mirković. 2009. Incrementality and prediction in human sentence processing. *Cognitive Science*, 33:583–809.

Asaf Bachrach. 2008. *Imaging Neural Correlates of Syntactic Complexity in a Naturalistic Context*. Ph.D. thesis, Massachusetts Institute of Technology.

Pierre Boullier. 1998. Proposal for a natural language processing syntactic backbone. Technical Report 3242, Projet Atoll, INRIA, Rocquencourt.

Jonathan Brennan, Yuval Nir, Uri Hasson, Rafael Malach, David J. Heeger, and Liinay Pylkkänen. 2010. Syntactic structure building in the anterior temporal lobe during natural story listening. *Forthcoming*.

Håkan Burden and Peter Ljunglöf. 2005. Parsing linear context-free rewriting systems. In *Ninth International Workshop on Parsing Technologies, IWPT'05*.

Craig G. Chambers, Michael K. Tanenhaus, Kathleen M. Eberhard, Hana Filip, and Greg N. Carlson. 2004. Actions and affordances in syntactic ambiguity resolution. *Journal of Experimental Psychology: Learning, Memory and Cognition*, 30(3):687–696.

Cristiano Chesi. 2007. An introduction to phase-based minimalist grammars: Why *move* is top-down from left-to-right. Technical report, Centro Interdepartmentale di Studi Cognitivi sul Linguaggio.

Vera Demberg and Frank Keller. 2009. A computational model of prediction in human parsing: Unifying locality and surprisal effects. In *Proceedings of the 29th meeting of the Cognitive Science Society (CogSci-09)*, Amsterdam.

Werner Frey and Hans-Martin Gärtner. 2002. On the treatment of scrambling and adjunction in minimalist grammars. In *Proceedings, Formal Grammar'02*, Trento.

Thomas Graf. 2011. Closure properties of minimalist derivation tree languages. In *Logical Aspects of Computational Linguistics, LACL'11*, Forthcoming.

Matthieu Guillaumin. 2004. Conversions between mildly sensitive grammars. UCLA and École Normale Supérieure. http://www.linguistics.ucla.edu/people/stabler/epssw.htm.

Nicholas J. Haddock. 1989. Computational models of incremental semantic interpretation. *Language and Cognitive Processes*, 4((3/4)):337–368.

John T. Hale. 2011. What a rational parser would do. *Cognitive Science*, 35(3):399–443.

Henk Harkema. 2001a. A characterization of minimalist languages. In *Proceedings, Logical Aspects of Computational Linguistics, LACL'01*, Port-aux-Rocs, Le Croisic, France.

Henk Harkema. 2001b. A characterization of minimalist languages. In Philippe de Groote, Glyn Morrill, and

Christian Retoré, editors, *Logical Aspects of Computational Linguistics*, Lecture Notes in Artificial Intelligence, No. 2099, pages 193–211, NY. Springer.

Henk Harkema. 2001c. *Parsing Minimalist Languages*. Ph.D. thesis, University of California, Los Angeles.

Aravind Joshi. 1985. How much context-sensitivity is necessary for characterizing structural descriptions. In D. Dowty, L. Karttunen, and A. Zwicky, editors, *Natural Language Processing: Theoretical, Computational and Psychological Perspectives*, pages 206–250. Cambridge University Press, NY.

Laura Kallmeyer. 2010. *Parsing beyond context-free grammars*. Springer, NY.

Makoto Kanazawa. 2009. A pumping lemma for well-nested multiple context free grammars. In *13th International Conference on Developments in Language Theory, DLT 2009*.

Yoshihide Kato and Shigeki Matsubara. 2009. Incremental parsing with adjoining operation. *IEICE Transactions on Information and Systems*, E92.D(12):2306–2312.

Jonathan King and Marcel Adam Just. 1991. Individual differences in syntactic processing: the role of working memory. *Journal of Memory and Language*, 30:580–602.

Gregory M. Kobele, Christian Retoré, and Sylvain Salvati. 2007. An automata-theoretic approach to minimalism. In J. Rogers and S. Kepser, editors, *Model Theoretic Syntax at 10, ESSLLI'07*.

Gregory M. Kobele. 2011. Minimalist tree languages are closed under intersection with recognizable tree languages. In *Logical Aspects of Computational Linguistics, LACL'11*, Forthcoming.

Thomas Mainguy. 2010. A probabilistic top-down parser for minimalist grammars. http://arxiv.org/abs/1010.1826v1.

Jens Michaelis. 1998. Derivational minimalism is mildly context-sensitive. In *Proceedings, Logical Aspects of Computational Linguistics, LACL'98*, pages 179–198, NY. Springer.

Jens Michaelis. 2001a. *On Formal Properties of Minimalist Grammars*. Ph.D. thesis, Universität Potsdam. *Linguistics in Potsdam 13*, Universitätsbibliothek, Potsdam, Germany.

Jens Michaelis. 2001b. Transforming linear context free rewriting systems into minimalist grammars. In P. de Groote, G. Morrill, and C. Retoré, editors, *Logical Aspects of Computational Linguistics*, LNCS 2099, pages 228–244, NY. Springer.

Kentaro Nakatani and Edward Gibson. 2008. Distinguishing theories of syntactic expectation cost in sentence comprehension: Evidence from Japanese. *Linguistics*, 46(1):63–86.

Brian Roark and Mark Johnson. 1999. Efficient probabilistic top-down and left-corner parsing. In *Proceedings of the 37th Annual Meeting of the Association for Computational Linguistics*, pages 421–428.

Brian Roark. 2001. Probabilistic top-down parsing and language modeling. *Computational Linguistics*, 27(2):249–276.

Brian Roark. 2004. Robust garden path parsing. *Natural Language Engineering*, 10(1):1–24.

William Schuler. 2010. Incremental parsing in bounded memory. In *Proceedings of the 10th International Workshop on Tree Adjoining Grammars and Related Frameworks, TAG+10*.

Hiroyuki Seki, Takashi Matsumura, Mamoru Fujii, and Tadao Kasami. 1991. On multiple context-free grammars. *Theoretical Computer Science*, 88:191–229.

Libin Shen and Aravind Joshi. 2005. Incremental LTAG parsing. In *Proceedings, Human Language Technology Conference and Conference on Empirical Methods in Human Language Processing*.

Edward P. Stabler. 2001. Recognizing head movement. In Philippe de Groote, Glyn Morrill, and Christian Retoré, editors, *Logical Aspects of Computational Linguistics*, Lecture Notes in Artificial Intelligence, No. 2099, pages 254–260. Springer, NY.

Edward P. Stabler. 2011. Computational perspectives on minimalism. In Cedric Boeckx, editor, *Oxford Handbook of Linguistic Minimalism*, pages 617–641. Oxford University Press, Oxford.

Sarah VanWagenen, Jonathan Brennan, and Edward P. Stabler. 2011. Evaluating parsing strategies in sentence processing. In *Proceedings of the CUNY Sentence Processing Conference*.

K. Vijay-Shanker and David Weir. 1994. The equivalence of four extensions of context free grammar formalisms. *Mathematical Systems Theory*, 27:511–545.

Éric Villemonte de la Clergerie. 2002. Parsing MCS languages with thread automata. In *Proceedings of the 6th International Workshop on Tree Adjoining Grammars and Related Frameworks, TAG+6*.

David Weir. 1988. *Characterizing Mildly Context-Sensitive Grammar Formalisms*. Ph.D. thesis, University of Pennsylvania, Philadelphia.

Stephen Wu, Asaf Bachrach, Carlos Cardenas, and William Schuler. 2010. Complexity metrics in an incremental right-corner parser. In *Proceedings of the 48th Annual Meeting of the Association for Computer Linguistics*, pages 1189–1198.

Exploring the relationship between learnability and linguistic universals

Anna N. Rafferty (rafferty@cs.berkeley.edu)
Computer Science Division, University of California, Berkeley, CA 94720 USA

Thomas L. Griffiths (tom_griffiths@berkeley.edu)
Department of Psychology, University of California, Berkeley, CA 94720 USA

Marc Ettlinger (marc@northwestern.edu)
Department of Communication Sciences and Disorders
Northwestern University, Evanston, IL 60208 USA

Abstract

Greater learnability has been offered as an explanation as to why certain properties appear in human languages more frequently than others. Languages with greater learnability are more likely to be accurately transmitted from one generation of learners to the next. We explore whether such a learnability bias is sufficient to result in a property becoming prevalent across languages by formalizing language transmission using a linear model. We then examine the outcome of repeated transmission of languages using a mathematical analysis, a computer simulation, and an experiment with human participants, and show several ways in which greater learnability may not result in a property becoming prevalent. Both the ways in which transmission failures occur and the relative number of languages with and without a property can affect whether the relationship between learnability and prevalence holds. Our results show that simply finding a learnability bias is not sufficient to explain why a particular property is a linguistic universal, or even frequent among human languages.

1 Introduction

A comparison of languages around the world reveals that certain properties are far more frequent than others, which are taken to reflect linguistic universals (Greenberg, 1963; Comrie, 1981; Croft, 2002). Understanding the origins of linguistic universals is an important project for linguistics, and understanding how they relate to human cognitive processes is an important project for cognitive science. One prominent explanation for the existence of these patterns is the presence of cognitive biases that make certain properties of language more easily learned than others (Slobin, 1973; Wilson, 2003; Finley & Badecker, 2007; Wilson, 2006). Under this hypothesis, certain properties are common across languages because they are more easily learned than others (a *learnability bias*) and are therefore more likely to be maintained when a language is passed from one generation to the next. These universals generally reflect tendencies, rather than properties that are present in each and every language (Croft, 2002).

Recent work in psycholinguistics has provided support for a relationship between learnability biases and the properties that are prevalent in human languages. A number of studies have shown that certain common phonological patterns, such as vowel harmony, voicing agreement and final devoicing are, indeed, more learnable than other unattested patterns (Finley & Badecker, 2007; Moreton, 2008; Becker, Ketrez, & Nevins, 2011). Based on these findings, it is tempting to argue that learnability biases alone might account for the prevalence of these properties in human languages. However, this argument assumes that more accurate learning of a language with a certain property is sufficient for that property to become widespread across languages and does not account for why a property might be prevalent but not universal across languages.

In this paper, we examine the assumption that greater learnability is sufficient for a property to become prevalent. We formalize language transmission using a simple linear model, and then show two basic scenarios in which greater learnability for a particular language does not result in that language becoming prevalent. We first perform a mathematical analysis to show that one way this can occur is for errors in transmission to favor particular languages over others. We next use a simulation to show another scenario in which greater learnability can fail to result in a dominant pattern: when the number of alternative languages is large. We conduct two experiments with human participants to illustrate the occurrence of this second scenario in the case of a particular property of human language, vowel harmony.

2 Linking Learnability and Transmission

Languages change over time due to transmission from generation to generation (e.g., Labov, 2001). Our goal is to understand how long-term trends of language change are related to cognitive, perceptual, and production biases observed in a single instance of transmission. We begin by formalizing transmission using a general mathematical model in order to uncover what long term trends emerge given that certain languages are more likely to be accurately transmitted than others.

We use a linear model of cultural transmission, in which it is assumed that each person learns a language from utterances produced by one person in the previous generation. This linear model of transmission has many specific instantiations in the literature on language evolution, such as the iterated learning model (Kirby, 2001; Griffiths & Kalish, 2007) or the replicator dynamics (Schuster & Sigmund, 1983; Komarova & Nowak, 2003). To specify this model, we first define the set of possible languages, denoted H. Each element $h \in H$ is one possible language. Transmission occurs when a new member of the population receives linguistic data (a set of utterances) from another member of the population and learns a language $h \in H$. We assume transmission occurs only from one person to another person, and that each person learns only one language. For example, someone who knows language j might speak to another member of the population, and based on hearing those utterances, the learner might also learn the language j. Alternatively, the learner might learn another language: The learner might not have heard enough language to fully specify j as the language or might have misheard something, and thus simply infers another language i that is consistent with the data she or he heard. More generally, we assume that for all $i, j \in H$, q_{ij} is the probability that someone will learn language i from someone who knows language j. These can be encoded in a transition matrix Q where the (i, j)th entry of the matrix corresponds to q_{ij} (see Figure 1).

(a)

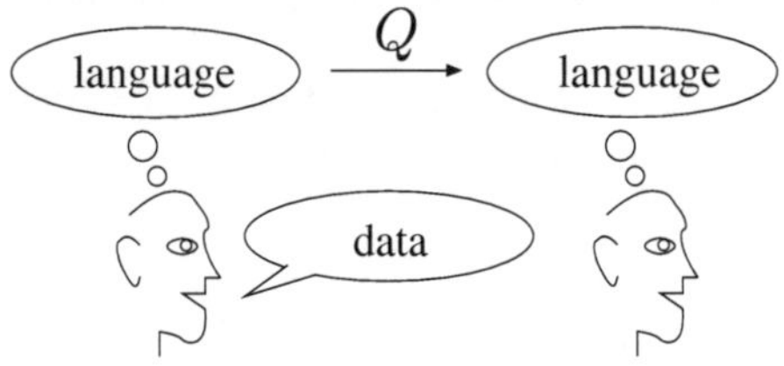

(b)

$$Q = \begin{bmatrix} 0.90 & 0.05 & 0.07 \\ 0.04 & 0.76 & 0.08 \\ 0.06 & 0.19 & 0.85 \end{bmatrix}$$

(c)

$$\pi = \begin{bmatrix} 0.39 \\ 0.20 \\ 0.41 \end{bmatrix}$$

Figure 1: (a) A general model of the cultural transmission of languages. A language is passed from one learner to another, and the matrix Q encodes the probability a learner will learn a particular language i from someone who knows language j. (b) An example transition matrix Q with three states. (c) The solution to the eigenvector equation $Q\pi = \pi$ for this transition matrix. π gives the equilibrium probability that a learner will learn a particular language when languages are transmitted via a process that has transition matrix Q.

Using this framework, we can formally define learnability biases and determine whether a learnability bias for some property necessarily implies that this property will be present in the majority of languages. As mentioned previously, we define learnability bias to mean that one type of language is more likely to be transmitted accurately to the next generation than another; this is similar to the notion of "cognitive bias" discussed in Wilson (2003) and is what is tested in experiments. Formally, a learnability bias for some language i over some other language j means that $q_{ii} > q_{jj}$. For example, one might expose one group of learners to language i and another group to language j. If more learners in the first group accurately learned the language they were exposed to, this would indicate a learnability bias for language i over language j.

We can extend the idea of a learnability bias to a property of a language, rather than a specific language, by applying a similar definition to sets of languages. Imagine there are two sets of languages, H_1 and H_2. These sets might be defined by classifying all languages with a particular property in H_1 and all languages without the property in H_2. One way of defining a learnability bias that favors a particular property is for each language with that property to be more likely to be transmitted successfully than each language without that property. That is, for all possible pairs $i \in H_1$ and $j \in H_2$, $q_{ii} > q_{jj}$. This would indicate a general learnability bias for languages in H_1 over languages in H_2.

Using this definition of a learnability bias, we can determine whether such a bias is sufficient to establish that the property will be present in the majority of languages. That is, if H_1 denotes the languages with the property of interest, we want to determine whether a learnability bias for languages in H_1 implies that after many generations, the majority of the languages in the population will be in H_1 and not in H_2. We can determine the consequences of many instances of language transmission in this model by appealing to existing results on the equilibrium of this linear dynamical system. As mentioned above, this linear transmission model is related to two kinds of models that have been used to study language evolution: If we assume that learners are organized in a chain, this linear model is called iterated learning (Kirby, 2001); alternatively, if we assume that there are an infinite number of learners in the population, the model is called the replicator dynamics (Schuster & Sigmund, 1983). In either case, the probability that a learner will learn language h, assuming the population has reached equilibrium, is given by the solution to the eigenvector equation $Q\pi = \pi$, normalized such that $\sum_{i=1}^{n} \pi_i = 1$ (for details, see Griffiths & Kalish, 2007). For languages in H_1 to occur the majority of the time, it thus must be the case that $\sum_{h \in H_1} \pi_h > \sum_{h \in H_2} \pi_h$.

We can now identify one context in which a learnability bias is not sufficient to ensure that a property will appear in the majority of languages. Consider the example transition matrix Q shown in Figure 1 (b). Let $H_1 = \{s_1\}$ and $H_2 = \{s_2, s_3\}$, where each state s_i represents a distinct language. We have that $q_{11} > q_{ii}$ for all $i \in H_2$: each state in H_2 has a lower self transition probability than state s_1, the only state in H_1. Thus, we have a learnability bias for state s_1 over all states in H_2. However, the eigenvector π shown in Figure 1 (c) indicates that the equilibrium of this system, which will be reached after languages are transmitted from person to person many times, favors state s_3 over the other states. Overall, $\sum_{h \in H_1} \pi_h = 0.39$ while $\sum_{h \in H_2} \pi_h = 0.61$: most of the learners will learn a language in H_2.[1]

Intuitively, this result comes from the fact that transmission failures tend to favor languages in H_2. A learner who learns from someone who speaks a language i in H_2 will rarely learn the language in H_1, although she may learn a different language than i in H_2. This pattern of transmission failures overwhelms the learnability bias that the language in H_1 has over the languages in H_2. Note that this pattern holds even given that $q_{1i} > q_{i1}$ for all $i \in H_2$, another common criterion for a learnability bias.

This result implies that if the linear transmission model is an accurate model for understanding human language evolution, then it is not sufficient to compare how accurately languages are maintained over a single generation in order to predict what trends will emerge after many generations. Instead, one must also look at what happens when languages are not maintained accurately. The ways in which mutations occur may be as important as the relative fidelities of transmission in determining long term trends. When one only looks for a learnability bias, the rate of different mutations is not accounted for, leaving open the possibility that predictions about long term trends will be incorrect.

3 Simulating Language Transmission

In the previous section, we used a simple linear transmission model to identify one context in which a learnability bias is not sufficient for languages with a certain property to become prevalent. We now explore a second context in which a learnability bias is not sufficient to guarantee that languages with a particular property become prevalent, using a simulation of language transmission. We use an iterated learning model in which our representation of language is inspired by the principles and parameters approach (Chomsky & Lasnik, 1993). Rafferty, Griffiths, and Klein (2009) present a model similar to the one we consider here and show that compa-

[1]While one might try to resolve this issue by collapsing all languages in H_2 into a single state in the Markov chain, such a transformation is possible only in cases where $q_{ij} = q_{ik}$ for all languages $j,k \in H_2$ and $i \notin H_2$ (Burke & Rosenblatt, 1958; Kemeny & Snell, 1960).

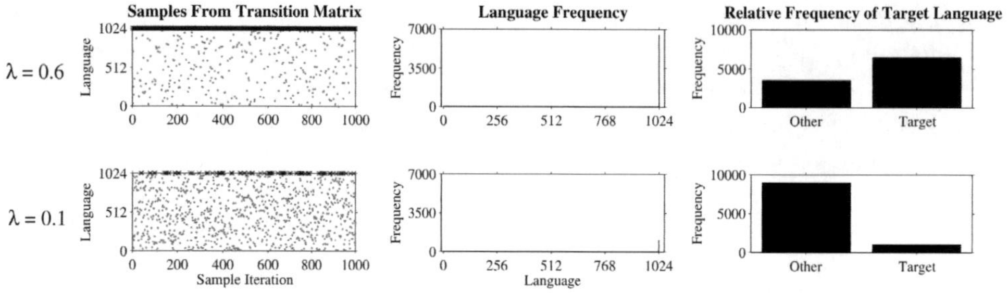

Figure 2: Model results for the frequency of the target language based on adjusting the bias towards that hypothesis. The rows in the above figure correspond to two possible values of λ; larger λ results in a higher prior probability on the target language. The leftmost column shows $1,000$ samples from the transition matrix, with black x marks corresponding to occurrences of the target language. The middle column corresponds to the frequency of each language in the full $10,000$ samples; the rightmost bar in each figure corresponds to the target language. The rightmost column shows the frequency of the target language versus all other languages for the same $10,000$ samples.

rable results hold using other representations of language, such as those based on optimality theory.

In order to define the transition matrix Q, we need to specify the process by which learners select a language. We assume that learners are Bayesian, meaning that they infer a language h based on the data d that they receive according to Bayes' rule. The *posterior probability* assigned to h after observing d is $p(h|d) \propto p(d|h)p(h)$, where $p(d|h)$ (the *likelihood*) indicates the probability of d being generated from h, and $p(h)$ (the *prior*) indicates the extent to which the learner was biased towards h before observing d. If we assume learners select hypotheses with probability equal to their posterior probability, we obtain a transition matrix Q with entries

$$\begin{aligned} q_{ij} &= p(h^{(t+1)} = i|h^{(t)} = j) \\ &= \sum_d p(h^{(t+1)} = i|d)p(d|h^{(t)} = j) \end{aligned}$$

where $h^{(t)}$ and $h^{(t+1)}$ are the languages of learners at iterations t and $t+1$ respectively.

To represent languages, we use binary vectors of length N. Each place corresponds to the setting for a particular parameter. We consider one particular setting of the parameters to be the target language and include a learnability bias for this language in the model; we then look at whether this language is more prevalent than other languages after many transmissions. In the iterated learning model that we use, learners are organized into a chain, with each learner learning from data generated by the previous learner (Kirby, 2001). The previous learner generates k pieces of data that match her or his language. These pieces of data each specify the correct parameter setting for one of the properties represented by the binary vector. The other $N-k$ properties are left unspecified in the data given to the next learner.

In order to define the transition probability between languages, we need to define the two terms in Bayes rule: the prior $p(h)$ and the likelihood $p(d|h)$. Intuitively, the prior probability distribution over languages corresponds to how much evidence is required for the learner to learn each hypothesis. If one hypothesis has a very high prior probability, only a small amount of evidence will be required to convince the learner that that hypothesis is the correct one. By controlling the prior probability of the target language versus the other languages, we can manipulate the learnability bias for the target language. We thus set the prior probability of the target language to λ and then divide the remaining probability mass of $1-\lambda$ uniformly across all of the languages (including the target language). The parameter λ thus controls the strength of the learnability bias for the target language, but this language is always favored for any λ greater than 0.

The likelihood $p(d|h)$ reflects the probability that a given hypothesis h would produce data d. We assume d is a string of length N that contains 0s, 1s, and ?s. A '?' in the ith position means that no information was given about the ith property. We also assume there is a probability ε that the chosen language will not match the data at each position; that is, with probability ε, the language chosen by the learner will have a 1 in the ith spot if the data had a 0 in that spot. This gives:

$$p(d|h) = \prod_{i=1,d_i \neq ?}^{N} \varepsilon^{I(h \vdash d_i)} (1-\varepsilon)^{I(h \nvdash d_i)}$$

where $h \vdash d_i$ means that h has the same setting of the ith property as d_i.

Given these specifications for the prior and the likelihood, we can calculate the $2^N \times 2^N$ transition matrix and sample from this matrix to simulate a sequence of learners each learning a language from the utterances produced by the previous learner. We let $N = 10$ and $k = 5$. As shown in Griffiths and Kalish (2007), in this model – iterated learning with Bayesian learners – the equilibrium π is simply the prior distribution $p(h)$. The distribution over languages is thus unaffected by the error parameter ε; this parameter only affects the time to reach equilibrium (Rafferty et al., 2009). We present results using $\varepsilon = 0.25$. Figure 2 shows how relative frequency of the target language is affected by changing the parameter λ, using $\lambda = 0.6$ and $\lambda = 0.1$. Frequencies are based on taking $11,000$ samples from the matrix and discarding the first $1,000$ to ensure that the population had reached equilibrium.

The middle column of Figure 2 shows that the frequency with which learners chose the target language was greater than that of the other languages for both values of λ. This is consistent with the target language having a higher prior probability than other languages. However, depending on the strength of the bias, this language may still not be chosen the majority of the time, as shown in the rightmost column of Figure 2. When λ is large, its probability overwhelms that of its competitors. However, if λ is relatively small, the combined frequencies of all other languages exceed that of the target language. Thus, despite being favored by a learnability bias, the target language is not chosen by the majority of learners. Like the previous example, this simulation demonstrates that learnability biases may not always lead to accurate prediction of long term trends. More specifically, it highlights that one must consider the size of the comparison set: If there are many alternate possible languages, learners may tend to learn one of these languages even if some particular language with a learnability bias is more frequent than any other given individual language.

4 Language Transmission in the Lab

While we have shown two scenarios in which a simple linear transmission model does not predict that learnability biases will necessarily lead to linguistic universals, human learners are not necessarily consistent with this model and could follow a different pattern. Thus, we conducted two experiments to determine if the same dissociation between individual bias and long-term change can be shown when teaching human learners an artificial grammar. In Experiment 1, we establish a learnability bias for a linguistic pattern that is common in the world's languages over an arbitrary pattern. In Experiment 2, we explore what happens when a language with the common pattern is transmitted multiple times among learners in the lab. Each learner learns a language and then produces data from this language to teach the next learner. By examining the languages that emerge after several transmissions, we will show that the learnability bias in Experiment 1 does not translate to the pattern becoming widespread across the learned languages in Experiment 2. This pattern is an instance of the scenario in which the many alternative languages overwhelm the language with the learnability bias.

In our experiments, we use the property of vowel harmony. Relatively common across the world's languages (van der Hulst & van de Weijer, 1995), vowel harmony is a linguistic pattern wherein the vowels in words in a language must share some phonological feature. For example, in Turkish, the plural suffix is *-lar* in *bash-lar* 'heads', but *-ler* in *bebek-ler* 'babies' so as to adhere to the requirement that words are front-back harmonic. In the former, both vowels are back vowels and in the latter, both vowels are front vowels. Harmony is well-suited for use in this case because English speakers have no familiarity with vowel harmony from their native language input and because previous work has shown that typologically attested vowel harmony patterns are generally more easily learned (Moreton, 2008; Finley & Badecker, 2009).

5 Experiment 1: Establishing a Bias

5.1 Methods

Participants. There were 40 participants who received either monetary compensation or course credit for their participation. All were native speakers of English.

Stimuli. A native speaker of English was recorded saying 160 CVCVC words. Each word began with one of 80 CVC stems, twenty each with the vowels /i/, /e/, /u/ and /o/ and random consonants. Each stem was recorded with both variants, or allomorphs, of a suffix, [it] and [ut]. Thus, half the words were front-harmonic (e.g., pel-it, bis-it) and half were front-disharmonic (e.g., pel-ut, bis-ut).

Procedure. The procedure followed a modified artificial grammar paradigm. Participants were assigned to one of two conditions: the harmonic condition or the height-front dependency condition, which is unattested. In both conditions, participants were exposed in training to 40 words from the language they were learning. In the harmonic condition, 40 harmonic words were selected. In the height-front dependency condition, words were selected such that mid-vowel stems received the front vowel suffix (e.g., pel-it, bod-it) and high-vowel stems received the back-vowel suffix (e.g., bis-ut, tug-ut). This rule was chosen arbitrarily from the space of possible languages to test the hypothesis that vowel harmony would have a learnability bias over other patterns.

Participants were familiarized with the words in the same way regardless of condition. They were given alternating blocks of passive listening and blocks in which for each trial, two words were played and they were required to choose which word they had previously heard. In the forced choice trials, the choice was between a word that had been played in the passive listening section and a word with the same prefix and the alternate allomorph. A total of five blocks of 40 trials each were included in training: three passive listening blocks with a forced choice block in between each.

Following the training trials, participants completed one block of 80 test trials. On each test trial, participants were asked to choose which of two words they thought was from the language they had learned in the training trials. In each trial, the two words both had the same stem and differed in the suffix. 40 of the test trials included words from training, and 40 were generalization trials involving novel words.

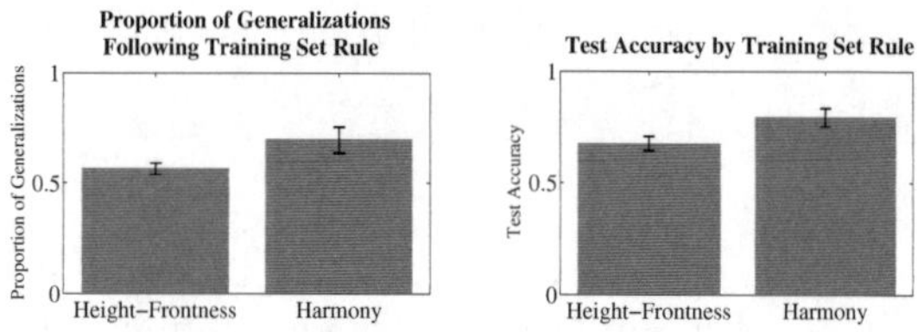

Figure 3: Results for harmonic versus height-frontness rule conditions. By condition, there are significant differences in the proportion of generalizations following the rule (0.70 for harmony rule versus 0.57 for height-frontness rule, $t(38) = 2.05, p < 0.05$; left) and in test accuracy (0.80 for harmony rule versus 0.68 for height-frontness rule, $t(38) = 2.23, p < 0.05$; right).

5.2 Results

As shown in Figure 3, we found a learnability bias for the harmonic language. Learners had significantly greater accuracy in test when they learned the vowel harmonic language than when they learned the height-front dependency language (80% correct for learners of the harmony rule versus 68% correct for the height-frontness rule, $t(38) = 2.23, p < 0.05$). Additionally, 70% of generalizations made by learners in the harmony rule condition followed the harmonic rule while only 57% of generalizations made by learners in the height-front dependency condition followed the height-frontness rule ($t(38) = 2.05, p < 0.05$).[2] The result of these two phenomena was that the final languages produced by the learners in the harmony condition had a greater prevalence of harmonic words than the final languages of learners in the height-frontness dependency had of adhering words.

These results establish that the probability of transitioning from a harmonic language to another language with a high proportion of harmonic words is higher than the probability of transitioning from a height-front dependency language to another language with a high proportion of adhering words. In

[2]For the second experiment, participants who had low accuracy (< 62.5% of previously heard words chosen in test as "from the language") were excluded. Performing this exclusion in this experiment preserves the same results: Mean accuracy of 87% for the harmonic condition versus 73% for the height-front dependency condition ($t(28) = 2.74, p < 0.025$), and 77% mean proportion of generalizations following the rule for the harmonic condition versus 58% for the height-front dependency condition ($t(28) = 2.43, p < 0.025$). This exclusion criterion resulted in removing five participants from each condition.

terms of the transition matrix, this corresponds to $q_{\ell_{\text{harm}},\ell_{\text{harm}}} > q_{\ell_{\text{h-f}},\ell_{\text{h-f}}}$, where ℓ_{harm} is the set of languages with a high proportion of harmonic words and $\ell_{\text{h-f}}$ is the set of languages with a high proportion of words that follow the height-frontness rule. In other words, the harmonic language is easier to learn than the height-front dependency language.

6 Experiment 2: Language Transmission

6.1 Methods

Participants. There were a total of 104 participants who received either monetary compensation or course credit for their participation. All were native speakers of English.

Stimuli. The same stimuli were used as in Experiment 1.

Procedure. The procedure for this experiment was similar to Experiment 1, but the way that words were chosen for training differed. For the first subject in each chain, a total of 40 prefixes were selected at random, and based on the starting condition of the chain, the allophone for each prefix was selected. For example, for the 50% harmonic starting condition, 40 prefixes were chosen and of those prefixes, half were chosen to have the appropriate allophone to make the word harmonic and half were chosen to have the allophone to make the word non-harmonic. For subsequent subjects in each chain, 40 words were chosen at random from those words which the previous subject had said was in the language. In order to exclude subjects who had not actually learned the language in training, subjects were not included in the chain if their accuracy in test on previously seen words was below 62.5%; this is the lowest level of accuracy that is significantly different (binomial test, $p < 0.05$) from chance guessing. Chains were started at 100%, 75%, 50%, 25%, and 0% harmonic. One chain with 10 subjects was run for each starting point except for 100%. Four chains of 10 subjects each were run at this starting point as this is the point of most interest: given a learnability bias, does the percentage of harmonic words in a language remain consistently large?

6.2 Results

While Experiment 1 showed a learnability bias for the harmonic language over an arbitrarily chosen language, the iterated learning chains in Experiment 2 did not favor the harmonic language. As shown in Figure 4, all chains tended toward languages with approximately 50% harmonic words, and after several generations, the chains that began with 100% harmonic words did not differ significantly from the other chains. There is also no difference in accuracy on the harmonic items over time, as shown in Figure 5. This is empirical evidence that the pattern shown in simulation can also occur with human learners: One language is more accurately transmitted than others, but due to the large number of other possible languages, this language does not predominate after many transmissions.

7 General Discussion

In this paper, we formalized language transmission using a linear model in order to examine whether a learnability bias for some property of language is sufficient for that property to become prevalent in human languages. We showed two ways in which a learnability bias for a property can exist but not cause that property to become prevalent. First, using a mathematical analysis, we showed that this can occur when transmission failures favor languages other than those that have greater learnability. This illustrates the importance of considering the entire transmission matrix, not just the probabilities of accurate transmissions that are considered when establishing a learnability bias.

Second, we showed that it is possible for the sheer number of other possible languages to overwhelm greater learnability for a particular language. We then illustrated that this second scenario might lead to incorrect predictions in an experimental context. In artificial language experiments, greater learnability is often established by comparing the accuracy of transmission for a language with the property of interest to an arbitrary language. However, in our experiment, we established such a learnability bias for vowel harmony, but this did not result in vowel harmony being maintained after many instances of transmission. This result seems to be due to the fact that numerous languages other than harmonic languages were possible, so learners tended to learn one of these many other languages.

One limitation of our analysis is the use of the

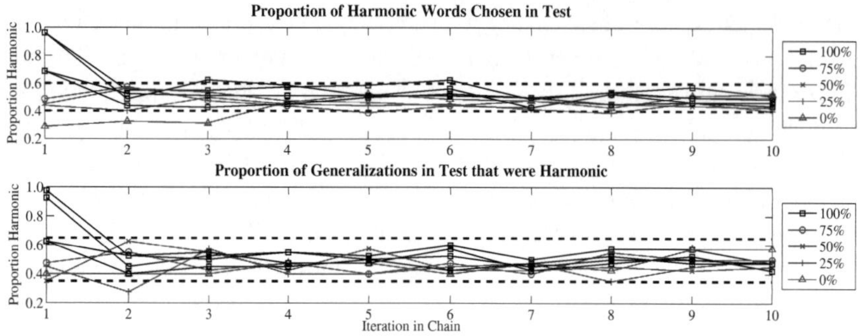

Figure 4: Iterated learning chain results. Dotted lines show the two-tailed 95% confidence interval for chance responding; confidence intervals differ between the two graphs because there are 40 opportunities to generalize versus 80 opportunities to choose harmonic words.

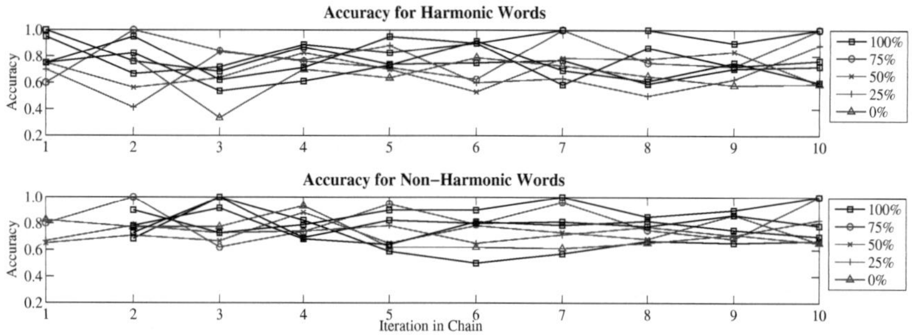

Figure 5: Accuracy on harmonic versus non-harmonic words by iteration. Overall, there is no difference in accuracy.

simple linear transmission model, in which each learner learns from one member of the previous generation. It is easy to imagine variants on this model that make more realistic assumptions about cultural transmission of languages. However, we suspect that these more complex models would not alter the conclusions that we have drawn here. For example, learning from multiple members of the previous generation tends to dilute the effects of learnability on the languages produced by a population (Smith, 2009; Burkett & Griffiths, 2010).

Overall, the result of a more complicated relationship between learnability biases and linguistic universals is congruent with the evidence that all languages do not exhibit all properties for which learnability biases have been found. Indeed, in historical linguistics, the general principle is one of language divergence, rather than convergence on some universal language (e.g., Greenberg, 1971). Given this relationship, one must rethink using experimental evidence for particular learnability biases to explain linguistic tendencies. Instead, one must either estimate all of the values in the transmission matrix, or actually simulate the process of multiple transmissions in the lab to establish whether a particular property with a learnability bias is actually maintained over many generations. While this process is dependent on assuming a particular model of how transmission occurs in populations, such as the linear iterated learning paradigm we used in our experiments, it provides a way of understanding what mutations are likely to occur and of exploring the long term trends that result from particular learnability biases. As we showed for vowel harmony, long term trends may not match what one predicted based on a learnability bias. Given such a result, one must look to factors other than the learnability bias to explain why a property is common across languages.

Acknowledgements. This work was supported by an NSF Graduate Research Fellowship to ANR, grant number BCS-0704034 from the NSF to TLG, and grant number T32 NS047987 from the NIH to ME.

References

Becker, M., Ketrez, N., & Nevins, A. (2011). The surfeit of the stimulus: Analytic biases filter lexical statistics in turkish laryngeal alternations. *Language*, *87*(1), 84-125.

Burke, C. J., & Rosenblatt, M. (1958). A Markovian function of a Markov chain. *The Annals of Mathematical Statistics*, *29*(4), 1112–1122.

Burkett, D., & Griffiths, T. (2010). Iterated learning of multiple languages from multiple teachers. In *The Evolution of Language: Proceedings of the 8th International Conference (EVOLANG8).*

Chomsky, N., & Lasnik, H. (1993). The theory of principles and parameters. In J. Jacobs, A. von Stechow, W. Sternefeld, & T. Vannemann (Eds.), *Syntax: An international handbook of contemporary research* (pp. 506–569). Berlin: Walter de Gruyter.

Comrie, B. (1981). *Language universals and linguistic typology*. Chicago: University of Chicago Press.

Croft, W. (2002). *Typology and universals*. Cambridge University Press.

Finley, S., & Badecker, W. (2007). Towards a substantively biased theory of learning. *Berkeley Linguistics Society*, *33*.

Finley, S., & Badecker, W. (2009). Artificial language learning and feature-based generalization. *Journal of Memory and Language*, *61*, 423–437.

Greenberg, J. (Ed.). (1963). *Universals of language*. Cambridge, MA: MIT Press.

Greenberg, J. (1971). *Language, culture, and communication*. Stanford: Stanford University Press.

Griffiths, T. L., & Kalish, M. L. (2007). A Bayesian view of language evolution by iterated learning. *Cognitive Science*, *31*, 441-480.

Kemeny, J., & Snell, J. (1960). *Finite markov chains*. Princeton, NJ: van Nostrand.

Kirby, S. (2001). Spontaneous evolution of linguistic structure: An iterated learning model of the emergence of regularity and irregularity. *IEEE Journal of Evolutionary Computation*, *5*, 102-110.

Komarova, N. L., & Nowak, M. A. (2003). Language dynamics in finite populations. *Journal of Theoretical Biology*, *221*, 445-457.

Labov, W. (2001). *Principles of linguistic change. Volume II: Social Factors*. Blackwell.

Moreton, E. (2008). Analytic bias and phonological typology. *Phonology*, *25*(1), 83–127.

Rafferty, A. N., Griffiths, T. L., & Klein, D. (2009). Convergence bounds for language evolution by iterated learning. *Proceedings of the Thirty-First Annual Conference of the Cognitive Science Society*.

Schuster, P., & Sigmund, K. (1983). Replicator dynamics. *Journal of Theoretical Biology*, *100*(3), 533 - 538.

Slobin, D. (1973). Cognitive prerequisites for the acquisition of grammar. In C. Ferguson & D. Slobin (Eds.), *Studies of child language development* (pp. 173–208).

Smith, K. (2009). Iterated learning in populations of Bayesian agents. In *Proceedings of the 31st Annual Conference of the Cognitive Science Society.*

van der Hulst, H., & van de Weijer, J. (1995). Vowel harmony. In J. Goldsmith (Ed.), *The Handbook of Phonological Theory* (pp. 495–534). Blackwell.

Wilson, C. (2003). Experimental investigation of phonological naturalness. *Proceedings of the 22nd West Coast Conference on Formal Linguistics*.

Wilson, C. (2006). Learning phonology with substantive bias: An experimental and computational study of velar palatalization. *Cognitive Science*, *30*, 945–982.

Composing and Updating Verb Argument Expectations: A Distributional Semantic Model

Alessandro Lenci
University of Pisa, Department of Linguistics
via S. Maria, 36
56126 Pisa (Italy)
alessandro.lenci@ling.unipi.it

Abstract

The aim of this paper is to present a computational model of the dynamic composition and update of verb argument expectations using Distributional Memory, a state-of-the-art framework for distributional semantics. The experimental results conducted on psycholinguistic data sets show that the model is able to successfully predict the changes on the patient argument thematic fit produced by different types of verb agents.

1 Introduction

A number of studies using different experimental paradigms (priming, self-paced reading, etc.) have shown that verbs (*eat*) activate expectations about nouns occurring as their arguments (*cheese*)(McRae et al., 1998), and vice versa (McRae et al., 2005). Nouns also activate expectations about other nouns occurring as co-arguments in the same event (*key – door*)(Hare et al., 2009). These behavioral effects support the hypothesis that in the mental lexicon verbs and their arguments are arranged into a web of *mutual expectations*. Verb argument expectations encoded in lexical representations are exploited by subjects to determine the plausibility of a noun as an argument of a particular verb (*thematic fit*, or *selectional preferences* in the linguistic literature), which has been proved to have important effects on human sentence processing (McRae et al., 1998).

In a recent work, Bicknell et al. (2010) bring evidence suggesting a more complex view of the organization and on-line use of verb argument expectations. In fact, the expectations about the likely fillers of a given verb argument (e.g., the patient role) depend on the way another verb argument (e.g., the agent role) is filled. For instance, if the agent noun is *journalist*, the most likely patient for the verb *check* is *spelling*, while if the agent noun is *mechanic*, the most likely patient for the same verb is *brakes*. As a consequence, thematic fit judgments are also sensitive to the way other roles of the same verb are filled. Bicknell et al. (2010) show that this fact has clear consequences for sentence processing, and argue that subjects dynamically compute and update verb argument expectations and thematic fit during on-line sentence comprehension, by integrating various types of knowledge about events and their arguments.

The aim of this paper is to present a computational model of the dynamic composition and update of verb argument expectations using *Distributional Memory* (DM)(Baroni and Lenci, 2010), a state-of-the-art Distributional Semantic Model (DSM). DSMs (aka *vector space models*) represent word meaning with vectors encoding corpus-based co-occurence statistics, under the assumption of the so-called *Distributional Hypothesis* (Miller and Charles, 1991; Sahlgren, 2006): Words occurring in similar contexts are also semantically similar (Landauer and Dumais, 1997; Padó and Lapata, 2007; Turney and Pantel, 2010). Thematic fit judgments have already been successfully modeled with DSMs (Erk et al., 2010), but to the best of our knowledge the problem of how thematic fit is dynamically updated depending on the way other arguments are filled has not been addressed yet. The core of our proposal is that Distributional Memory can be used to represent the subject's expectations about the most likely words co-occurring in given syntactic role. We will add to the original Distributional Memory framework a model for verb argument expectation composition called ECU, *Expectation Composition and Update*. Specifically, we will show how the expectations of an agent-verb pair about their patient noun argument can be compositionally derived from the DM representation of the verb and the DM representation of its agent. ECU is evaluated on the data set used in Bicknell et al. (2010), and the experimental results show that it is able to successfully predict the changes on the patient thematic fit with a verb, depending on different agent fillers. More generally, we want to argue that the ECU model proposed here can represent a general and viable approach to address compositionality in distributional semantics.

After reviewing some related work in section 2, we present Distributional Memory (section 3) and its use to model verb-argument composition (section 4). Experiments and evaluation are reported in section 5.

2 Background and related work

Elman (2009) argues that the information on preferred fillers of one verb argument depends on what the filler is of one of the other arguments. For instance, the most likely patient of *cut* is *wood*, when the agent is *lumberjack*, but it is *meat*, when the agent is *butcher*. This claim finds an empirical confirmation in the experiments reported by Bicknell et al. (2010), in which subjects are presented with sentence pairs like the following ones:

(1) The **journalist**$_{AG}$ checked the **spelling**$_{PA}$ of his latest report. (*congruent condition*)

(2) The **mechanic**$_{AG}$ checked the **spelling**$_{PA}$ of his latest report. (*incongruent condition*)

Each pair contains the same verb and patient argument, while differing for the agent argument. In the congruent condition, the patient is a preferred argument of the verb, given the agent, e.g. spelling is something which is typically checked by a journalist. In the incongruent condition, the patient is not a preferred argument of the verb, given its agent, e.g. spelling is not something that is typically checked by a mechanic, who rather checks brakes, engines, etc. Thematic fit judgments used to determine congruent and incongruent agent-verb-patient tuples were collected in an off-line norming study. Bicknell et al. (2010) report that self-paced reading times were shorter at the word directly following the patient for the congruent than the incongruent items. Similar results were obtained in an event-related brain potential (ERP) experiment, in which an N400 effect was observed immediately at the patient noun in the incongruent condition. In eye-tracking experiments, Kamide et al. (2003) also demonstrated that the thematic fit of an object depended on the other verb argument fillers.

The conclusion drawn by Bicknell et al. (2010) is that verb argument expectations and thematic fit are not simply stored in the lexicon, but are rather dynamically updated during sentence comprehension, by integrating various types of knowledge. In fact, if the verb expectations about an argument role depend on the nouns filling its other arguments, the hypothesis that they are compositionally updated is highly plausible, since, "it is difficult to envision how the potentially unbounded number of contexts that might be relevant could be anticipated and stored in the lexicon" (Elman 2009: 21).

Thematic fit judgments have been successfully modeled in distributional semantics. Erk et al. (2010) propose the Exemplar-Based Model of Selectional Preferences, in turn based on Erk (2007). The thematic fit of a noun n as an argument of a verb v is measured with the similarity in a vector space between n and a set of noun exemplars occurring in the same argument role of v. A related approach is adopted by Baroni and Lenci (2010), the main difference being that the thematic fit of n is measured by comparing its vector with a "prototype" vector obtaining by averaging over the vectors of the most typical arguments of v. In both cases, the distributional measure of thematic fit is shown to be highly correlated with human plausibility judgements. Their success notwithstanding, these models fall short of accounting for the dynamical and context-sensitive nature of thematic fit. In the next section, we will extend the Baroni and Lenci (2010) approach with a model for verb-argument composition, which is able to account for the argument interdependency phenomena shown by the experiments in Bicknell et al (2010).

If verb argument expectations are likely to be dynamically computed integrating knowledge of the verb with information about its fillers, modeling thematic fit with DSM requires us to address compositional representations. DSMs have mostly addressed semantic issues related to the representation of the content of single words. However, growing efforts have recently been devoted to the problem of how to build distributional semantic representations of complex expressions (e.g., phrases, sentences, etc.) by composing the distributional representations of their component lexical items (Kintsch, 2001; Clark and Pulman, 2007; Widdows, 2008; Mitchell and Lapata, 2010). Different proposals to address compositionality in DSM exist, but the most common approach is to model semantic composition as vector composition. Mitchell and Lapata (2010) systematically explore various vector composition functions (e.g., vector addition, vector product, and other more sophisticated variants thereof), which are used to build distributional vector representations for verb-noun and adjective-noun phrases. The various models for vector composition are then evaluated in a phrase similarity task.

Erk and Padó (2008) address a partially different and yet crucial aspect of compositionality, i.e., the fact that when words are composed, they tend to affect each other's meanings. The meaning of *run* in *The horse runs* is in fact different from its meaning in *The water runs* (Kintsch, 2001). Erk and Padó (2008) claim that words are associated with various types of expectations (typical events for nouns, and typical arguments for verbs)(McRae et al., 1998; McRae et al., 2005) that influence each other when words compose, thereby altering their meaning. They model this context-sensitive compositionality by distinguishing the lemma vector of a word w_1 (i.e. its out-of-context representation), from its vector in the context of another word w_2. The vector-in-context for w_1 is obtained by combining the lemma vector of w_1 with the lemma vectors of the expectations activated by w_2. For instance, the vector-in-context assigned to *run* in *The horse runs* is obtained by combining the lemma vector of *run* with the lemma vectors of the most typical verbs in which *horse* appears as a subject (e.g. *gallop*, *trot*, etc.). Like in Mitchell and Lapata (2010), various functions to build vectors in contexts are tested. Erk and Padó (2008) evaluate their model for context-sensitive vector representation to predict verb similarity in context (e.g. *slump* in the context of *shoulder* is more similar to *slouch* than to *decline*) and to rank paraphrases.

Our model draws close inspiration from Erk and Padó (2008), with which it shares the importance of verb argument expectations. However, differently from them, we want to model how the combination of a verb with an argument affects its expectations about the likely fillers of its other arguments. While Erk and Padó (2008) test their model on a standard word similarity task (i.e. they measure the similarity between the vector-in-context of a verb with the vector of another "landmark" verb), we evaluate our model for compositionality in distributional semantics in a thematic fit task. Indeed, to the best of our knowledge this is the first time in which the issues of thematic fit and compositionality in DSMs are addressed together.

3 Distributional Memory

Distributional Memory (DM) (Baroni and Lenci, 2010) is a framework for distributional semantics aiming at generalizing over different existing typologies of semantic spaces. Distributional Memory represents corpus-extracted distributional facts as a *weighted tuple structure* T, a set of weighted word-link-word tuples $\langle\langle w_1, l, w_2\rangle, \sigma\rangle$, such that w_1 and w_2 belong to W, a set of content words (e.g. nouns, verbs, etc.), and l belongs to L, a set of syntagmatic co-occurrence links between words in a text (e.g. syntactic dependencies, lexicalized patterns, etc.). For instance, the tuple $\langle\langle book, \texttt{obj}, read\rangle, \sigma\rangle$ encodes the piece of distributional information that *book* co-occurs with *read* in the corpus, and `obj` specifies the type of syntagmatic link between these words, i.e. direct object. The score σ is some function of the co-occurrence frequency of the tuple in a corpus and is used to characterize its statistical salience.

Distributional Memory belongs to the family of so-called *structured DSMs*, which take into account the crucial role played by syntactic structures in shaping the distributional properties of words. To qualify as context of a target item, a word must be linked to it by some (interesting) lexico-syntactic relation, which is also typically used to distinguish the type of this co-occurrence (Lin, 1998; Padó and Lapata, 2007). Differently from other structured DSMs, the tuple structure T is formally represented as a 3-way geometrical object, namely a *third order labeled tensor*. A tensor is a multi-way array (Turney, 2007; Kolda and Bader, 2009), i.e. a generalization of vectors (first order tensors) and matrices (second order tensors). Different semantic spaces are then generated "on demand" through *tensor matricization*, projecting the tuple tensor onto 2-way matrices, whose rows and columns represent semantic spaces to deal with different semantic tasks.

For instance, the space $W_1 \times LW_2$ is formed by vectors for words and the dimensions represent the attributes of these words in terms of lexico-syntactic relations with lexical collocates, such as $\langle$*obj, read*$\rangle$, or $\langle$*use, pen*$\rangle$. Consistently, this space is most suitable to address tasks involving the measurement of the "attributional similarity" between words (Turney, 2006), such as synonym detection or modeling selectional preferences. Instead, the space $W_1W_2 \times L$ contains vectors associated with word pairs, whose dimensions are links between these pairs. This space is thus suitable to address tasks involving the measurement of so-called "relational similarity" (Turney, 2006), such as analogy detection or relation classification (cf. Baroni and Lenci 2010 for more details about the Distributional Memory spaces and tasks). Crucially, these spaces are now alternative "views" of the same underlying distributional memory formalized in the tensor. Many semantic tasks (such as analogical similarity, selectional preferences, property extraction, synonym detection, etc.), which are tackled in the literature with different, often unrelated semantic spaces, are addressed in DM with the same distributional tensor, harvested once and for all from the corpus. This is the reason why Distributional Memory is claimed to be a general purpose resource for semantic modeling.

Depending on the selection of the sets W and L and of the scoring function σ, different DM models can be generated. The Distributional Memory instantiation chosen for the experiments reported in this paper is *TypeDM*, whose links include lexicalized dependency paths and lexico-syntactic shallow patterns, with a scoring function based on pattern type frequency.[1] We have chosen TypeDM, because it is the best performing DM model across the various semantic tasks addressed in Baroni and Lenci (2010). The TypeDM tensor contains about 130M non-zero tuples automatically extracted from a corpus of about 2.83 billion tokens, obtained by concatenating the the Web-derived ukWaC corpus (about 1,915 billion tokens),[2] a mid-2009 dump of the English Wikipedia (about 820 million tokens),[3] and the British National Corpus (about 95 million tokens).[4] The resulting concatenated corpus was tokenized, POS-tagged and lemmatized with the TreeTagger[5] and dependency-parsed with the MaltParser.[6]

The TypeDM word set (W_{TypeDM}) contains 30,693 lemmas (20,410 nouns, 5,026 verbs and 5,257 adjectives). These are the top 20,000 most frequent nouns and top 5,000 most frequent verbs and adjectives in the corpus, augmented with lemmas in various standard test sets in distributional semantics, such as the TOEFL and SAT lists. The TypeDM link set (L_{TypeDM}) contains 25,336 direct and inverse links formed by (partially lexicalized) syntactic dependencies and patterns. This is a sample of the links in L_{TypeDM}:

- **obj**: *The journalist is checking his article* → $\langle$*article,* `obj`*, check*$\rangle$
- **verb**: *The journalist is checking his article* → $\langle$*journalist,* `verb`*, article*$\rangle$
- **sbj_tr**: *The journalist is checking his article* → $\langle$*journalist,* `sbj_tr`*, check*$\rangle$
- **preposition:** *I saw a journalist with a pen* → $\langle$*pen,* `with`*, journalist*$\rangle$
- **such_as:** "*NOUN such as NOUN*" and "*such NOUN as NOUN*": *animals such as cats* → $\langle$*animal,* `such_as`*+ns+ns, cat*$\rangle$

[1] The TypeDM tensor is publicly available at http://clic.cimec.unitn.it/dm

[2] http://wacky.sslmit.unibo.it/

[3] http://en.wikipedia.org/wiki/Wikipedia:Database_download

[4] http://www.natcorp.ox.ac.uk

[5] http://www.ims.uni-stuttgart.de/projekte/corplex/TreeTagger/

[6] http://w3.msi.vxu.se/~nivre/research/MaltParser.html

The first two links above are the most relevant ones for the purposes of the present paper: `obj` links a transitive verb and its direct object, and `verb` is a lexically underspecified link between a subject noun and a complement noun of the same verb.

The scoring function σ is the *Local Mutual Information* (LMI) (Evert, 2005) computed on link type frequency (negative LMI values are raised to 0):

$$\text{LMI} = O_{ijk} \log \frac{O_{ijk}}{E_{ijk}} \tag{1}$$

O_{ijk} and E_{ijk} are respectively the observed and expected frequency of a triple $\langle w_i, l_j, w_k \rangle$.

4 Composing verb argument expectations

In this section, we address the fact that the information on preferred fillers of one verb argument depends on the filler of its other arguments by proposing a model for *Expectation Composition and Update* (ECU), which will then be computationally formalized with Distributional Memory.

ECU relies on the hypothesis that nouns and verbs are linked in a web of mutual expectations. Verbs are associated with expectations about their likely arguments, and nouns have expectations about the events they are involved with and also about other nouns co-occuring in the same events (cf. section 1). We argue that, when words compose (e.g. a verb and a noun), their expectations are integrated and updated. Specifically, we focus here on how the composition of a verb and its agent argument determines an update of the verb expectations for its patient argument. Let $EX_{PA}(v)$ be the expectations of a verb v about its patient arguments, i.e. a set of nouns likely to occur as verb patients. For instance, $EX_{PA}(check)$ = *mistakes, engines, books*, etc. Let $EX(n_{AG})$ be the expectations about typical events performed and typical entities acted upon by the agent noun. For instance, $EX(mechanic)$ = *mechanics fix cars, mechanics check oil*, etc. ECU is formally defined as follows:

$$EX_{PA}(\langle n_{AG}, v \rangle) = f(EX(n_{AG}), EX_{PA}(v)) \tag{2}$$

f is some function for expectation composition and update (cf. below). ECU assumes that the result of semantically composing the verb and its agent argument is an update of the verb expectations about its patient argument. $EX_{PA}(\langle n_{AG}, v \rangle)$ are the updated expectations of v about its patient arguments, resulting from the composition of its original expectations with the agent's expectations. For instance, the result of composing *check* with the agent argument *mechanic* is a new set of expectations $EX_{PA}(\langle mechanic, check \rangle)$ formed by objects that are likely checked by mechanics, such as *cars, engines, wheels*, etc. These updated expectations are a function of the typical patients of checking events, and of the typical patients of events performed by mechanics.

4.1 Modeling ECU with Distributional Memory

The tuple structure of the DM tensor is well suited to represent the web of mutual expectations in which lexical items are arranged. In fact, given a word w, the expectations of w, $EX(w)$, can be defined as the subset of the DM tensor formed by the tuples $\langle \langle w_1, l, w_2 \rangle, \sigma \rangle$, such that $w = w_1$ or $w = w_2$. The tuple score σ determines the statistical salience and typicality of a particular expectation.

To model ECU with TypeDM, we approximate the patient semantic role with the syntactic dependency DM link of `obj` (cf. section 3). The expectations about the typical patient arguments of a verb v ($EX_{PA}(v)$) thus correspond to the set of TypeDM tuples $\langle n_i$, `obj`, $v\rangle$: e.g, $EX_{PA}(check)$ = ⟨*mistake*, `obj`, *check*⟩, ⟨*engine*, `obj`, *check*⟩, etc. We model $EX(n_{AG})$ with the set of DM tuples $\langle n_{AG}$, `verb`, $n_j \rangle$, which characterize the typical patients (i.e., direct objects) of events performed by the agent noun n_{AG}: e.g, $EX(mechanic)$ = ⟨*mechanic*, `verb`, *car*⟩, ⟨*mechanic*, `verb`, *oil*⟩, ⟨*mechanic*, `verb`, *engine*⟩, etc.

The expectation composition function f of equation 2 is modeled as a tensor updating function: f modifies the TypeDM tensor by updating the scores of the relevant subset of tuples. Following current compositionality models in distributional semantics (cf. Mitchell and Lapata 2010), we focus here on two alternative versions of f:

check	$\langle journalist, check\rangle$	$\langle mechanic, check\rangle$
site	article	car
page	book	tyre
website	information	work
box	question	price
detail	fact	vehicle
link	report	job
list	site	system
file	source	bike
record	content	value
information	account	problem

Table 1: Original TypeDM expectations for *check* and their compositional updates obtained with f = **PRODUCT**

SUM
For each tuple $\langle\langle n_i, \texttt{obj}, v\rangle, \sigma_i\rangle \in EX_{PA}(v)$, $\langle\langle n_i, \texttt{obj}, v\rangle, \sigma_u\rangle \in EX_{PA}(\langle n_{AG}, v\rangle)$, and

$$\sigma_u = \begin{cases} \sigma_i + \sigma_j & \text{if } \langle\langle n_{AG}, \texttt{verb}, n_j\rangle, \sigma_j\rangle \\ & \in EX(n_{AG}) \text{ and } n_i = n_j \\ \sigma_i & \text{otherwise} \end{cases} \quad (3)$$

PRODUCT
For each tuple $\langle\langle n_i, \texttt{obj}, v\rangle, \sigma_i\rangle \in EX_{PA}(v)$, $\langle\langle n_i, \texttt{obj}, v\rangle, \sigma_u\rangle \in EX_{PA}(\langle n_{AG}, v\rangle)$, and

$$\sigma_u = \begin{cases} \sigma_i * \sigma_j & \text{if } \langle\langle n_{AG}, \texttt{verb}, n_j\rangle, \sigma_j\rangle \\ & \in EX(n_{AG}) \text{ and } n_i = n_j \\ 0 & \text{otherwise} \end{cases} \quad (4)$$

The idea underlying both types of tensor updating functions is that the verb expectations about its likely patients are modified with the score of the tuples representing objects that are typical patients of events performed by the agent noun. With **SUM**, expectation composition is a linear function of the score of the tuples in $EX_{PA}(v)$ and in $EX(n_{AG})$: $EX_{PA}(\langle n_{AG}, v\rangle)$ contains all the tuples belonging to $EX_{PA}(v)$, but their score is added to the score of the tuples in $EX(n_{AG})$ sharing the same object noun. With the **PRODUCT** function, the updated expectations only include the tuples in $EX_{PA}(v)$ sharing the same objects with a tuple in $EX(n_{AG})$. The score of these tuples is the product of the original tuple score, while the score of the other tuples in $EX_{PA}(v)$ is set to 0.

Table 1 reports a sample output of the application of ECU to the TypeDM tensor. The left column contains the objects of the top-scoring tuples of $EX_{PA}(check)$ in the original TypeDM tensor (ordered by decreasing values of σ). The central column contains the top-scoring nouns in $EX_{PA}(\langle journalist, check\rangle)$, compositionally derived by updating $EX_{PA}(check)$ with $EX(journalist)$: the nouns are ordered by decreasing value of σ modified according to the **PRODUCT** composition function. We can notice that the updated verb argument expectations include nouns consistent with what journalists typically check. The right column instead contains the top-scoring nouns in $EX_{PA}(\langle mechanic, check\rangle)$, derived from updating $EX_{PA}(check)$ with $EX(mechanic)$: the composition function is still the **PRODUCT**. The difference with the central column is striking: the top-scoring nouns in the updated verb argument expectations are now related to what mechanics typically check.

5 Experiments and evaluation

The ECU model for the compositional update of verb-argument expectations has been evaluated by measuring the thematic fit between an agent-verb pair ($\langle n_{AG}, v\rangle$) and a patient noun argument (n_{PA}) of the same verb. Thematic fit is computed with the verb expectations in $EX_{PA}(\langle n_{AG}, v\rangle)$, which in turned have been obtained by composing $EX(n_{AG})$ and $EX_{PA}(v)$ with either of the two functions described in section 4. In the following subsections, we illustrate the data sets used for the experiments, the procedure to compute the compositional thematic fit in TypeDM, and the results of the experiments.

5.1 Data sets

Two data sets of agent-verb-patient triples from Bicknell et al. (2010) have been used to test ECU:

- **bicknell.64** - 64 test triples used in the self-paced reading and ERP experiments in Bicknell et al. (2010);
- **bicknell.100** - 100 test triples, a superset of bicknell.64.

Triples are organized in pairs, each sharing the same verb, but differing for the agent and patient nouns:

- *journalist*$_{AG}$ - *check* - *spelling*$_{PA}$
- *mechanic*$_{AG}$ - *check* - *brake*$_{PA}$

Patients in each triple were produced by 47 subjects as the prototypical (*congruent*) arguments of the verbs, given a certain agent. The patient noun in one triple is *incongruent* for the other triple with the same verb: e.g., *brake* is the incongruent patient for the *mechanic*$_{AG}$ - *check* pair. The bicknell.100 dataset contains all the triples produced in the original norming study. The bicknell.64 data set is a subset of the normed triples selected by Bicknell et al. (2010) after removing test items that were potentially problematic for the behavioral experiments.

5.2 Procedure

The thematic fit of a noun n_{PA} as the patient of $\langle n_{AG}, v\rangle$ is measured with the cosine between the vector of n_{PA} in the TypeDM $W_1{\times}LW_2$ space and the "prototype" vector in the same space built with the vectors of the top-k expected objects belonging to $EX(n_{AG}, v)$. This is an extension of the approach to selectional preferences modeling presented in Baroni and Lenci (2010) (in turn inspired to Erk 2007). These are the steps used to compute the compositional thematic fit in the TypeDM $W_1{\times}LW_2$ space:

1. we select a set of k of prototypical patient nouns n_{PA} for $\langle n_{AG}, v\rangle$ (in the reported experiments we set $k = 20$). The selected nouns are the n_i in the k tuples $\langle\langle n_i, \texttt{obj}, v\rangle, \sigma_u\rangle \in EX_{PA}(\langle n_{AG}, v\rangle)$ with the highest score σ. The patient nouns in the datasets are excluded;

2. the vectors in the $W_1{\times}LW_2$ TypeDM space of the selected nouns are normalized and summed. The result is a centroid vector representing an abstract "patient prototype vector" for $\langle n_{AG}, v\rangle$;

3. for each n_{AG} - v - n_{PA} test triple (e.g., *journalist*$_{AG}$ - *check* - *spelling*$_{PA}$), we measure i.) the cosine between n_{PA} and the "patient prototype vector" for the congruent $\langle n_{AG}, v\rangle$ pair, (e.g., *journalist*$_{AG}$ - *check*) and ii.) the cosine between n_{PA} and the "patient prototype vector" for the incongruent $\langle n_{AG}, v\rangle$ pair, belonging to the other triple with the same verb v (e.g., *mechanic*$_{AG}$ - *check*).

For each test triple, we score a "hit" if n_{PA} has a higher thematic fit (i.e., cosine) with the congruent $\langle n_{AG}, v\rangle$ pair, than with the incongruent one. For instance, if $cosine(\langle journalist, check\rangle, spelling) > cosine(\langle mechanic, check\rangle, spelling)$, we score a "hit", otherwise we score a "fail".

5.3 Results

Experiments to model the verb-argument compositional thematic fit have been carried out with the two ECU functions, **SUM** and **PRODUCT**, each tested on both datasets. Model performance has been evaluated with "hit" accuracy, i.e. the percentage of "hits" scored on each data set. As a baseline, we have simply adopted the random accuracy. The results of the ECU models are reported in table 2.

We can notice that when the verb-argument expectations are compositionally updated with the **PRODUCT** function, the model is able to significantly outperform the baseline accuracy with both data sets. Conversely, **SUM** is never able to go beyond the baseline. This is remindful of the results reported by Erk and Padó (2008) and Mitchell and Lapata (2010), in which multiplicative vector composition achieves better performance in the (verb in context or phrase) similarity tasks than (at least simple) additive functions. In fact, the advantage of the multiplicative function is that it allows the composition process to highlight the dimensions shared by the vectors of the component words, thereby emphasizing context effects. Something similar can be argued to explain the results of the current experiments. With **PRODUCT** the expectations of $EX_{PA}(\langle n_{AG}, v\rangle)$ are a non-linear function of the expectations about patient nouns shared by v and n_{AG}. Therefore, the objects that are likely to be checked by a mechanic depend on the things that are both typical patients of checking events and typical patients of actions performed by a mechanic. This results in a stronger thematic fit in the congruent condition than in the incongruent one.

We also carried out experiments to investigate whether the choice of the parameter k (the number of nouns selected to build the "prototype patient vector") affects the model performance. However, we obtained no significant difference with respect to the values reported in table 2.

data set	ECU function	accuracy	p-value
bicknell.64	SUM	40.62%	
bicknell.64	PRODUCT	84.37%	3.798e-08 ***
bicknell.100	SUM	37.5%	
bicknell.100	PRODUCT	73%	4.225e-06 ***
baseline		50%	

Table 2: Results of the thematic fit experiments (p-values computed with a χ^2 test).

6 Conclusions and further directions of research

Psycholinguistic evidence has proved that verb argument thematic fit is highly context-sensitive. In fact, subjects' sensitivity to the likelihood of a noun as a verb argument strongly depends on the nouns filling other arguments of the same verb. These data hint at a dynamic process underlying verb argument expectation and thematic fit computation, resulting from the compositional integration of the verb expectations with those activated by its arguments. In this paper, we have presented ECU, a distributional semantic model for the compositional update of verb argument expectations. ECU has been applied to Distributional Memory, a state-of-the-art Distributional Semantic Model, whose core tensor of corpus-derived tuples is particularly suited to represent word expectations. ECU has been tested sucesfully in an experiment to measure the thematic fit between an agent-verb pair ($\langle n_{AG}, v \rangle$) and a patient noun argument (n_{PA}) of the same verb, with the data set used in the psycholinguistic experiments reported in Bicknell et al. (2010). The good results we have obtained prove that DSMs can provide interesting computational models of the compositional update of thematic fit. Of course, other factors besides verb-argument knowledge may also contribute to the context-sensitive nature of thematic fit. However, it is worth noticing that one of the hypotheses advanced by Bicknell et al. (2010) to explain their experimental results is indeed that subjects use their knowledge of statistical linguistic regularities. This is exactly the type of knowledge that is represented in the Distributional Memory tensor structure and is exploited by ECU.

Starting from the experimental results in Bicknell et al. (2010) on sentence on-line processing, in this paper we have addressed the issue of how the agent of a verb modulates the subjects' expectations about its patients. On the other hand, there is broad evidence that the meaning of a verb is predominantly modulated by its object. This suggests that ECU should also be applied to model how the preferences about the agent argument are determined by the choice of the verb object. We leave this issue for future research.

Besides being a computational model for thematic fit, we also claim that the ECU approach has a more general relevance for the issue of how to address compositionality in DSMs. In fact, let us assume that part of the semantic content of a word consists of expectations about likely co-occurring words, which in turn can be modeled with subsets of a distributional tuple tensor. We can therefore claim that (at least part of) the effect of the semantic composition of words is to update their expectations about other co-occurring words, like ECU does. We have seen here that this hypothesis finds a nice confirmation with verb-argument composition. We believe that an interesting empirical question is to investigate to what extent this hypothesis can be generalized to other cases of compositionality.

In the future, we also plan to experiment with other types of expectation composition functions. Moreover we will extend the ECU model to tackle context-sensitive effects in the thematic fit with respect to other types of verb argument relations, besides agent and patient ones. In fact, Matsuki et al. (submitted) have reported that patient and instrument verb arguments show interdependency effects similar to the ones between agents and patients that we have addressed in this paper.

Acknowledgments

I am very grateful to Ken McRae for providing the data set used in this paper. I also thank Marco Baroni - the co-author of Distributional Memory - and the two anonymous reviewers for their helpful comments. The usual disclaimers apply.

References

Marco Baroni and Alessandro Lenci. 2010. Distributional Memory : A general framework for corpus-based semantics. *Computational Linguistics*, 36(4): 673–721.

Klinton Bicknell, Jeffrey L. Elman, Mary Hare, Ken McRae, and Marta Kutas. 2010. Effects of event knowledge in processing verbal arguments. *Journal of Memory and Language*, 63(4): 489–505.

Stephen Clark and Stephen Pulman. 2007. Combining symbolic and distributional models of meaning. In *Proceedings of the AAAI Spring Symposium on Quantum Interaction*: 52–55.

Jeffrey L. Elman. 2009. On the meaning of words and dinosaur bones: Lexical knowledge without a lexicon. *Cognitive Science*, 33(4): 547–582.

Katrin Erk. 2007. A simple, similarity-based model for selectional preferences. In *Proceedings of ACL*: 216–223.

Katrin Erk and Sebastian Padó. 2008. A structured vector space model for word meaning in context. In *Proceedings of EMNLP 08*: 897–906.

Katrin Erk, Sebastian Padó, and Ulrike Padó. 2010. A flexible, corpus-driven model of regular and inverse selectional preferences. *Computational Linguistics*, 36(4): 723–763.

Stefan Evert. 2005. *The Statistics of Word Cooccurrences*. Ph.D. dissertation, Stuttgart University.

Mary Hare, Michael Jones, Caroline Thomson, Sarah Kelly,and Ken McRae. 2009. Activating event knowledge. *Cognition*, 111(2): 151–167.

Yuki Kamide, Gerry T.M. Altmann, and Sarah L. Haywood. 2003. The time-course of prediction in incremental sentence processing: Evidence from anticipatory eye movements. *Journal of Memory and Language*, 49: 133–156.

Walter Kintsch. 2001. Predication. *Cognitive Science*, 25(2): 173–202.

Tamara Kolda and Brett Bader. 2009. Tensor decompositions and applications. *SIAM Review*, 51(3): 455–500.

Thomas Landauer and Susan Dumais. 1997. A solution to Plato's problem: The latent semantic analysis. theory of acquisition, induction, and representation of knowledge. *Psychological Review*, 104(2): 1–31.

Dekang Lin 1998. Automatic retrieval and clustering of similar words. In *Proceedings of COLING-ACL*: 768–774.

Kazunaga Matsuki, Tracy Chow, Mary Hare, Jeffrey L. Elman, Christoph Scheepers, and Ken McRae. submitted for publication. Event-based plausibility immediately influences on-line language comprehension

Ken McRae, Michael J. Spivey-Knowlton, and Michael K.Tanenhaus. 1998. Modeling the influence of thematic fit (and other constraints) in on-line sentence comprehension *Journal of Memory and Language*, 38: 283–312.

Ken McRae, Mary Hare, Jeffrey L. Elman, and Todd Ferretti. 2005. A basis for generating expectancies for verbs from nouns *Memory & Cognition*, 33(7): 1174–1184.

George Miller and Walter Charles. 1991. Contextual correlates of semantic similarity *Language and Cognitive Processes*, 6: 1–28.

Jeff Mitchell and Mirella Lapata. 2010. Composition in distributional models of semantics. *Cognitive Science*, 34(8): 1388–1429.

Sebastian Padó and Mirella Lapata. 2007. Dependency-based construction of semantic space models. *Computational Linguistics*, 33(2): 161–199.

Magnus Sahlgren. 2006. *The Word-Space Model*. Ph.D. dissertation, Stockholm University.

Peter D. Turney. 2006. Similarity of semantic relations. *Computational Linguistics*, 32(3): 379–416.

Peter D. Turney. 2007. Empirical evaluation of four tensor decomposition algorithms. *Technical Report ERB-1152, NRC.*

Peter D. Turney, Patrick Pantel. 2010. From frequency to meaning : Vector space models of semantics. *Journal of Artificial Intelligence Research*, 37: 141–188.

Dominic Widdows. 2008. Semantic vector products: Some initial investigations. In *Proceedings of the Second AAAI Symposium on Quantum Interaction*: 1–8.

WM load influences the interpretation of referring expressions

Jacolien van Rij
University of Groningen
J.C.van.Rij@rug.nl

Hedderik van Rijn
University of Groningen
D.H.van.Rijn@rug.nl

Petra Hendriks
University of Groningen
P.Hendriks@rug.nl

Abstract

This paper presents a study of the effect of working memory load on the interpretation of pronouns in different discourse contexts: stories with and without a topic shift. We present a computational model (in ACT-R, Anderson, 2007) to explain how referring subjects are used and interpreted. We furthermore report on an experiment that tests predictions that follow from simulations. The results of the experiment support the model predictions that WM load only affects the interpretation of pronouns in stories with a topic shift, but not in stories without a topic shift.

1 Introduction

How do listeners interpret a potentially ambiguous referring expression? To describe a particular event, object or character, often different referring expressions can be used. Some referring expressions are more specific than others. For example, a proper name such as 'Eric' is more specific than the personal pronoun 'he', which can refer to any of the male characters in a given linguistic context.

Generally, pronouns are used and interpreted as referring to the most salient character or object (the *topic*) in the linguistic context (a.o., Ariel, 1990; Gundel, Hedberg, & Zacharski, 1993). In contrast, full noun phrases or proper names are used to introduce new characters or to refer to less salient characters. Different factors have been found to affect the saliency of characters or objects in the linguistic context (see Arnold, 1998, for a review), among others the grammatical role. The subject of the previous sentence is likely to be the current topic (Grosz, Weinstein, & Joshi, 1995). As a result, listeners will often interpret a pronoun as referring to the previous subject (a.o., McDonald & MacWhinney, 1995; Stevenson, Crawley, & Kleinman, 1994).

However, for children up to the age of 7, the grammatical role seems to be a less important cue than for adults. Manipulating the discourse structure, Koster and colleagues showed that children interpret subject pronouns in a different way than adults do (Koster, Hoeks, & Hendriks, in press). They presented adults and children with prerecorded short stories about two characters of the same gender. Two types of stories were tested, stories with and without a topic shift. In the stories with topic shift the topic shifted halfway by changing the grammatical role of the characters (see Table 1): the second character becomes the subject of next sentences, rather than the first character. In all stories the final sentence started with a potentially ambiguous pronoun ('he' or 'she').

Story with topic shift (+TS)	
1.	Eric/gaat/voetballen/in de sporthal. 'Eric is going to play soccer in the sports hall.'
2.	Philip/vraagt/Eric/om mee te rijden/naar de training. 'Philip asks Eric to carpool to the training.'
3.	Philip/haalt/Eric/na het eten/met de auto op. 'Philip picks up Eric after dinner by car.'
4.	Hij/voetbalt/al twintig jaar. 'He has played soccer for twenty years.'
Story without topic shift (-TS)	
1.	Eric/gaat/voetballen/in de sporthal. 'Eric is going to play soccer in the sports hall.'
2.	Eric/vraagt/Philip/om mee te rijden/naar de training. 'Eric asks Philip to carpool to the training.'
3.	Eric/haalt/Philip/na het eten/met de auto op. 'Eric picks up Philip after dinner by car.'
4.	Hij/voetbalt/al twintig jaar. 'He has played soccer for twenty years.'
Q	Wie voetbalt al twintig jaar? 'Who has played soccer for twenty years?'

Table 1: Example of the Dutch sentences (and the English translations) of a story with and without topic shift.

Adult listeners interpreted this pronoun as referring to the second character in stories with a topic shift, and as referring to the first character in stories without a topic shift. Children, on the other hand, did not distinguish between these two types of stories: they showed a small preference for the first character as the referent of the pronoun. Koster et al. found that children with a higher auditory working memory capacity performed more adult-like, which raises the question whether limited WM capacity causes decreased performance.

We have implemented a cognitive model to investigate the effect of WM load on the interpretation of subject pronouns in discourse. To test the prediction following from our model that WM load can decrease adults' comprehension of stories with a topic shift, we also performed an experiment.

2 Modeling pronoun interpretation

We have implemented a cognitive model within the cognitive architecture ACT-R (Anderson, 2007) that can simulate both the use and interpretation of referring subjects (Van Rij, Van Rijn, & Hendriks, submitted). Here we focus on the interpretation of subject pronouns.

2.1 Computational simulation

To simulate the results of Koster et al. (in press), the model is presented with stories of 6 sentences, with or without a topic shift. The stories are provided to the model word by word. During on-line sentence processing the model builds a (simplified) representation of the preceding discourse: every character in the story is represented in the declarative memory. Each representation (referred to as "chunk") has a certain amount of activation that reflects the saliency of the character in the current discourse. The model determines the referent of the potentially ambiguous pronoun in the final sentence, by selecting the chunk with the highest level of activation as the current discourse topic and as the referent of the pronoun.

Explaining children's and adults' performance

In ACT-R, the activation of chunks reflects the chunk's history, because activation is dependent on the frequency of use (the more frequently used, the higher the activation) and the recency of the last retrieval (the more recent the last retrieval, the higher the activation). The activation of chunks decays with time, but is increased when the chunk is retrieved. In addition to this base-level activation, spreading activation can temporarily boost the activation of a chunk in a particular context, reflecting the usefulness of that chunk in that context[1]. Chunks that are currently being processed spread activation to other, connected chunks in declarative memory. As the amount of spreading activation determines the ability to maintain goal-relevant information, differences in spreading activation account for individual differences in working memory capacity (Daily, Lovett, & Reder, 2001). In our model, the subject of the previous sentence spreads activation to all discourse elements associated with it.

To explain the difference between children's and adults' interpretation of subject pronouns, we manipulated the amount of spreading-activation from the previous subject. If the amount of spreading activation is high, the chunk representing the subject spreads a large amount of activation and discourse elements that are associated with the subject become more activated in comparison with the other discourse elements. As a result, the model will retrieve the subject of the previous sentence as the current discourse topic. However, if the subject spreads a small amount of activation, reflecting a low WM capacity, then there will be no effect on the discourse elements associated with the subject. In that case, the effects of frequency and recency will be the main determinants of which referent is retrieved.

Figure 1 shows the effect of WM capacity (i.e., the amount of spreading activation) on the activation of the two referents in the stories that were provided to the model. The second character, referent 'b', is introduced in the third sentence. The +TS condition starts to differ from the – TS condition in sentence 4, where the second character be-

[1] In ACT-R the activation of chunk i is defined by: $A_i = \ln\left(\sum_{k=1}^{n} t_k^{-0.5}\right) + \sum_{j=1}^{m} W_j S_{ji} + \varepsilon_i$, with n being the number of presentations of chunk i, and t_k the time since the kth presentation, m the number of chunks that are connected with chunk i, W_j the amount of activation that is spread from chunk j, S_{ji} the strength of association between j and i, and ε_i noise.
The activation of a chunk determines the time it takes to retrieve it from declarative memory: $T = e^{-A_i}$.

comes the subject in the +TS stories but not the –TS stories (cf. Koster et al., in press). With a high WM capacity, the model selects the subject of the previous sentence as the referent of the pronoun in sentence 6, because this discourse element clearly has the highest activation (Figure 1, right). However, with a low WM capacity, the model will show a much-reduced preference for the second character as the referent of the pronoun, and often chooses the first character. Similarly to children's performance, the models' interpretation of pronouns is not affected by grammatical role (Figure 1, left).

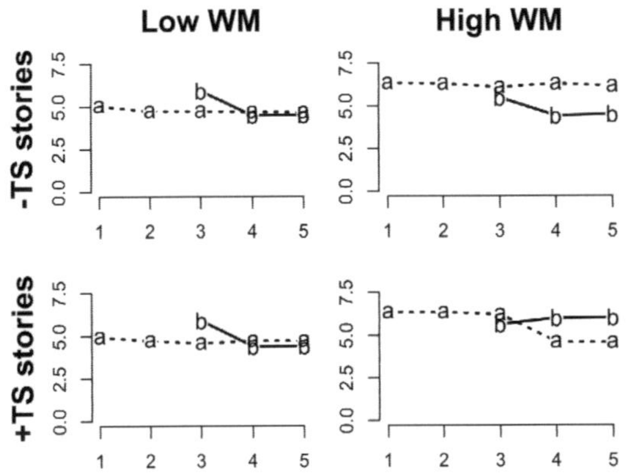

Figure 1. Mean levels of activation of the first character (a) and the second character (b) in stories with (+TS) and without (-TS) a topic shift, measured at the end of each of 5 sentences (x-axis). In sentence 6, the model selects the character with the highest activation as the referent of the pronoun.

Prediction of the model

On the basis of these simulations we propose that an individual's WM capacity determines how much the grammatical structure of the previous sentence plays a role in resolving a potentially ambiguous subject pronoun. If this hypothesis is correct, we expect that adults show difficulties in detecting a topic shift when their WM is taxed by having to perform a memory task in parallel. This prediction follows directly from the ACT-R model: goal-relevant information spreads a proportion of the total spreading activation to other chunks in the declarative memory. If the number of sources from which activation is spread increases, the amount of spreading activation that is received by individual chunks decreases. In a high WM load situation, more information needs to be maintained in an activated state and as a result, the subject of the previous sentence spreads less activation to the discourse elements associated with the subject. Therefore, the model predicts that adult listeners or readers show more child-like performance in high WM load conditions: they will more often select the first character as the current discourse topic. In addition, the model predicts that it will take more time to retrieve a discourse element in a high WM load condition, because the retrieval time is determined by the level of activation (the lower the activation, the longer it takes to retrieve the information).

3 Experiment

We performed a dual-task experiment to test our prediction that adult listeners will show difficulties with the comprehension of a topic shift if they have less WM capacity available. To manipulate WM load, participants were asked to perform a combined task: memorizing a sequence of digits for later recall and performing a moving-window task (Just, Carpenter, & Woolley, 1982).

3.1 Methods

Digit task

At the start of each trial, participants were presented with a sequence of either three or six digits (low and high WM load conditions) that they had to memorize. Digits were shown for 1 second each in the center of a computer screen. After completing the moving-window task, the participants recalled the memorized digits. The digits were pseudo-randomly chosen from 1 to 9, while ensuring that not all the digits were the same.

Moving-window task

After the presentation of the digits, the moving-window task started. In this task, participants had to read stories of four sentences each (see Table 1), followed by a comprehension question. The sentences were presented one by one and were subdivided into smaller word clusters (indicated by dashes in Table 1). Using a typical moving-window paradigm (Just et al., 1982), only the letters of one single word cluster were visible at a time. All other letters were replaced by a dot. By pressing a button, the participant could move the window to the next word cluster. After reading the four-sentence story in this way, a question was presented in the center of the screen, and two answer alternatives were presented in the bottom corners of the screen. Participants had to press the corresponding button to answer the question. After answering the question, they had to type in the digits that were presented at the beginning of the trial.

At the end of each trial, participants only received feedback on the digit task to ensure sufficient focus on the WM task. We collected different measures per trial: the reading times per region, accuracy and reaction times for the questions and the number of errors in reproducing the digits.

Design

Stories. In every story two characters of the same gender played a role, of which the first names started with a different letter. All names consisted of 4-8 characters, and two syllables. Importantly, the final sentence started with a subject pronoun *hij* ('he') or *zij* ('she') that was ambiguous: the pronoun could refer to both characters, so that the only clue to the interpretation of the pronouns was the structure of the story.

We designed two variants of every test story (see Table 1), in which we manipulated whether there was a shift of topic. The topic shift is realized by making the second character ('Philip') the subject of the second sentence. If there was no topic shift, we expected participants to prefer the firstly introduced character as the referent of the ambiguous pronoun, but if there was a topic shift, we expected participants to prefer the second character. At the end of every test story a question was presented to elicit the preferred interpretation of the ambiguous pronoun.

Lists. The presented materials were part of a larger experiment, in which we additionally tested another two variants of every story. In total, 64 test stories were designed in four different variants. Four lists of 64 test stories were constructed, so that every list received a different variant of the test stories and thus contained 16 test stories per condition. Besides the test stories, the lists also contained 128 filler items (the same for all lists), so that the lists consisted of 192 items in total. The filler stories had the same structure as the test stories, so 64 filler stories per condition. The filler stories were followed by a question about the first or second sentence of the story to avoid reading strategies and to mask the experimental manipulations. Half of the filler questions asked about one of the characters, the other half asked about a non-referent (what- or where-question). Note that in contrast to the test questions, that were designed to elicit an interpretational preference, filler questions were not ambiguous and could be unambiguously scored as right or wrong.

Here, we report on 2 times 32 test items, and the 64 filler items with the same two discourse structures. One test story (both variants) was removed from the data, because of a technical problem during presentation.

Procedure

Participants were randomly assigned to one of the four lists. The experiment consisted of two blocks: a low WM load block (3 digits) and a high WM load block (6 digits). The order of blocks was counterbalanced; within blocks the items were randomly distributed. Participants first received instructions, followed by a practice trial suited for the current WM load condition. Between the two blocks participants received instructions for the other digit task.

Participants

Sixty-two first-year psychology students (17 men, 40 women; mean age 20) participated in the experiment in exchange for course credits. Five participants could not complete the experiment because of technical problems. Another 5 participants were excluded from data analysis, because they answered less than 75% of the filler questions correctly in the low WM load condition, and/or performed at chance level in one of the two types of filler questions. Data of 52 participants (15 men, 37 women) was used for the statistical analyses.

3.2 Results

In this section we first discuss the performance on the digit tasks, followed by the off-line story comprehension results, i.e., answers on the questions and the related reaction times, and the self-paced reading data.

Digit task results

Participants made more errors on the digit-task in the high WM load condition than in the low WM load condition (percentage correct trials: 3-digits=77.2%, 6-digits=52.0%, mean errors per trial: 3-digits=0.343, 6-digits=0.852), indicating that the 6-digit condition was indeed more difficult. We did not find any effect of story condition on the number of errors in the digit task or on the percentages correct trials.

Off-line results

Answers. Figure 2 shows the preference for either the first or second character as the referent of the ambiguous pronoun at the end of the test stories.

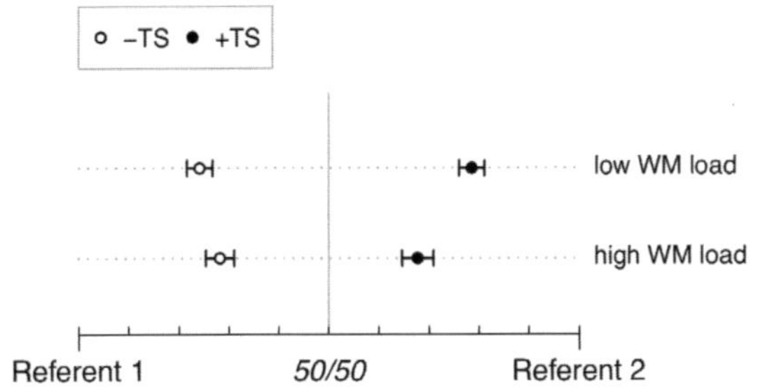

Figure 2: Referent preference for stories without (-TS) and with (+TS) topic shift (± SE), plotted separately for both WM load conditions.

Figure 2 shows that participants were sensitive to the topic-shift manipulation. In both WM load conditions, the expected referent was preferred (i.e., Referent 1 in –TS, and Referent 2 in +TS).

We examined the effects of *Topic shift*, *WM load*, and *Trial position*, the position of the trial in the experiment, on the choice for the first character (yes or no) using logistic mixed-effects models (cf. Baayen, 2008). More complex models that included additional predictors did not show qualitatively different effects. In all the presented models, participant and item (i.e., all variants of a story were labeled as the same item) were included as crossed-random effects.

We compared different models using a stepwise variable deletion procedure, starting with the complete interaction model. For every model comparison, we examined whether the difference in -2 log likelihood is significant, given the difference in degrees of freedom using the chi-square distribution. If this difference is significant, the reduced model has a significantly lower goodness-of-fit, indicating that the deletion of the variable or interaction is not justified. As removing the 3-way interaction did not show a significant difference with the complete interaction model, we selected the model without this three-way interaction as the baseline (or full model). Figure 3 summarizes the model comparisons performed to investigate whether WM load and the type of story affect the choice for the first character (left graph). All two-way interactions (*Topic shift* by *Trial position*, *Trial position* by *WM load*, and importantly *Topic shift* by *WM load*) needed to be included in the statistical model.

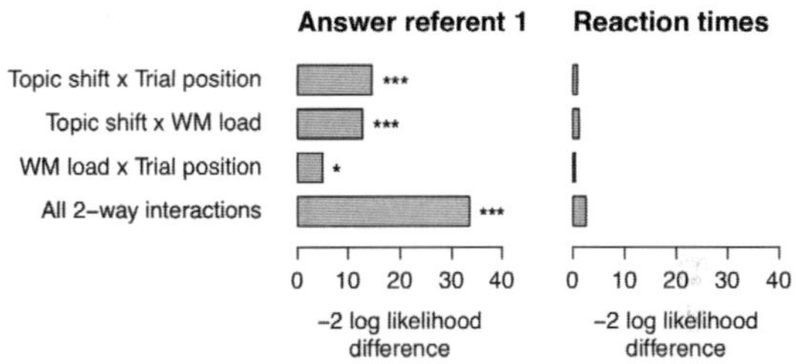

Figure 3. Explained variance in -2 log likelihood of interactions compared to a full model (see text). The statistical significance is calculated with a χ^2-test (with 1,1,1, or 3 degrees of freedom respectively). ('*' p<.05, '**' p<.01, '***' p<.001)

The best model showed that, in stories with topic shift (+TS), the first character was selected more often in the high WM load condition than in the low WM load condition (β=0.844, z=3.57; p<.001), in line with the assumption that decreasing working memory capacity reduces pronoun resolution performance. The model showed no general effect of WM load (β=0.308, z=1.10; p>.1). Thus, no differential effect for WM load condition was found for the condition without topic shift. In addition, participants were more likely to select the first character in stories with a topic shift as the experiment progressed (β=0.008, z=3.81; p<.001), but in the high WM load condition this effect was reduced (β=-0.005, z=-2.28; p=.023).

Reaction times. In the same way as we analyzed the choice of referent, we analyzed the log-transformed reaction times after excluding the short outliers (<= 50ms; less than 1% of the data). However, we did not find any significant interaction (see Figure 3). The best fitting model, which included the main effects, but no interactions, only showed a significant contribution of *Trial position*: Participants became faster in answering during the experiment (β=-0.002, t=-5.97; p<.001).

To summarize, we found that WM load affects the comprehension of stories with a topic shift, but not the stories without a topic shift: participants more often select the first character as the referent of the ambiguous pronoun in the high WM load condition. However, we did not find a difference in reaction times between the two types of stories, suggesting that the questions after stories with a topic shift are not more difficult to answer. These findings support our prediction that adults will show difficulties in processing a topic shift if they experience more WM load.

3.3 Reading time data

Before analyzing the reading time data we removed missing data (2%), short outliers (smaller than 50 ms, 19%) and used a log-transform to reduce the effect of the long outliers (cf. Baayen & Milin, 2010). The relatively large amount of short outliers was caused by a technical problem. As the outliers were equally distributed over the story conditions and the WM load conditions ($\chi^2(1)$=0.925, p>.1), it is unlikely that this influences our results in qualitative ways.

We compared linear mixed-effects models in the same way as before to test the effects of *Topic shift*, *WM load*, and *Trial position* for all moving-window regions on the log-transformed reading times. More complex models that included additional predictors did not show qualitatively different effects. We found no significant 3-way or 2-way interactions in the analyzed regions that needed to be included in the statistical model. We therefore only report on the main-effects model.

Sentence 1. The first sentence of the story is identical in both variants of the stories (-TS and +TS). Figure 4 displays reading times of the first three regions for the two working memory conditions, collapsed over the two story types. The main-effects model showed an effect of *Trial position* (participants read faster as the experiment progressed, β=-0.004, t=-13.00; p<.001), an effect of *WM load* (increased reading time in high WM condition, β=0.245, t=9.44; p<.001), but no effect of *Topic shift* (β=0.012, t=0.48; p>.1). Similar results were found for region 2.

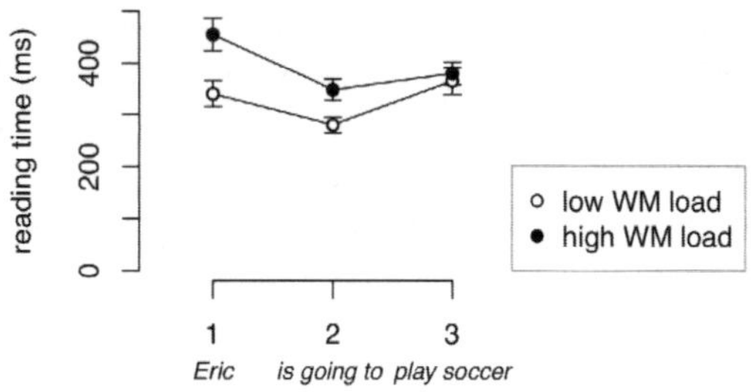

Figure 4. Reading times (raw data) of the first three regions of sentence 1 (±SE). (English translation of an example sentence from Table 1)

Sentence 2. In the stories with a topic shift (+TS), the topic shift is initiated in the second sentence, by introducing a new character in subject position. Therefore, we would expect to see differences in reading times between the two story types. In addition, we expected to find an interaction between *WM load* and *Topic shift*, as an early measure of the effect of *WM load* on the off-line data: in the high WM load condition, the previous subject has less influence, therefore we would expect the difference in reading times to be reduced. However, we did not find any significant interaction.

Figure 5 shows the normalized effects of regions 1-4 of the second sentence (normalized by the first region). For region 1, the main effects model revealed that participants became faster over the course of the experiment (β=-0.004, t=-12.21; p<.001). However, *Topic shift* (β=0.024, t=0.83; p>.1) and *WM load* (β=-0.010, t=-0.33; p>.1) did not contribute to the fit of the data.

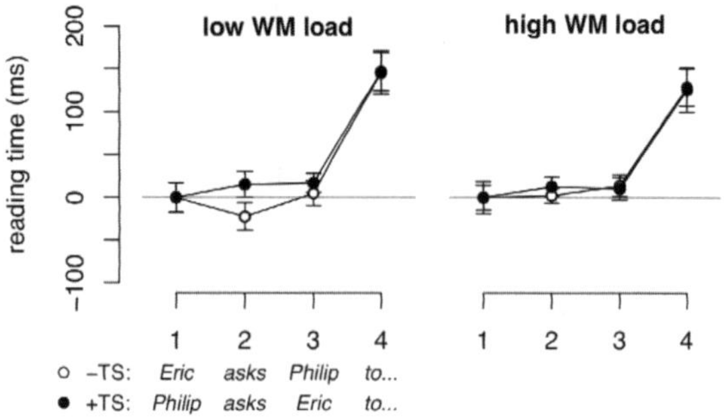

Figure 5. Normalized reading times (difference with region 1) of the first four regions of sentence 2 (±SE). (English translations of example sentences from Table 1)

For analyzing the reading times of region 2 we removed possible confounding effects at the beginning of the sentence, such as the effect of *Trial position*, by taking the difference in reading time between the second and first region.[2] The main-effects model for analyzing region 2 without *Trial position* showed a significant increase in reading time for the stories with a topic shift in comparison with the stories without a topic shift (β=0.085, t=2.79; p=0.004), indicating that participants expected to see the subject of the previous sentence instead of a new referent. However, there was no significant contribution of *WM load*. Analyzing the remaining regions of sentence 2 did not show an effect of *Topic shift* or *WM load*. In sentences 3 and 4, we did not find significant effects of *Topic shift* or *WM load*, nor an interaction between these two factors.

To summarize, we found an effect of *WM load* in the first sentence and an effect of *Topic shift* in the second sentence. The longer reading times on the first sentence in the high WM load condition probably reflect some final rehearsing of the digits. However, after this first sentence, no effect of WM load is found.

4 Discussion

We predicted, on the basis of our cognitive model, that adults will show more difficulties in processing a topic shift in higher WM load conditions. We performed a dual-task experiment to investigate this prediction. We hypothesized that as WM load increased, adult readers would show a significant decrease in their preferences for the second character as the referent of a pronoun in the stories with a topic shift. In addition, we expected an increase in reading times in stories with a topic shift as a result of the topic shift, but we expected that this increase would diminish in the high WM load condition.

The off-line data support the prediction of the model: participants selected the first character as the referent of the ambiguous pronoun significantly more often in the high WM load condition. No differences in reaction times were found, suggesting that the comprehension questions were similarly difficult to answer for the two types of stories.

With respect to the reading times, we found an increase in reading times immediately after presenting a new referent in subject position, which indicates that readers expected to see the subject of the previous sentence instead of a new referent. However, we did not measure a significant interaction between WM load and type of story. Different explanations are possible for why this interaction did not reach significance, contrary to our expectations. It could be that WM load does not affect the processing of the sentence, but only affects the updating of the discourse representation with new sentence information. In that case, sentence wrap-up effects could have masked the effects of WM load. An alternative explanation is that the moving-window task is not suited to detect the effect of WM load. It is reasonable to assume that the effect of WM load on the topic shift is spread out over different regions, and is thus more difficult to detect. ERP studies provide support for this explanation, because for unexpected noun phrases readers show an ERP effect 300-600 ms after the determiner of the unexpected noun phrase (Otten & Van Berkum, 2009), which is much longer than it took participants in our experiment to read one region.

The link between WM capacity and language processing is not new. For example, within the context of ACT-R, Lewis and Vasishth (2005) have explained difficulties in sentence processing, which have been attributed to WM load, by ACT-R's fluctuating activation and similarity-based interference in the retrieval of chunks. The fluctuating activation of chunks also plays a role in our account of the interpretation of pronouns in discourse. This implementation is consistent with the memory account of Foraker and McElree (2007) that characterizes the prominence of discourse elements as differences in strength of their representations in memory (in contrast with a.o. Grosz et al., 1995; Gundel et al., 1993). Our implementation is similar to the account of Reitter, Keller and Moore (2011), who use ACT-R's spreading activation mechanism to explain short-term priming of syntactical structures. In addition, to explain the difference between children's and adults' performance, we implemented the WM theory of Daily, Lovett, and Reder (2001), who manipulated the amount of spreading activation to account for

[2] Analysis of the absolute reading times revealed the same effects. The reading times of region 1 were included in the analysis of the absolute reading times.

individual differences in working memory capacity on digit span tasks.

Our account is also in line with previously proposed computational models in different frameworks that explain the relation between WM capacity and language processing, such as CC READER (Just & Carpenter, 1992), or 4CAPS (Just & Varma, 2007). In these models, WM capacity is implemented as a limited amount of activation that is used for storage of intermediate results and for computation. The amount of activation is different for individuals. If more capacity is required for processing or storage than is available, this will result in longer processing times or retrieval errors. On the basis of this theory, Daneman and Carpenter (1980) predicted longer reading times on discourse pronouns for readers with a low WM capacity. In contrast, MacDonald and Christiansen (2002) have argued against the limited capacity theory of Just and Carpenter: they propose instead that differences in WM capacity are differences in skill that arise from variations in exposure to the language, and biological differences. However, our data that shows that WM load can affect the interpretation of stories with a topic shift, is difficult to explain in terms of language skills.

To conclude, on the basis of earlier research (Koster et al., in press) we hypothesized that limited WM capacity might cause decreased comprehension of stories with a topic shift. To investigate how WM capacity affects the comprehension of the discourse structure, we implemented a cognitive model. Our model implied that sufficient WM capacity is necessary for an adult-like interpretation of a potentially ambiguous subject pronoun. With sufficient WM capacity, information about the grammatical roles of the referents in the previous sentence determines the interpretation of the ambiguous pronoun, but readers or listeners without sufficient WM capacity rely more on the base level activation of discourse elements. To test whether adults' performance would decrease when their WM is taxed, we performed a dual-task experiment in which we manipulated the WM load. The results confirmed that with higher WM load, adults are less likely to distinguish between stories with and without a topic shift, similarly to children. Thus WM load can affect the interpretation of ambiguous subject pronouns.

References

Anderson, J. R. (2007). *How Can the Human Mind Occur in the Physical Universe?* New York: Oxford University Press, USA.

Ariel, M. (1990). *Accessing Noun-Phrase Antecedents.* London: Routledge.

Arnold, J. E. (1998). *Reference Form and Discourse Patterns.* Unpublished Ph.D. thesis, Stanford University.

Baayen, R. H. (2008). *Analyzing Linguistic Data: A Practical Introduction to Statistics Using R*: Cambridge University Press.

Baayen, R. H., & Milin, P. (2010). Analyzing Reaction Times. *International Journal of Psychological Research, 3*(2), 12-28.

Daily, L. Z., Lovett, M. C., & Reder, L. M. (2001). Modeling individual differences in working memory performance: A source activation account. *Cognitive Science, 25*(3), 315.

Daneman, M., & Carpenter, P. (1980). Individual differences in working memory and reading. *Journal of verbal learning and verbal behavior, 19*(4), 450-466.

Foraker, S., & McElree, B. (2007). The role of prominence in pronoun resolution: Active versus passive representations. *Journal of Memory and Language, 56*(3), 357-383.

Grosz, B. J., Weinstein, S., & Joshi, A. K. (1995). Centering: a framework for modeling the local coherence of discourse. *Computational Linguistics, 21*(2), 203-225.

Gundel, J. K., Hedberg, N., & Zacharski, R. (1993). Cognitive status and the form of referring expressions in discourse. *Language, 69*(2), 274-307.

Just, M. A., & Carpenter, P. A. (1992). A capacity theory of comprehension: Individual differences in working memory. *Psychological Review, 99*(1), 122-149.

Just, M. A., Carpenter, P. A., & Woolley, J. D. (1982). Paradigms and processes in reading comprehension. *Journal of Experimental Psychology, 111*(2), 228-238.

Just, M. A., & Varma, S. (2007). The organization of thinking: What functional brain imaging reveals about the neuroarchitecture of complex cognition. *Cognitive, Affective, & Behavioral Neuroscience, 7*(3), 153-191.

Koster, C., Hoeks, J., & Hendriks, P. (in press). Comprehension and production of subject pronouns: Evidence for the asymmetry of grammar. In A. Grimm, A. Müller, C. Hamann & E. Ruigendijk (Eds.), *Production-comprehension asymmetries in child language*. Berlin: De Gruyter.

Lewis, R. L., & Vasishth, S. (2005). An activation-based model of sentence processing as skilled memory retrieval. *Cognitive Science, 29*(3), 375-419.

MacDonald, M. C., & Christiansen, M. H. (2002). Reassessing working memory: Comment on Just and Carpenter (1992) and Waters and Caplan (1996). *Psychological Review, 109*(1), 35-54.

McDonald, J. L., & MacWhinney, B. (1995). The time course of anaphor resolution: Effects of implicit verb causality and gender. *Journal of Memory and Language, 34*(4), 543-566.

Otten, M., & Van Berkum, J. J. A. (2009). Does working memory capacity affect the ability to predict upcoming words in discourse? *Brain research, 1291*, 92-101.

Reitter, D., Keller, F., & Moore, J. D. (2011). A Computational Cognitive Model of Syntactic Priming. *Cognitive Science, 35*.

Stevenson, R. J., Crawley, R. A., & Kleinman, D. (1994). Thematic roles, focus and the representation of events. *Language and Cognitive Processes, 9*(4), 519-548.

Van Rij, J., Van Rijn, H., & Hendriks, P. (submitted). Production and comprehension of referring subjects: A computational model of the interaction between linguistic and cognitive constraints.

Chameleons in imagined conversations: A new approach to understanding coordination of linguistic style in dialogs

Cristian Danescu-Niculescu-Mizil and Lillian Lee
Department of Computer Science, Cornell University
cristian@cs.cornell.edu, llee@cs.cornell.edu

Abstract

Conversational participants tend to immediately and unconsciously adapt to each other's language styles: a speaker will even adjust the number of articles and other function words in their next utterance in response to the number in their partner's immediately preceding utterance. This striking level of coordination is thought to have arisen as a way to achieve social goals, such as gaining approval or emphasizing difference in status. But has the adaptation mechanism become so deeply embedded in the language-generation process as to become a reflex? We argue that fictional dialogs offer a way to study this question, since authors create the conversations but don't receive the social benefits (rather, the imagined characters do). Indeed, we find significant coordination across many families of function words in our large movie-script corpus. We also report suggestive preliminary findings on the effects of gender and other features; e.g., surprisingly, for articles, on average, characters adapt more to females than to males.

1 Introduction

"...it is dangerous to base any sociolinguistic argumentation on the evidence of language in fictional texts only" (Bleichenbacher (2008), crediting Mareš (2000))

The chameleon effect is the "nonconscious mimicry of the postures, mannerisms, facial expressions, and other behaviors of one's interaction partners" (Chartrand and Bargh, 1999).[1] For example, if one conversational participant crosses their arms, their partner often unconsciously crosses their arms as well. The effect occurs for language, too, ranging from matching of acoustic features such as accent, speech rate, and pitch (Giles et al., 1991; Chartrand and van Baaren, 2009) to lexico-syntactic priming across adjacent or nearby utterances (Bock, 1986; Pickering and Garrod, 2004; Ward and Litman, 2007; Reitter et al., 2011).

Our work focuses on adjacent-utterance coordination with respect to classes of function words. To exemplify the phenomenon, we discuss two short conversations.

• *First example:* The following exchange from the movie "The Getaway" (1972) demonstrates quantifier coordination.

Doc: At [least] you were outside.
Carol: It doesn't make [much] difference where you are [...]

Note that "Carol" used a quantifier, one that is different than the one "Doc" employed. Also, notice that "Carol" could just as well have replied in a way that doesn't include a quantifier, for example, "It doesn't really matter where you are...".

• *Second example:* Levelt and Kelter (1982) report an experiment involving preposition coordination. Shopkeepers who were called and asked "[At] what time does your shop close?" were significantly more likely to say "[At] five o'clock" than "five o'clock".[2]

[1]The term is a reference to the movie *Zelig*, wherein a "human chameleon" uncontrollably takes on the characteristics of those around him. The term is meant to contrast with "aping", a word connoting intentional imitation.

Related terms include adaptation, alignment, entrainment, priming, and Du Bois' dialogic syntax.

[2]This is an example of lexical matching manifested as part of syntactic coordination.

Coordination of function-word class has been previously documented in several settings (Niederhoffer and Pennebaker, 2002; Taylor and Thomas, 2008; Ireland et al., 2011; Gonzales et al., 2010), the largest-scale study being on Twitter (Danescu-Niculescu-Mizil et al., 2011).

Problem setting People don't consciously track function words (Levelt and Kelter, 1982; Segalowitz and Lane, 2004; Petten and Kutas, 1991) — it's not easy to answer the question, "how many prepositions were there in the sentence I just said?". Therefore, it is quite striking that humans nonetheless instantly adapt to each other's function-word rates. Indeed, there is active debate regarding what mechanisms cause nonconscious coordination (Ireland et al., 2011; Branigan et al., 2010).

One line of thought is that convergence represents a social strategy[3] whose aim is to gain the other's social approval (Giles, 2008; Street and Giles, 1982) or enhance the other's comprehension (Clark, 1996; Bortfeld and Brennan, 1997).[4] This hypothesis is supported by studies showing that coordination is affected by a number of social factors, including relative social status (Natale, 1975; Gregory and Webster, 1996; Thakerar et al., 1982) and gender role (Bilous and Krauss, 1988; Namy et al., 2002; Ireland and Pennebaker, 2010).

But an important question is whether the adaptation mechanism has become so deeply embedded in the language-generation process as to have transformed into a reflex not requiring any social triggering.[5] Indeed, it has been argued that unconscious mimicry is partly innate (Chartrand and Bargh, 1999), perhaps due to evolutionary pressure to foster relationships (Lakin et al., 2003).

To answer this question, we take a radical approach: we consider a setting in which the persons *generating* the coordinating dialog are different from those *engaged* in the dialog (and standing to reap the social benefits) — imagined conversations, specifically, scripted movie dialogs.

[3]In fact, social signaling may also be the evolutionary cause of chameleons' color-changing ability (Stuart-Fox et al., 2008).

[4]For the purpose of our discussion, we are conflating social-approval and audience-design hypotheses under the category of *social strategy*.

[5]This hypothesis relates to characterizations of alignment as an unmediated mechanism (Pickering and Garrod, 2004).

Life is beautiful, but cinema is paradise A priori, it is not clear that movie conversations would exhibit convergence. Dialogs between movie characters are not truthful representations of real-life conversations. They often are "too carefully polished, too rhythmically balanced, too self-consciously artful" (Kozloff, 2000), due to practical and artistic constraints and scriptwriting practice (McKee, 1999). For example, mundane phenomena such as stuttering and word repetitions are generally nonexistent on the big screen. Moreover, writers have many goals to accomplish, including the need to advance the plot, reveal character, make jokes as funny as possible, and so on, all incurring a cognitive load.

So, the question arises: do scripted movie dialogs, in spite of this quasi-artificiality and the aforementioned generation/engagement gap, exhibit the real-life phenomenon of stylistic convergence? When imagining dialogs, do scriptwriters (nonconsciously[6]) adjust the respondent's replies to echo the initiator's use of articles, prepositions, and other apparently minor aspects of lexical choice? According to our results, this is indeed the case, which has fascinating implications.

First, this provides evidence that coordination, assumed to be driven by social motivations, has become so deeply embedded into our ideas of what conversations "sound like" that the phenomenon occurs even when the person generating the dialog is not the recipient of the social benefits.[7]

Second, movies can be seen as a controlled environment in which preconceptions about the relation between communication patterns and the social features of the participants can be studied. This gives us the opportunity to understand how people (scriptwriters) nonconsciously *expect* convergence to relate to factors such as gender, status and relation type. Are female characters thought to accommodate more to male characters than vice-versa?

Furthermore, movie scripts constitute a corpus that is especially convenient because meta-features

[6]The phenomenon of real-life language convergence is not widely known among screenplay authors (Beth F. Milles, professor of acting and directing, personal communication).

[7]Although some writers may perhaps imagine themselves "in the shoes" of the recipients, recall that authors generally don't include in their scripts the repetitions and ungrammaticalities of "real-life" speech.

like gender can be more or less readily obtained.

Contributions We check for convergence in a corpus of roughly 250,000 conversational exchanges from movie scripts (available at `http://www.cs.cornell.edu/~cristian/movies`). Specifically, we examine the set of nine families of stylistic features previously utilized by Ireland et al. (2011), and find a statistically significant convergence effect for all these families. We thereby provide evidence that language coordination is so implanted within our conception of conversational behavior that, even if such coordination is socially motivated, it is exhibited even when the person generating the language in question is not receiving any of the presumed social advantages.

We also study the effects of gender, narrative importance, and hostility. Intriguingly, we find that these factors indeed "affect" movie characters' linguistic behavior; since the characters aren't real, and control of stylistic lexical choice is largely non-conscious, the effects of these factors can only be springing from patterns existing in the scriptwriters' minds.

Our findings, by enhancing our understanding of linguistic adaptation effects in stylistic word choice and its relation to various socially relevant factors, may in the future aid in practical applications. Such an understanding would give us insight into how and what kinds of language coordination yield more satisfying interactions — convergence has been already shown to enhance communication in organizational contexts (Bourhis, 1991), psychotherapy (Ferrara, 1991), care of the mentally disabled (Hamilton, 1991), and police-community interactions (Giles et al., 2007). Moreover, a deeper understanding can aid human-computer interaction by informing the construction of natural-language generation systems, since people are often more satisfied with encounters exhibiting appropriate linguistic convergence (Bradac et al., 1988; van Baaren et al., 2003), even when the other conversational participant is known to be a computer (Nass and Lee, 2000; Branigan et al., 2010).

2 Related work not already mentioned

Linguistic style and human characteristics Using stylistic (i.e., non-topical) elements like articles and prepositions to characterize the utterer in some way has a long history, including in authorship attribution (Mosteller and Wallace, 1984; Juola, 2008), personality-type classification (Argamon et al., 2005; Oberlander and Gill, 2006; Mairesse et al., 2007), gender categorization (Koppel et al., 2002; Mukherjee and Liu, 2010; Herring and Paolillo, 2006), identification of interactional style (Jurafsky et al., 2009; Ranganath et al., 2009), and recognizing deceptive language (Hancock et al., 2008; Mihalcea and Strapparava, 2009).

Imagined conversations There has been work in the NLP community applying computational techniques to fiction, scripts, and other types of text containing imagined conversations. For example, one recent project identifies conversational networks in novels, with the goal of evaluating various literary theories (Elson et al., 2010; Elson and McKeown, 2010). Movie scripts were used as word-sense-disambiguation evaluation data as part of an effort to generate computer animation from the scripts (Ye and Baldwin, 2006). Sonderegger (2010) employed a corpus of English poetry to study the relationship between pronunciation and network structure. Rayson et al. (2001) computed part-of-speech frequencies for imaginative writing in the British National Corpus, finding a typology gradient progressing from conversation to imaginative writing (e.g., novels) to task-oriented speech to informative writing. The data analyzed by Oberlander and Gill (2006) consisted of emails that participants were instructed to write by imagining that they were going to update a good friend on their current goings-on.

3 Movie dialogs corpus

To address the questions raised in the introduction, we created a large set of imagined conversations, starting from movie scripts crawled from various sites.[8] Metadata for conversation analysis and duplicate-script detection involved mostly-automatic matching of movie scripts with the IMDB movie database; clean-up resulted in 617 unique titles tagged with genre, release year, cast lists, and

[8]The source of these scripts and more detail about the corpus are given in the README associated with the Cornell movie-dialogs corpus, available at `http://www.cs.cornell.edu/~cristian/movies`.

IMDB information. We then extracted 220,579 conversational exchanges between pairs of characters engaging in at least 5 exchanges, and automatically matched these characters to IMDB to retrieve gender (as indicated by the designations "actor" or "actress") and/or billing-position information when possible (≈9000 characters, ≈3000 gender-identified and ≈3000 billing-positioned). The latter feature serves as a proxy for narrative importance: the higher up in the credits, the more important the character tends to be in the film.

To the best of our knowledge, this is the largest dataset of (metadata-rich) imaginary conversations to date.

4 Measuring linguistic style

For consistency with prior work, we employed the nine LIWC-derived categories (Pennebaker et al., 2007) deemed by Ireland et al. (2011) to be processed by humans in a generally non-conscious fashion. The nine categories are: articles, auxiliary verbs, conjunctions, high-frequency adverbs, impersonal pronouns, negations, personal pronouns, prepositions, and quantifiers (451 lexemes total).

It is important to note that language coordination is multimodal: it does not necessarily occur simultaneously for all features (Ferrara, 1991), and speakers may converge on some features but diverge on others (Thakerar et al., 1982); for example, females have been found to converge on pause frequency with male conversational partners but diverge on laughter (Bilous and Krauss, 1988).

5 Measuring convergence

Niederhoffer and Pennebaker (2002) use the correlation coefficient to measure accommodation with respect to linguistic style features. While correlation at first seems reasonable, it has some problematic aspects in our setting (we discuss these problems later) that motivate us to employ an alternative measure.

We instead use a convergence measure introduced in Danescu-Niculescu-Mizil et al. (2011) that quantifies how much a given feature family t serves as an *immediate trigger* or stimulus, meaning that one person's utterance exhibiting such a feature triggers the appearance of that feature in the respondent's immediate reply.

For example, we might be studying whether one person A's inclusion of articles in an utterance triggers the usage of articles in respondent B's reply. Note that this differs from asking whether B uses articles more often when talking to A than when talking to other people (it is not so surprising that people speak differently to different audiences). This also differs from asking whether B eventually starts matching A's behavior in later utterances within the same conversation. We specifically want to know whether each utterance by A triggers an *immediate* change in B's behavior, as such instantaneous adaptation is what we consider the most striking aspect of convergence, although immediate and long-term coordination are clearly related.

We now describe the statistic we employ to measure the extent to which person B accommodates to A. Consider an arbitrary conversational exchange started by A, and let a denote A's initiating utterance and $b_{\hookrightarrow a}$ denote B's reply to a.[9] Note that we use lowercase to emphasize when we are talking about individual utterances rather than all the utterances of the particular person, and that thus, the arrow in $b_{\hookrightarrow a}$ indicates that we mean the reply to the specific single utterance a. Let a^t be the indicator variable for a exhibiting t, and similarly for $b^t_{\hookrightarrow a}$. Then, we define the convergence $Conv_{A,B}(t)$ of B to A as:

$$P(b^t_{\hookrightarrow a} = 1 | a^t = 1) - P(b^t_{\hookrightarrow a} = 1). \quad (1)$$

Note that this quantity can be negative (indicating *divergence*). The overall degree $Conv(t)$ to which t serves as a trigger is then defined as the expectation of $Conv_{A,B}(t)$ over all initiator-respondent pairs:

$$Conv(t) \stackrel{def}{=} E_{\text{pairs}(A,B)}(Conv_{A,B}(t)). \quad (2)$$

Comparison with correlation: the importance of asymmetry[10] Why do we employ $Conv_{A,B}$, Equation (1), instead of the well-known correlation coefficient? One reason is that correlation fails to

[9] We use "initiating" and "reply" loosely: in our terminology, the conversation ⟨A: "Hi." B: "Eaten?" A: "Nope."⟩ has two exchanges, one initiated by A's "Hi", the other by B's "Eaten?".

[10] Other asymmetric measures based on conditional probability of occurrence have been proposed for adaptation within monologues (Church, 2000) and between conversations (Stenchikova and Stent, 2007). Since our focus is different, we control for different factors.

capture an important asymmetry. The case where $a^t = 1$ but $b^t_{\hookrightarrow a} = 0$ represents a true failure to accommodate; but the case where $a^t = 0$ but $b^t_{\hookrightarrow a} = 1$ should not, at least not to the same degree. For example, a may be very short (e.g., "What?") and thus not contain an article, but we don't assume that this completely disallows B from using articles in their reply. In other words, we are interested in whether the presence of t acts as a trigger, not in whether $b_{\hookrightarrow a}$ exhibits t if and only if a does, the latter being what correlation detects.[11]

It bears mentioning that since a^t and $b^t_{\hookrightarrow a}$ are binary, a simple calculation shows that the covariance[12] $cov(a^t, b^t_{\hookrightarrow a}) = Conv_{A,B}(t) \cdot P(a^t = 1)$. But, the two terms on the right hand side are not independent: raising $P(a^t = 1)$ could cause $Conv_{A,B}(t)$ to decrease by affecting the first term in its definition, $P(b^t_{\hookrightarrow a} = 1 | a^t = 1)$ (see eq. 1).

6 Experimental results

6.1 Convergence exists in fictional dialogs

For each ordered pair of characters (A, B) and for each feature family t, we estimate equation (1) in a straightforward manner: the fraction of B's replies to t-manifesting A utterances that themselves exhibit t, minus the fraction of all replies of B to A that exhibit t.[13] Fig. 1 compares the average values of these two fractions (as a way of putting convergence values into context), showing positive differences for all of the considered families of features (statistically significant, paired t-test $p < 0.001$); this demonstrates that movie characters do indeed converge to each other's linguistic style on all considered trigger families.[14]

[11] One could also speculate that it is easier for B to (unconsciously) pick up on the presence of t than on its absence.

[12] The covariance of two random variables is their correlation times the product of their standard deviations.

[13] For each t, we discarded pairs of characters where some relevant count is < 10, e.g., where B had fewer than 10 replies manifesting the trigger.

[14] We obtained the same qualitative results when measuring convergence via the correlation coefficient, doing so for the sake of comparability with prior work (Niederhoffer and Pennebaker, 2002; Taylor and Thomas, 2008).

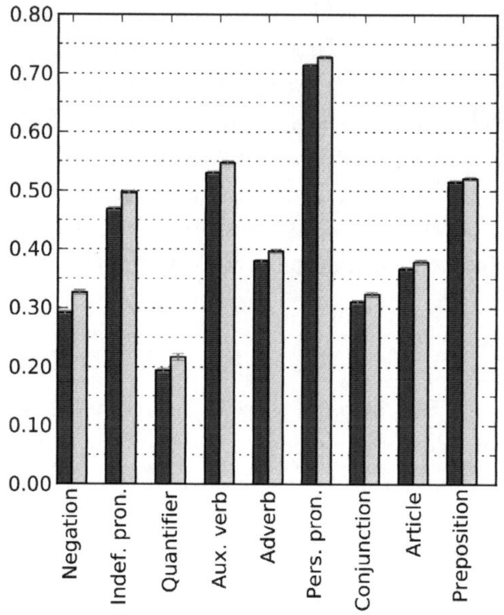

Figure 1: Implicit depiction of convergence for each trigger family t, illustrated as the difference between the means of $P(b^t_{\hookrightarrow a} = 1 | a^t = 1)$ (right/light-blue bars) and $P(b^t_{\hookrightarrow a} = 1)$ (left/dark-blue bars). (This implicit representation allows one to see the magnitude of the two components making up our definition of convergence.) The trigger families are ordered by decreasing convergence. All differences are statistically significant (paired t-test). In all figures in this paper, error bars represent standard error, estimated via bootstrap resampling (Koehn, 2004). (Here, the error bars, in red, are very tight.)

Movies vs. Twitter One can ask how our results on movie dialogs correspond to those for real-life conversations. To study this, we utilize the results of Danescu-Niculescu-Mizil et al. (2011) on a large-scale collection of Twitter exchanges as data on real conversational exchanges. Figure 2 depicts the comparison, revealing two interesting effects. First, Twitter users coordinate more than movie characters on all the trigger families we considered, which does show that the convergence effect is stronger in actual interchanges. On the other hand, from the perspective of potentially using imagined dialogs as proxies for real ones, it is intriguing to see that there is generally a correspondence between how much convergence occurs in real dialogs for a given feature family and how much convergence occurs for that feature in imagined dialogs, although conjunctions and articles show a bit less convergence in fictional

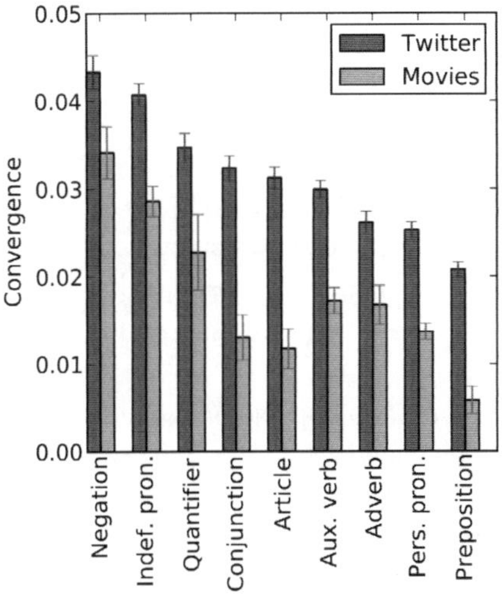

Figure 2: Convergence in Twitter conversations (left bars) vs. convergence in movie dialogs (right bars; corresponds to the difference between the two respective bars in Fig. 1) for each trigger family. The trigger families are ordered by decreasing convergence in Twitter.

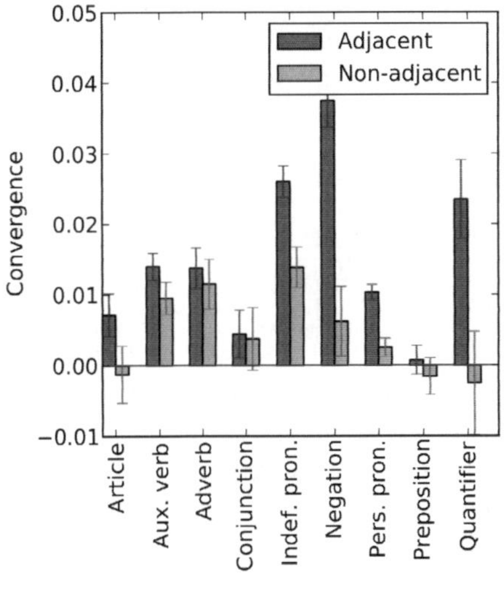

Figure 3: Immediate vs. within-conversation effects (for conversations with at least 5 utterances). Suppose that we have a conversation $a_1\, b_2\, a_3\, b_4\, a_5 \ldots$. The lefthand/dark-green bars show the usual convergence measure, which involves the utterance pair a_1 and b_2. The righthand/mustard-green bars show convergence based on pairs like a_1 and b_4 — utterances in the same conversation, but not adjacent. We see that there is a much stronger triggering effect for immediately adjacent utterances.

exchanges than this pattern would suggest.

6.2 Potential alternative explanations

Immediate vs. within-conversation effects An additional natural question is, how much are these accommodation effects due to an immediate triggering effect, as opposed to simply being a by-product of utterances occurring within the same conversation? For instance, could the results be due just to the topic of the conversation?

To answer this question requires measuring "convergence" between utterances that are not adjacent, but are still in the same conversation. To this end, we first restricted attention to those conversations in which there were at least five utterances, so that they would have the structure $a_1\, b_2\, a_3\, b_4\, a_5 \ldots$. We then measure convergence not between adjacent utterances, like a_1 and b_2, but where we skip an utterance, such as the pair a_1, b_4 or b_2, a_5. This helps control for topic effects, since b_4 and a_1 are still close and thus fairly likely to be on the same subject.[15]

Figure 3 shows that the level of convergence always falls off after the skipped utterance, sometimes dramatically so, thus demonstrating that the level of immediate adaptation effects we see cannot be solely explained by the topic of conversation or other conversation-level effects. These results accord with the findings of Levelt and Kelter (1982), where interposing "interfering" questions lowered the chance of a question's preposition being echoed by the respondent, and Reitter et al. (2006), where the effects of structural priming were shown to decay quickly with the distance between the priming trigger and the priming target.

Towards the same end, we also performed randomization experiments in which we shuffled the order of each participant's utterances in each conversation, while maintaining alternation between speakers. We again observed drop-offs in this randomized condition in comparison to immediate convergence, the main focus of this paper.

Self-coordination Could our results be explained entirely by the script author converging to their own self, given that self-alignment has been documented

[15] It is true that they might be on different topics, but in fact even b_2 might be on a different subject from a_1.

(Pickering and Garrod, 2004; Reitter et al., 2006)? If that were the case, then the *characters* that the author is writing about should converge to themselves no more than they converge to different characters. But we ran experiments showing that this is not the case, thus invalidating this alternative hypothesis. In fact, characters converge to themselves much more than they converge to other characters.

6.3 Convergence and imagined relation

We now analyze how convergence patterns vary with the type of relationship between the (imagined) participants. Note that, given the multimodal character of convergence, treating each trigger family separately is the most appropriate way to proceed, since in past work, for the same experimental factor (e.g., gender), different features converge differently (refer back to §4). For clarity of exposition, we discuss in detail only the results for the *Articles* feature family; but the results for all trigger families are summarized in Fig. 7, discussed later.

Imagined gender Fig. 4(a) shows how convergence on article usage depends on the gender of the initiator and respondent. Females are more influential than males: movie characters of either gender accommodate more to female characters than to male characters (compare the **F**emale **init**iator bar with the **M**ale **init**iator bar, statistically significant, independent t-test, $p < 0.05$). Also, female characters seem to accommodate slightly more to other characters than male characters do (though not statistically significantly so in our data).

We also compare the amount of convergence between all the possible types of gendered initiator-respondent pairs involved (Fig. 4(b)). One can observe, for example, that male characters adapt less in same-gender situations (**M**ale-**M**ale conversations) than in mixed-gender situations (**F**emale initiator-**M**ale respondent), while the opposite is true for female characters (**F**emale-**F**emale vs. **M**ale-**F**emale).

Interpreting these results lies beyond the scope of this paper. We note that these results could be a correlate of many factors, such as the roles that male and female characters are typically assigned in movie scripts.[16]

Narrative importance Does the relative importance bestowed by the scriptwriter to the characters affect the amount of linguistic coordination he or she (nonconsciously) embeds in their dialogs? Fig. 5 shows that, on average, the lead character converges to the second-billed character more than vice-versa (compare left bar in **1st resp.** group with left bar in **2nd resp.** group).

One possible confounding factor is that there is significant gender imbalance in the data (82% of all lead characters are males, versus only 51% of the secondary characters). Could the observed difference be a direct consequence of the relation between gender and convergence discussed above? The answer is no: the same qualitative observation holds if we restrict our analysis to same-gender pairs (compare the righthand bars in each group in Fig. 5[17]).

It would be interesting to see whether these results could be brought to bear on previous results regarding the relationship between social status and convergence, but such interpretation lies beyond the scope of this paper, since the connection between billing order and social status is not straightforward.

Quarreling The level of contention in conversations has also been shown to be related to the amount of convergence (Giles, 2008; Niederhoffer and Pennebaker, 2002; Taylor and Thomas, 2008). To test whether this tendency holds in the case of imagined conversations, as a small pilot study, we manually classified the conversations between 24 main pairs of characters from romantic comedies[18] as: *quarreling*, *some quarreling* and *no quarreling*. Although the experiment was too small in scale to provide statistical significance, the results (Fig. 6) suggest that indeed the level of convergence is affected by

[16]A comparison to previously reported results on real-life gender effects is not straightforward, since they pertain to different features; Ireland and Pennebaker (2010) show that females match their linguistic style more than males, where style matching is averaged over the same 9 trigger families we employ (they do not report gender effect for each family separately).

[17]Figure 5 also shows that our convergence measure does achieve negative values in practice, indicating divergence. Divergence is a rather common phenomenon which deserves attention in future work; see Danescu-Niculescu-Mizil et al. (2011) for an account.

[18]We chose the romantic comedy genre since it is often characterized by some level of contention between the two people in the main couple.

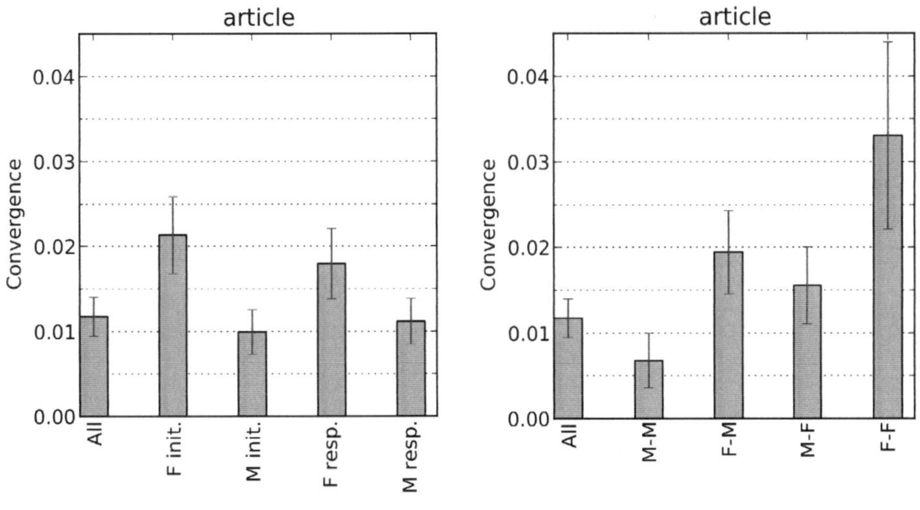

(a) (b)

Figure 4: Relation between *Article* convergence and imagined gender. (a) compares cases when the **init**iator and **resp**ondent are **M**ale or **F**emale; (b) compares types of gendered **initiator-respondent** relations: **M**ale-**M**ale, **F**emale-**M**ale, **M**ale-**F**emale, **F**emale-**F**emale. For comparison, the **All** bars represents the general *Article* convergence (illustrated in Fig. 1 as the difference between the two respective bars).

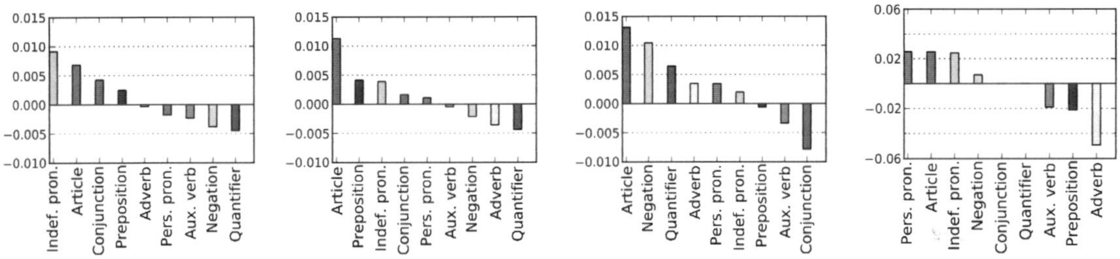

(a) **F resp.** minus **M resp.** (b) **F init.** minus **M init.** (c) **1st resp.** minus **2nd resp.** (d) **Quarrel** minus **No quarrel**

Figure 7: Summary of the relation between convergence and imagined gender (a and b), billing order (c), and quarreling (d). The bars represent the *difference* between the convergence observed in the respective cases; e.g., the **Article** (red) bar in (a) represents the difference between the **F resp.** and the **M resp.** bars in Fig. 4(a). In each plot, the trigger families are sorted according to the respective difference, but the color assigned to each family is consistent across plots. The scale of (d) differs from the others.

the presence of controversy: *quarreling* exhibited considerably more convergence for articles than the other categories (the same holds for personal and indefinite pronouns; see Fig. 7). Interestingly, the reverse is true for adverbs; there, we observe divergence for contentious conversations and convergence for non-contentious conversations (detailed plot omitted due to space constraints). This corresponds to Niederhoffer and Pennebaker's (2002) observations made on real conversations in their study of the Watergate transcripts: when the relationship between the two deteriorated, Richard Nixon converged more to John Dean on articles, but diverged on other features.[19]

Results for the other features Our results above suggest some intriguing interplay between convergence and gender, status, and level of hostility in imagined dialogs, which may shed light on how people (scriptwriters) nonconsciously *expect* con-

[19] Adverbs were not included in their study.

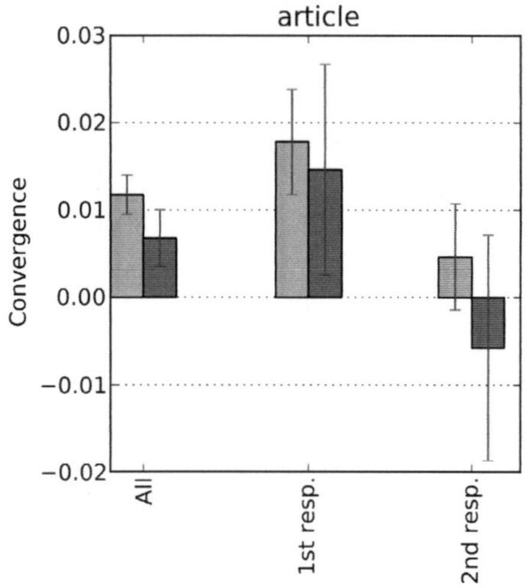

Figure 5: Comparison of the convergence of first-billed (lead) characters to second-billed characters (left bar in **1st resp.** group) to that of second-billed characters to leads (left bar in **2nd resp.** group); righthand bars (dark green) in each group show results for Male-Male pairs only.

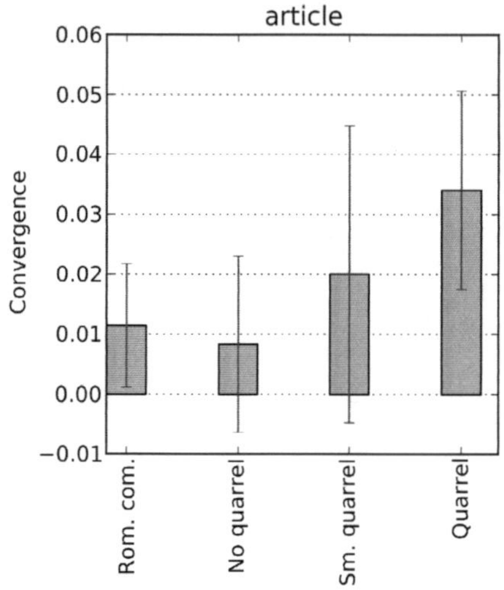

Figure 6: Relation between contention and convergence. The third bar combines *quarreling* and *some quarreling* to ameliorate data sparsity. For comparison, **Rom. com.** shows convergence calculated on all the conversations of the 24 romantic-comedy pairs considered in this experiment.

vergence to relate to such factors. (Interpreting these sometimes apparently counterintuitive findings is beyond the scope of this paper, but represents a fascinating direction for future work.) Fig. 7 shows how the nature of these relations depends on the trigger family considered. The variation among families is in line with the previous empirical results on the multimodality of convergence in real conversations, as discussed in §4.

7 Summary and future work

We provide some insight into the causal mechanism behind convergence, a topic that has generated substantial scrutiny and debate for over 40 years (Ireland et al., 2011; Branigan et al., 2010). Our work, along with Elson and McKeown (2010), advocates for the value of fictional sources in the study of linguistic and social phenomena. To stimulate such studies, we render our metadata-rich corpus of movie dialog public.

In §1, we described some practical applications of a better understanding of the chameleon effect in language; it boils down to improving communication both between humans and between humans and computers. Also, our results on contention could be used to further automatic controversy detection (Mishne and Glance, 2006; Gómez et al., 2008). Moreover, if we succeeded in linking our results on narrative importance to relative social status, we might further the development of systems that can infer social relationships in online social networks when conversational data is present but other, more explicit cues are absent (Wyatt et al., 2008; Bramsen et al., 2011). Such systems could be valuable to the rapidly expanding field of analyzing social networks.

Acknowledgments Many thanks for their help are due to Claire Cardie, Catalin Draghici, Susan Dumais, Shimon Edelman, Michael Gamon, Jon Kleinberg, Magdalena Narożniak, Alex Niculescu-Mizil, Myle Ott, Bo Pang, Morgan Sonderegger, plus NLP seminar participants Eric Baumer, Bin Lu, Chenhao Tan, Lu Wang, Bishan Yang, Ainur Yessenalina, and Marseille, and the anonymous reviewers (who went far beyond the call of duty!). Supported by NSF IIS-0910664, the Yahoo! FREP program, and a Yahoo! Key Scientific Challenges award.

References

Shlomo Argamon, Sushant Dhawle, and Moshe Koppel. 2005. Lexical predictors of personality type. *Proceedings of the 2005 Joint Annual Meeting of the Interface and the Classification Society of North America*.

Frances Bilous and Robert Krauss. 1988. Dominance and accommodation in the conversational behavior of same- and mixed-gender dyads. *Language and Communication*, 8:183–194.

Lukas Bleichenbacher. 2008. *Multilingualism in the movies: Hollywood characters and their language choices*. francke verlag, Jan.

J. Kathryn Bock. 1986. Syntactic persistence in language production. *Cognitive Psychology*, 18(3):355 – 387.

Heather Bortfeld and Susan E. Brennan. 1997. Use and acquisition of idiomatic expressions in referring by native and non-native speakers. *Discourse Processes*, 23(2):119–147.

Richard Y. Bourhis. 1991. Organizational communication and accommodation: Toward some conceptual and empirical links. In Howard Giles, Justine Coupland, and Nikolas Coupland, editors, *Contexts of Accommodation*. Cambridge University Press.

James J. Bradac, Anthony Mulac, and Ann House. 1988. Lexical diversity and magnitude of convergent versus divergent style shifting: Perceptual and evaluative consequences. *Language and Communication*, 8:213–228, Nov.

Philip Bramsen, Martha Escobar-Molana, Ami Patel, and Rafael Alonso. 2011. Extracting social power relationships from natural language. In *Proceedings of ACL HLT*.

Holly P. Branigan, Martin J. Pickering, Jamie Pearson, and Janet F. McLean. 2010. Linguistic alignment between people and computers. *Journal of Pragmatics*, 42(9):2355–2368.

Tanya L. Chartrand and John A. Bargh. 1999. The chameleon effect: The perception-behavior link and social interaction. *J. Personality and Social Psychology*, 76(6):893–910.

Tanya L. Chartrand and Rick van Baaren. 2009. Chapter 5: Human mimicry. In Mark P. Zanna, editor, *Advances in Experimental Social Psychology*, volume 41, pp. 219–274. Academic Press.

Kenneth W. Church. 2000. Empirical estimates of adaptation: the chance of two noriegas is closer to p/2 than p2. In *Proceedings of COLING*, pp. 180–186.

Herbert H. Clark. 1996. *Using language*. Cambridge University Press, second edition.

Cristian Danescu-Niculescu-Mizil, Michael Gamon, and Susan Dumais. 2011. Mark my words! Linguistic style accommodation in social media. In *Proceedings of WWW*.

David Elson and Kathleen McKeown. 2010. Automatic attribution of quoted speech in literary narrative. In *Proceedings of AAAI*.

David Elson, Nicholas Dames, and Kathleen McKeown. 2010. Extracting social networks from literary fiction. In *Proceedings of the 48th Annual Meeting of the Association for Computational Linguistics*, pp. 138–147.

Kathleen Ferrara. 1991. Accommodation in therapy. In *Accommodation theory: Communication, context, and consequences*. Cambridge University Press.

Howard Giles, Justine Coupland, and Nikolas Coupland. 1991. Accommodation theory: Communication, context, and consequences. In *Accommodation theory: Communication, context, and consequences*. Cambridge University Press.

Howard Giles, Michael Willemyns, Cynthia Gallois, and Michelle Anderson. 2007. Accommodating a new frontier: The context of law enforcement. In Klaus Fiedler, editor, *Social Communication*, Frontiers of Social Psychology, chapter 5, pp. 129–162.

Howard Giles. 2008. Communication accommodation theory. In *Engaging theories in interpersonal communication: Multiple perspectives*. Sage Publications.

Vicenç Gómez, Andreas Kaltenbrunner, and Vicente López. 2008. Statistical analysis of the social network and discussion threads in Slashdot. In *Proceedings of WWW*, pp. 645–654.

Amy L. Gonzales, Jeffrey T. Hancock, and James W. Pennebaker. 2010. Language style matching as a predictor of social dynamics in small groups. *Communication Research*, 37(1):3–19, Feb.

Stanford W. Gregory and Stephen Webster. 1996. A nonverbal signal in voices of interview partners effectively predicts communication accommodation and social status perceptions. *J. Personality and Social Psychology*, 70(6):1231–1240.

Heidi Hamilton. 1991. Accommodation and mental disability. In *Accommodation theory: Communication, context, and consequences*. Cambridge University Press.

Jeffrey T. Hancock, Lauren E. Curry, Saurabh Goorha, and Michael Woodworth. 2008. On lying and being lied to: A linguistic analysis of deception in computer-mediated communication. *Discourse Processes*, 45(1):1–23.

Susan C. Herring and John C. Paolillo. 2006. Gender and genre variation in weblogs. *Journal of Sociolinguistics*, Jan.

Walter Hill. 1972. *The Getaway*. Directed by Sam Peckinpah.

Molly E. Ireland and James W. Pennebaker. 2010. Language style matching in writing: Synchrony in essays, correspondence, and poetry. *J. Personality and Social Psychology*, 99(3):549–571.

Molly E. Ireland, Richard B. Slatcher, Paul W. Eastwick, Lauren E. Scissors, Eli J. Finkel, and James W. Pennebaker. 2011. Language style matching predicts relationship initiation and stability. *Psychological Science*, 22:39–44.

Patrick Juola. 2008. *Authorship Attribution*. Now Publishers.

Dan Jurafsky, Rajesh Ranganath, and Dan McFarland. 2009. Extracting social meaning: Identifying interactional style in spoken conversation. In *Proceedings of the NAACL*, pp. 638–646.

Philipp Koehn. 2004. Statistical significance tests for machine translation evaluation. *Proceedings of EMNLP*, pp. 388–395.

Moshe Koppel, Shlomo Argamon, and Anat Shimoni. 2002. Automatically categorizing written texts by author gender. *Literary and Linguistic Computing*.

Sarah Kozloff. 2000. *Overhearing Film Dialogue*. University of California Press.

Jessica L. Lakin, Valerie E. Jefferis, Clara Michelle Cheng, and Tanya L. Chartrand. 2003. The chameleon effect as social glue: Evidence for the evolutionary significance of nonconscious mimicry. *Journal of Nonverbal Behavior*, 27:145–162.

Willem J.M. Levelt and Stephanie Kelter. 1982. Surface form and memory in question answering. *Cognitive Psychology*, 14(1):78–106.

François Mairesse, Marilyn A. Walker, Matthias R. Mehl, and Roger K. Moore. 2007. Using linguistic cues for the automatic recognition of personality in conversation and text. *JAIR*, pp. 457–500.

Petr Mareš. 2000. Fikce, konvence a realita: K vícejazyčnosti v uměleckých textech [fiction, convention, and reality: On multilingualism in literary texts]. *Slovo a slovesnost*, 61(1):47–53.

Robert McKee. 1999. *Story: Substance, Structure, Style, and the Principles of Screenwriting*. Methuen.

Rada Mihalcea and Carlo Strapparava. 2009. The lie detector: Explorations in the automatic recognition of deceptive language. In *Proceedings of the ACL-IJCNLP 2009 Conference Short Papers*, pp. 309–312.

Gilad Mishne and Natalie Glance. 2006. Leave a reply: An analysis of weblog comments. *Third annual workshop on the Weblogging ecosystem*.

Frederick Mosteller and David L. Wallace. 1984. *Applied Bayesian and Classical Inference: The Case of the Federalist Papers*. Springer-Verlag.

Arjun Mukherjee and Bing Liu. 2010. Improving gender classification of blog authors. *EMNLP*.

Randall Munroe. 2010. http://xkcd.com/813/.

Laura L. Namy, Lynne C. Nygaard, and Denise Sauerteig. 2002. Gender differences in vocal accommodation. *J. Language and Social Psychology*, 21(4):422–432.

Clifford Nass and Kwan Min Lee. 2000. Does computer-generated speech manifest personality? An experimental test of similarity-attraction. In *Proceedings of CHI*, pp. 329–336.

Michael Natale. 1975. Convergence of mean vocal intensity in dyadic communication as a function of social desirability. *J. Personality and Social Psychology*, 32(5):790–804.

Kate G. Niederhoffer and James W. Pennebaker. 2002. Linguistic style matching in social interaction. *J. Language and Social Psychology*.

Jon Oberlander and Alastair J. Gill. 2006. Language with character: A stratified corpus comparison of individual differences in e-mail communication. *Discourse Processes*, 42(3):239–270.

James W. Pennebaker, Roger J. Booth, and Martha E. Francis. 2007. Linguistic inquiry and word count (LIWC): A computerized text analysis program. http://www.liwc.net/.

Cyma Van Petten and Marta Kutas. 1991. Influences of semantic and syntactic context on open- and closed-class words. *Memory and Cognition*, 19(1):95–112.

Martin Pickering and Simon Garrod. 2004. Toward a mechanistic psychology of dialogue. *Behavioral and Brain Sciences*, 27(02):169–190.

Rajesh Ranganath, Dan Jurafsky, and Dan McFarland. 2009. It's not you, it's me: Detecting flirting and its misperception in speed-dates. In *Proceedings of EMNLP*, pp. 334–342.

Paul Rayson, Andrew Wilson, and Geoffrey Leech. 2001. Grammatical word class variation within the British National Corpus Sampler. *Language and Computers*, 36:295–306(12).

David Reitter, Johanna D. Moore, and Frank Keller. 2006. Priming of syntactic rules in task-oriented dialogue and spontaneous conversation. In *Proceedings of the Conference of the Cognitive Science Society*.

David Reitter, Frank Keller, and Johanna D. Moore. 2011. A Computational Cognitive Model of Syntactic Priming. *Cognitive Science*.

Sidney J. Segalowitz and Korri Lane. 2004. Perceptual fluency and lexical access for function versus content words. *Behavioral and Brain Sciences*, 27(02):307–308.

Morgan Sonderegger. 2010. Applications of graph theory to an English rhyming corpus. *Computer Speech & Language*, In Press, Corrected Proof.

Svetlana Stenchikova and Amanda Stent. 2007. Measuring adaptation between dialogs. In *Proc. of the 8th SIGdial Workshop on Discourse and Dialogue*.

Richard L. Street and Howard Giles. 1982. Speech accommodation theory. In *Social cognition and communication*. Sage Publications.

Devi Stuart-Fox and Adnan Moussalli. 2008. Selection for social signalling drives the evolution of chameleon colour change. *PLoS Biol*, 6(1):e25, 01.

Paul J. Taylor and Sally Thomas. 2008. Linguistic style matching and negotiation outcome. *Negotiation and Conflict Management Research*, 1(3):263–281.

Jitendra N. Thakerar, Howard Giles, and Jenny Cheshire. 1982. Psychological and linguistic parameters of speech accommodation theory. In C. Fraser and K.R. Scherer, editors, *Advances in the Social Psychology of Language*. Cambridge.

Rick B. van Baaren, Rob W. Holland, Bregje Steenaert, and Ad van Knippenberg. 2003. Mimicry for money: Behavioral consequences of imitation. *Journal of Experimental Social Psychology*, 39(4):393–398.

Arthur Ward and Diane Litman. 2007. Dialog convergence and learning. In *Artificial Intelligence in Education (AIED)*, pp. 262–269.

Danny Wyatt, Jeff Bilmes, Tanzeem Choudhury, and James A. Kitts. 2008. Towards the automated social analysis of situated speech data. In *Proceedings of Ubicomp*, pp. 168–171.

Patrick Ye and Timothy Baldwin. 2006. Verb sense disambiguation using selectional preferences extracted with a state-of-the-art semantic role labeler. In *Proceedings of the Australasian Language Technology Workshop 2006*, pp. 139–148.

Classification of atypical language in autism

Emily T. Prud'hommeaux, Brian Roark, Lois M. Black, and Jan van Santen
Center for Spoken Language Understanding
Oregon Health & Science University
20000 NW Walker Rd., Beaverton, Oregon 97006
{emily,roark,lmblack,vansanten}@cslu.ogi.edu

Abstract

Atypical or idiosyncratic language is a characteristic of autism spectrum disorder (ASD). In this paper, we discuss previous work identifying language errors associated with atypical language in ASD and describe a procedure for reproducing those results. We describe our data set, which consists of transcribed data from a widely used clinical diagnostic instrument (the ADOS) for children with autism, children with developmental language disorder, and typically developing children. We then present methods for automatically extracting lexical and syntactic features from transcripts of children's speech to 1) identify certain syntactic and semantic errors that have previously been found to distinguish ASD language from that of children with typical development; and 2) perform diagnostic classification. Our classifiers achieve results well above chance, demonstrating the potential for using NLP techniques to enhance neurodevelopmental diagnosis and atypical language analysis. We expect further improvement with additional data, features, and classification techniques.

1 Introduction

Atypical language and communication have been associated with autism spectrum disorder (ASD) since Kanner (1943) first gave the name *autism* to the disorder. The Autism Diagnostic Observation Schedule (ADOS) (Lord et al., 2002) and other widely used diagnostic instruments include unusual word use as a diagnostic criterion. The broad and conflicting definitions used in diagnostic instruments for ASD, however, can lead to difficulty distinguishing the language peculiarities associated with autism.

The most recent and the most systematic study of unusual word use in ASD (Volden and Lord, 1991) found that certain types of atypical word use were significantly more prevalent in ASD speech than in the speech of children with typical development (TD). Although the results provided interesting information about unusual language in ASD, the process of coding these types of errors was laborious and required substantial linguistic and clinical expertise.

In this paper, we first use our own data to reproduce a subset of the results reported in Volden and Lord (1991). We then present a method of automatically identifying the types of errors associated with ASD using spoken language features and machine learning techniques. These same features are then used to differentiate subjects with ASD or a developmental language disorder (DLD) from those with TD. Although these linguistic features yield strong classification results, they also reveal a number of obstacles to distinguishing language characteristics associated with autism from those associated with language impairment.

2 Previous Work

Since it was first recognized as a neurodevelopmental disorder, autism has been associated with language described variously as: "seemingly nonsensical and irrelevant", "peculiar and out of place in ordinary conversation" (Kanner, 1946); "stereotyped", "metaphorical", "inappropriate" (Bartak et al., 1975); and characterized by "a lack of ease in the use of words" (Rutter, 1965) and "the use of standard, familiar words or phrases in idiosyncratic but meaningful way" (Volden and Lord, 1991). The three most common instruments used in ASD diagnosis – the Autism Diagnostic Observation Schedule (ADOS) (Lord et al., 2002), the Autism Diagnostic Interview-Revised (ADI-R) (Lord et al., 1994), and the Social Communication Questionnaire (SCQ) (Rutter et al., 2003) – make reference to these language particularities in their scoring algorithms. Unfortunately, the guidelines for identifying this unusual language are often vague (SCQ: "odd", ADI-R: "idiosyncratic", ADOS: "unusual") and sometimes contradictory (ADOS: "appropriate" vs. ADI-R: "inappropriate"; ADOS: "phrases...they could not have heard" vs. SCQ: "phrases that he/she has heard other people use").

In what is one of the only studies focused specifically on unusual word use in ASD, Volden and Lord (1991) transcribed two 10-minute speech samples from the ADOS for 20 school-aged, high-functioning children with autism and 20 with typical development. Utterances containing non-English words or the unusual use of a word or phrase were flagged by student workers and then categorized by the authors into one of three classes according to the type of error:

- Developmental syntax error: a violation of a syntactic rule normally acquired in early childhood, such as the use of object pronoun in subject position or an overextension of a regular morphological rule, e.g., *What does cows do?*
- Non-developmental syntax error: a syntactic error not commonly observed in the speech of children acquiring language, e.g., *But in the car it's some.*
- Semantic error: a syntactically intact sentence with an odd or unexpected word given the context and intended meaning, e.g., *They're siding the table.*

The authors found that high-functioning children with ASD produced significantly more non-developmental and semantic errors than children with typical development. The number of developmental syntax errors was not significantly different between these two groups.

Although there has been virtually no previous work on automated analysis of unannotated transcripts of the speech of children with ASD, automatically extracted language features have shown promise in the identification of other neurological disorders such as language impairment and cognitive impairment. Gabani et al. (2009) used part-of-speech language models to derive perplexity scores for transcripts of the speech of children with and without language impairment. These scores offered significant diagnostic power, achieving an F1 measure of roughly 70% when used within an support vector machine (SVM) for classification. Roark et al. (in press) extracted a much larger set of language complexity features derived from syntactic parse trees from transcripts of narratives produced by elderly subjects for the diagnosis of mild cognitive impairment. Selecting a subset of these features for classification with an SVM yielded accuracy, as measured by the area under the receiver operating characteristic curve, of 0.73.

Language models have also been applied to the task of error identification, but primarily in writing samples of ESL learners. Gamon et al. (2008) used word-based language models to detect and correct common ESL errors, while Leacock and Chodorow (2003) used part-of-speech bigram language models to identify potentially ungrammatical two-word sequences in ESL essays. Although these tasks differ in a number of ways from our tasks, they demonstrate the utility of using both word and part-of-speech language models for error detection.

3 Data Collection

3.1 Subjects

Our first objective was to gather data in order reproduce the results reported in Volden and Lord (1991). As shown in Table 1, the participants in our study were 50 children ages 4 to 8 with a performance IQ greater than 80 and a diagnosis of either typical

Diagnosis	Count	Age (s.d.)	IQ (s.d.)
TD	17	6.24 (1.38)	125.7 (11.63)
ASD	20	6.38 (1.25)	108.9 (16.41)
DLD	13	7.01 (1.10)	100.6 (10.95)

Table 1: Count, mean age and IQ by subject group.

development (TD, n=17), autism spectrum disorder (ASD, n=20), or developmental language disorder (DLD, n=13).

Developmental language disorder (DLD), also sometimes known as specific language impairment (SLI), is generally defined as the delayed or impaired acquisition of language without accompanying comparable delays or deficits in hearing, cognition, and socio-emotional development (McCauley, 2001). The language impairments that characterize DLD are not related to articulation or "speech impediments" but rather are associated with more profound problems producing and often comprehending language in terms of its pragmatics, syntax, semantics, and phonology. The DSM-IV-TR (American Psychiatric Association, 2000) includes neither DLD nor SLI as a disorder, but for the purposes of this work, DLD corresponds to the DSM's designations *Expressive Language Disorder* and *Mixed Expressive-Receptive Language Disorder*.

For this study, a subject received a diagnosis of DLD if he or she met one of two commonly used criteria: 1) The Tomblin Epi-SLI criteria (Tomblin, et al., 1996), in which diagnosis of language impairment is indicated when scores in two out of five domains (vocabulary, grammar, narrative, receptive, and expressive) are greater than 1.25 standard deviations below the mean; and 2) The CELF-Preschool-2/CELF-4 criteria, in which diagnosis of language impairment is indicated when one out of three index scores and one out of three spontaneous language scores are more than one standard deviation below the mean.

A diagnosis of ASD required a previous medical, educational, or clinical diagnosis of ASD, which was then confirmed by our team of clinicians according to the criteria of the DSM-IV-TR (American Psychiatric Association, 2000), the revised algorithm of the ADOS (Lord et al., 2002), and the SCQ parental interview (Rutter et al., 2003). Fifteen of the 20 ASD subjects participating in this study also met at least one of the above described criteria for DLD.

3.2 Data Preparation

The ADOS (Lord et al., 2002), a semi-structured series of activities designed to reveal behaviors associated with autism, was administered to all 50 subjects. Five of the ADOS activities that require significant amounts spontaneous speech (Make-Believe Play, Joint Interactive Play, Description of a Picture, Telling a Story From a Book, and Conversation and Reporting) were then transcribed at the utterance level for all 50 speakers. All utterances from the transcripts longer than four words (11,244) were presented to individuals blind to the purposes of the study, who were asked to flag any sentence with atypical or unusual word use. Those sentences were then classified by the authors as having no errors or one of the three error types described in Volden and Lord. Examples from our data are given in Table 2.

3.3 Reproducing Previous Results

In order to compare our results to those reported in Volden and Lord, we calculated the rates of the three types of errors for each subject, as shown in Table 2. With a two-sample (TD v. ASD) t-test, the rates of nondevelopmental and semantic errors were significantly higher in the ASD group than in the TD group, while there was no significant difference in developmental errors between the two groups. These results reflect the same trends observed in Volden and Lord, in which the raw counts of both developmental and semantic errors were higher in the ASD group.

Using ANOVA for significance testing over all three diagnostic groups, we found that the rate of developmental errors was significantly higher in the DLD group than in the other groups. The difference in semantic error rate between TD and ASD using the t-test was preserved, but the difference in nondevelopmental error rate was lost when comparing all three diagnostic groups with ANOVA, as shown in Figure 1.

Error	Example
Dev.	I have a games. The baby drinked it. The frogs was watching TV.
Nondev.	He locked him all of out. Would you like to be fall down? He got so the ball went each way.
Sem.	Something makes my eyes poke. It smells like it's falling on your head. All the fish are leaving in the air.

Table 2: Examples of error types.

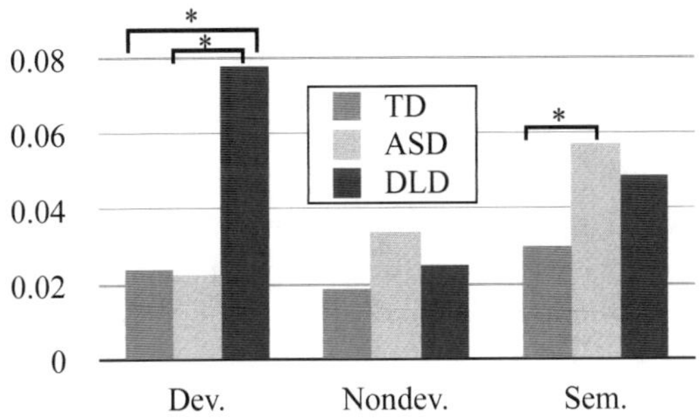

Figure 1: Error rates by diagnostic group (*p <0.05).

The process of manually identifying sentences with atypical or unusual language was relatively painless, but determining the specific error types is subjective and time-consuming, and requires a great deal of expertise. In addition, although we do observe significant differences between groups, it is not clear whether the differences are sufficient for diagnostic classification or discrimination.

We now propose automatically extracting from the transcripts various measures of linguistic likelihood, complexity, and surprisal that have the potential to objectively capture qualities that differentiate 1) the three types of errors described above, and 2) the three diagnostic groups discussed above. In the next three sections, we will discuss the various linguistic features we extract; methods for using these features to classify each sentence according to its error type for the purpose of automatic error-detection; and methods for using these features, calculated for each subject, for diagnostic classification.

4 Features

N-gram cross entropy. Following previous work in both error detection (Gamon et al., 2008; Leacock and Chodorow, 2003) and neurodevelopmental diagnostic classification (Gabani et al., 2009), we begin with simple bigram language model features. A bigram language model provides information about the likelihood of a given item (e.g., a word or part of speech) in a sentence given the previous item in that sentence. We suspect that some of the types of unusual language investigated here, in particular those seen in the syntactic errors shown in Table 2, are characterized by unlikely words (*drinked*) and word or part-of-speech sequences (*a games*, *all of out*) and hence might be distinguished by language model-based scores.

We build a word-level bigram language model and a part-of-speech level bigram language model from the Switchboard (Godfrey et al., 1992) corpus. We then automatically generate part-of-speech tags for each sentence (where the tags were derived from the best scoring output of the full syntactic parser mentioned below), and then apply the two models to each sentence. For each sentence, we calculate its cross entropy and perplexity. For a word string $w_1 \dots w_n$ of length n, the cross entropy H is

$$H(w_1 \dots w_n) \quad = \quad -\frac{1}{n} \log \mathrm{P}(w_1 \dots w_n) \quad (1)$$

where $\mathrm{P}(w_1 \dots w_n)$ is calculated as the product of the n-gram probabilities of each word in the string. The corresponding measure can be calculated for the POS-tag sequence, based on an n-gram model of tags. Perplexity is simply 2^H.

While we would prefer to use a corpus that is closer to the child language that we are attempting to model, we found the conversational style of the Switchboard corpus to be the most effective large corpus that we had at our disposal for this study. As the size of our small corpus grows, we intend to make use of the text to assist with model building, but for this study, we used all out-of-domain data for n-gram language models and parsing models. Using Switchboard also allowed us to use the same corpus to train both n-gram and parsing models.

Surprisal-based features. Surprisal, or the unexpectedness of a word or syntactic category in a given context, is often used as a psycholinguistic measure of sentence-processing difficulty (Hale, 2001; Boston et al., 2008). Although surprisal is usually discussed in the context of cognitive load for language processing, we hoped that it might also capture some of the language characteristics of the semantic errors like those in Table 2, which often contain common words used in surprising ways, and the nondevelopmental syntax errors, which often include strings of function words presented in an order that would be difficult to anticipate.

To derive surprisal-based features, each sentence is parsed using the Roark (2001) incremental top-down parser relying on a model built again on the Switchboard corpus. The incremental output of the parser shows the surprisal for each word, as well as other scores, as presented in Roark et al. (2009). For each sentence, we collected the mean surprisal (equivalent to the cross entropy given the model); the mean syntactic surprisal; and the mean lexical surprisal. The lexical and syntactic surprisal are a decomposition of the total surprisal into that portion due to probability mass associated with building non-terminal structure (syntactic surprisal) and that portion due to probability mass associated with building terminal lexical items in the tree (lexical surprisal). We refer the reader to that paper for further details.

Other linguistic complexity measures The non-developmental syntax errors in Table 2 are characterized by their ill-formed syntactic structure. Following Roark et al. (in press), in which the authors explored the relationship between linguistic structural complexity and cognitive decline, and Sagae (2005), in which the authors used automatic syntactic annotation to assess syntactic development, we also investigated the following measures of linguistic complexity: words per clause, tree nodes per word, dependency length per word, and Ygnve and Frazier scores per word. Each of these scores can be calculated from a provided syntactic parse tree, and to generate these we made use of the Charniak parser (Charniak, 2000), also trained on the Switchboard treebank.

Briefly, words per clause is the total number of words divided by the total number of clauses; and tree nodes per word is the total number of nodes in the parse tree divided by the number of words. The dependency length for a word is the distance (in word tokens) between that word and its governor, as determined through standard head-percolation methods from the output of the Charniak parser. We calculate the mean of this length over all words in the utterance. The Yngve score of a word is the size of the stack of a shift-reduce parser after that word; and the Frazier score essentially counts how many intermediate nodes exist in the tree between the word and its lowest ancestor that is either the root or has a left sibling in the tree. We calculate the mean of both of these scores over the utterance. We refer the reader to the above cited paper for more details on these measures.

As noted in Roark et al. (in press), some of these measures are influenced by particular characteristics of the Penn Treebank style trees – e.g., flat noun phrases, etc. – and measures vary in the degree to which they capture divergence from typical structures. Some (including Yngve) are sensitive to the breadth of trees (e.g., flat productions with many children); others (including Frazier) are sensitive to depth of trees. This variability is a key reason for including multiple, complementary features, such as both Frazier and Yngve scores, to capture more subtle syntactic characteristics than would be available from any of these measures alone.

Although we were not able to measure parsing accuracy on our data set and how it might affect the reliability of these features, Roark et al. (in press) did investigate this very issue. They found that all of the above described syntactic measures, when they were derived from automatically generated parse trees, correlated very highly (greater than 0.9) with those measures when they were derived from manually generated parse trees. For the moment, we assume that the same principle holds true for our data set, though we do intend both to verify this assumption and to supplement our parsing models with data from child speech. Based on manual inspection of parser output, the current parsing model does seem to be recovering largely valid structures.

5 Error Classification

The values for 8 of the 12 features were significantly different over the three error classes, as measured by one-way ANOVA: words per clause, Yngve, dependency, word cross-entropy all significant at $p < 0.001$; Frazier, nodes per word at $p < 0.01$; overall surprisal and lexical surprisal at $p < 0.05$. We built classification and regression trees (CART) using the Weka data mining software (Hall et al., 2009) using all of the 12 features described above to predict which error each sentence contained, and we report the accuracy, weighted F measure, and area under the receiver operating characteristic curve (AUC).

Including all 12 features in the CART using 10-fold cross validation resulted in an AUC of 0.68, while using only those features with significant between-group differences yielded an AUC of 0.65.

Classifier	Acc.	F1	AUC
Baseline 1	41%	0.24	0.5
Baseline 2	33%	0.32	0.5
All features	53%	0.53	0.68
Feature subset	49%	0.49	0.65

Table 3: Error-type classification results.

These are both substantial improvements over a baseline with an unbalanced corpus in which the most frequent class is chosen for all input items (Baseline 1) or a baseline with a balanced corpus in which class is chosen at random (Baseline 2), which both have an AUC of 0.5. The results for each of these classifiers, provided in Table 3, show potential for automating the identification of error type.

6 Diagnostic Classification

In Section 3, we found a number of significant differences in error type production rates across our three diagnostic groups. Individual rates of error production, however, provide almost no classification power within a CART (AUC = 0.51). Perhaps the phenomena being observed in ASD and DLD language are related to subtle language features that are less easily identified than simply the membership of a sentence in one of these three error categories.

Given the ability of our language features to discriminate error types moderately well, as shown in Section 5, we decided to extract these same 12 features from every sentence longer than 4 words from the entire transcript for each of the subjects. We then took the mean of each feature over all of the sentences for each speaker. These per-speaker feature vectors were used for diagnostic classification within a CART.

We first performed classification over the three diagnostic groups using the full set of 12 features described in Section 4. This results in only modest gains in performance over the baseline that uses error rates as the only features. We then used ANOVA to determine which of the 12 features differed significantly across the three groups. Only four features were found to be significantly different across the three groups (words per clause, Yngve, dependency, word cross entropy), and none of them different significantly between the ASD group and the DLD group. As expected, classification did not improve with this feature subset, as reported in Table 4.

Features	Acc.	F1	AUC
Error rates	33%	0.32	0.51
All features	42%	0.38	0.59
Feature subset	40%	0.37	0.6

Table 4: All subjects: Diagnostic classification results.

Recall that 15 of the 20 ASD subjects also met at least one criterion for a developmental language disorder. Perhaps the language peculiarities we observe in our subjects with ASD are related in part to language characteristics of DLD rather than ASD. We now attempt to tease apart these two sources of unusual language by investigating three separate classification tasks: TD vs. ASD, TD vs. DLD, and ASD vs. DLD.

6.1 TD vs. ASD

We perform classification of the TD and ASD subjects with three feature sets: 1) per-subject error rates; 2) all 12 features described in Section 4; and 3) the subset of significantly different features. We found that 7 of the 12 features explored in Section 4 differed significantly between the TD group and the ASD group: words per clause, Yngve, dependency, word cross-entropy, overall surprisal, syntactic surprisal, and lexical surprisal. Classification results are shown in Table 5. We see that using the automatically derived linguistic features improves classification substantially over the baseline using per-subject error rates, particularly when we use the feature subset. Note that the best classification accuracy results are comparable to those reported in related work on language impairment and mild cognitive impairment described in Section 2.

6.2 TD vs. DLD

We perform classification of TD and DLD subjects with the same three feature sets used for the TD vs. ASD classification. We found that 6 of the 12

Features	Acc.	F1	AUC
Error rates	62%	0.62	0.56
All features	62%	0.62	0.65
Feature subset	68%	0.67	0.72

Table 5: TD vs. ASD: Diagnostic classification results.

Features	Acc.	F1	AUC
Error rates	67%	0.67	0.72
All features	80%	0.79	0.75
Feature subset	77%	0.75	0.66

Table 6: TD vs. DLD: Diagnostic classification results.

features explored in Section 4 different significantly between the TD group and the ASD group: words per clause, Yngve, dependency, word cross-entropy, overall surprisal, and lexical surprisal. Note that this is a subset of the features that differed between the TD group and ASD group. Classification results are shown in Table 6. Interestingly, using per-subject error rates for classification of TD and DLD subjects was quite robust. Using all of the features improved classification somewhat, while using only a subset resulted in degraded performance. We see that the discriminative power of these features is superior to that reported in earlier work using LM-based features for classification of specific language impairment (Gabani et al., 2009).

6.3 ASD vs. DLD

Finally, we perform classification of the ASD and DLD subjects using only the first two features sets, since there were no features found to be even marginally significantly different between these two groups. Classification results, which are dismal for both feature sets, are shown in Table 7.

6.4 Discussion

It seems quite clear that the error rates, feature values, and classification performance are all being influenced by the fact that a majority of the ASD subjects also meet at least one criterion for a developmental language disorder. Neither error rates nor feature values could discriminate between the ASD and DLD group. Nevertheless we see that our ASD group and DLD group do not follow the same patterns in their error production or language feature scores. Clearly there are differences in the language patterns of the two groups that are not being captured with any of the methods discussed here.

Features	Acc.	F1	AUC
Error rates	55%	0.52	0.48
All features	58%	0.44	0.40

Table 7: ASD vs. DLD: Diagnostic classification results.

We also observe that the error rates themselves, while sometimes significantly different across groups as originally observed in Volden and Lord, do not perform well as diagnostic features for ASD in our framework. Volden and Lord did not attempt classification in their study, so it is not known whether the authors would have encountered the same problem. There are, however, a number of possible explanations for a discrepancy between our results and theirs. First, our data was gathered from pre-school and young school-aged children, while the Volden and Lord subjects were generally teenagers and young adults. The way in which their spoken language samples were elicited allowed Volden and Lord to use raw error counts rather than error rates. There may also have been important differences in the way we carried out the manual error identification process, despite our best efforts to replicate their procedure. Further development of our classification methods and additional data collection are needed to determine the utility of error type identification for diagnostic purposes.

7 Future Work

Although our classifiers using automatically extracted features were generally robust, we expect that including additional classification techniques, subjects (especially ASD subjects without DLD), and features will further improve our results. In particular, we would like to explore semantic and lexical features that are less dependent on linear order and syntactic structure, such as Resnik similarity and features derived using latent semantic analysis.

We also plan to expand the training input for the language model and parser to include children's speech. The Switchboard corpus is conversational speech, but it may fail to adequately model many linguistic features characteristic of small children. The CHILDES database of children's speech, although it is not large enough to be used on its own for our analysis and would require significant manual syntactic annotation, might provide enough data for us to adapt our models to the child language domain.

Finally, we would like to investigate how informative the error types are and whether they can be reliably coded by multiple judges. When we examined the output of our error-type classifier, we noticed that many of the misclassified examples could be construed, upon closer inspection, as belonging to multiple error classes. The sentence *He's flying in a lily-pond*, for instance, could contain a developmental error (i.e., the child has not yet acquired the correct meaning of *in*) or a semantic error (i.e., the child is using the word *flying* instead of *swimming*). Without knowing the context in which the sentence was uttered, it is not possible to determine the type of error through any manual or automatic means. The seemingly large number of misclassifications of sentences like this indicates the need for further investigation of the existing coding procedure and in-depth classification error analysis.

8 Conclusions

Our method of automatically identifying error type shows promise as a supplement to, or substitute for, the time-consuming and subjective manual coding process described in Volden and Lord (Volden and Lord, 1991). However, the superior performance of our automatically extracted language features suggests that perhaps it may not be the errors themselves that characterize the speech of children with ASD and DLD but rather a preference for certain structures and word sequences that sometimes manifest themselves as clear language errors. Such variations in complexity and likelihood might be too subtle for humans to reliably observe.

In summary, the methods explored in this paper show potential for improving diagnostic discrimination between typically developing children and those with these neurodevelopmental disorders. Further research is required, however, in finding the most reliable markers that can be derived from such spoken language samples.

Acknowledgments

This work was supported in part by NSF Grant #BCS-0826654; an Innovative Technology for Autism grant from Autism Speaks; and NIH NIDCD grant #1R01DC007129-01. Any opinions, findings, conclusions or recommendations expressed in this publication are those of the authors and do not necessarily reflect the views of the NSF, Autism Speaks, or the NIH. Thanks to Meg Mitchell and Cheryl Greene for their assistance with this project.

References

American Psychiatric Association. 2000. *DSM-IV-TR: Diagnostic and Statistical Manual of Mental Disorders.* American Psychiatric Publishing, Washington, DC, 4th edition.

Laurence Bartak, Michael Rutter, and Anthony Cox. 1975. A comparative study of infantile autism and specific developmental receptive language disorder. I. The children. *British Journal of Psychiatry*, 126:27145.

Mariss Ferrara Boston, John Hale, Reinhold Kliegl, and Shravan Vasishth. 2008. Surprising parser actions and reading difficulty. In *Proceedings of ACL-08:HLT, Short Papers*.

Eugene Charniak. 2000. A maximum-entropy-inspired parser. In *Proceedings of the 1st Conference of the North American Chapter of the ACL*, pages 132–139.

Keyur Gabani, Melissa Sherman, Thamar Solorio, and Yang Liu. 2009. A corpus-based approach for the prediction of language impairment in monolingual english and spanish-english bilingual children. In *Proceedings of NAACL-HLT*, pages 46–55.

Michael Gamon, Jianfeng Gao, Chris Brockett, and Re Klementiev. 2008. Using contextual speller techniques and language modeling for ESL error correction. In *Proceedings of IJCNLP*.

John J. Godfrey, Edward Holliman, and Jane McDaniel. 1992. SWITCHBOARD: telephone speech corpus for research and development. In *Proceedings of ICASSP*, volume 1, pages 517–520.

John T. Hale. 2001. A probabilistic Earley parser as a psycholinguistic model. In *Proceedings of the 2nd meeting of NAACL*.

Mark Hall, Eibe Frank, Geoffrey Holmes, Bernhard Pfahringer, Peter Reutemann, and Ian H. Witten. 2009. The WEKA data mining software: An update. *SIGKDD Explorations*, 11(1).

Leo Kanner. 1943. Autistic disturbances of affective content. *Nervous Child*, 2:217–250.

Leo Kanner. 1946. Irrelevant and metaphorical language. *American Journal of Psychiatry*, 103:242–246.

Claudia Leacock and Martin Chodorow. 2003. Automated grammatical error detection. In M.D. Shermis and J. Burstein, editors, *Automated essay scoring: A cross-disciplinary perspective*. Lawrence Erlbaum Associates, Inc., Hillsdale, NJ.

Catherine Lord, Michael Rutter, and Anne LeCouteur. 1994. Autism diagnostic interview-revised: A revised version of a diagnostic interview for caregivers of individuals with possible pervasive developmental disorders. *Journal of Autism and Developmental Disorders*, 24:659–685.

Catherine Lord, Michael Rutter, Pamela DiLavore, and Susan Risi. 2002. *Autism Diagnostic Observation Schedule (ADOS)*. Western Psychological Services, Los Angeles.

Rebecca McCauley. 2001. *Assessment of language disorders in children*. Lawrence Erlbaum Associates, Mahwah, NJ.

Brian Roark, Asaf Bachrach, Carlos Cardenas, and Christophe Pallier. 2009. Deriving lexical and syntactic expectation-based measures for psycholinguistic modeling via incremental top-down parsing. In *Proceedings of EMNLP*, pages 324–333.

Brian Roark, Margaret Mitchell, John-Paul Hosom, Kristina Hollingshead, and Jeffrey Kaye. in press. Spoken language derived measures for detecting mild cognitive impairment. *IEEE Transactions on Audio, Speech and Language Processing*.

Brian Roark. 2001. Probabilistic top-down parsing and language modeling. *Computational Linguistics*, 27(2):249–276.

Michael Rutter, Anthony Bailey, and Catherine Lord. 2003. *Social Communication Questionnaire (SCQ)*. Western Psychological Services, Los Angeles.

Michael Rutter. 1965. Speech disorders in a series of autistic children. In A. Franklin, editor, *Children with communication problems*, pages 39–47. Pitman.

Kenji Sagae, Alon Lavie, and Brian MacWhinney. 2005. Automatic measurement of syntactic development in child language. In *Proceedings of the 43rd Annual Meeting of the ACL*.

Joanne Volden and Catherine Lord. 1991. Neologisms and idiosyncratic language in autistic speakers. *Journal of Autism and Developmental Disorders*, 21:109–130.

Colourful Language: Measuring Word–Colour Associations

Saif Mohammad
Institute for Information Technology
National Research Council Canada
Ottawa, Ontario, Canada, K1A 0R6
saif.mohammad@nrc-cnrc.gc.ca

Abstract

Since many real-world concepts are associated with colour, for example *danger* with red, linguistic information is often complimented with the use of appropriate colours in information visualization and product marketing. Yet, there is no comprehensive resource that captures concept–colour associations. We present a method to create a large word–colour association lexicon by crowdsourcing. We focus especially on abstract concepts and emotions to show that even though they cannot be physically visualized, they too tend to have strong colour associations. Finally, we show how word–colour associations manifest themselves in language, and quantify usefulness of co-occurrence and polarity cues in automatically detecting colour associations.[1]

1 Introduction

Colour is a vital component in the successful delivery of information, whether it is in marketing a commercial product (Sable and Akcay, 2010), designing webpages (Meier, 1988; Pribadi et al., 1990), or visualizing information (Christ, 1975; Card et al., 1999). Since real-world concepts have associations with certain colour categories (for example, *danger* with red, and *softness* with pink), complimenting linguistic and non-linguistic information with appropriate colours has a number of benefits, including: (1) strengthening the message (improving semantic coherence), (2) easing cognitive load on the receiver, (3) conveying the message quickly, and (4) evoking the desired emotional response. Consider, for example, the use of red in stop signs. Drivers are able to recognize the sign faster, and it evokes a subliminal emotion pertaining to danger, which is entirely appropriate in the context. The use of red to show areas of high crime rate in a visualization is another example of good use of colour to draw emotional response. On the other hand, improper use of colour can be more detrimental to understanding than using no colour (Marcus, 1982; Meier, 1988).

Most languages have expressions involving colour, and many of these express sentiment. Examples in English include: *green with envy*, *blue blood* (an aristocrat), *greener pastures* (better avenues), *yellow-bellied* (cowardly), *red carpet* (special treatment), and *looking through rose-tinted glasses* (being optimistic). Further, new expressions are continually coined, for example, *grey with uncertainty* from Bianca Marsden's poem *Confusion*.[2] Thus, knowledge of concept–colour associations may also be useful for automatic natural language systems such as textual entailment, paraphrasing, machine translation, and sentiment analysis.

A word has strong association with a colour when the colour is a salient feature of the concept the word refers to, or because the word is related to a such a concept. Many concept–colour associations, such as *swan* with white and *vegetables* with green, involve physical entities. However, even abstract notions and emotions may have colour as-

[1] This paper is an extended, non-archival, version of the short paper—Mohammad (2011). It provides additional details on the analysis of crowdsourced data, and experiments on the manifestations of word–colour associations in WordNet and in text. It also proposes a polarity-based automatic method.

[2] http://www.biancaday.com/confusion.html

sociations (*honesty*–white, *danger*–red, *joy*–yellow, *anger*–red). Further, many associations are culture-specific (Gage, 1969; Chen, 2005). For example, *prosperity* is associated with red in much of Asia.

Unfortunately, there exists no lexicon with any significant coverage that captures concept–colour associations, and a number of questions remain unanswered, such as, the extent to which humans agree on these associations, and whether physical concepts are more likely to have a colour association than abstract ones. We expect that the word–colour associations manifest themselves as co-occurrences in text and speech, but there have been no studies to show the extent to which words co-occur more with associated colours than with other colours.

In this paper, we describe how we created a large word–colour association lexicon by crowdsourcing with effective quality control measures (Section 3). We used a word-choice question to guide the annotators toward the desired senses of the target words, and also to determine if the annotators know the meanings of the words.

We conducted several experiments to measure the consensus in word–colour associations, and how these associations manifest themselves in language. Specifically, we show that:

- More than 30% of terms have a strong colour association (Sections 4).
- About 33% of thesaurus categories have strong colour associations (Section 5).
- Abstract terms have colour associations almost as often as physical entities do (Section 6).
- There is a strong association of emotions and polarities with colours (Section 7).
- Word-colour association manifests itself as closeness in WordNet (to a smaller extent), and as high co-occurrence in text (to a greater extent) (Section 8).

Finally, we present an automatic method to determine word–colour association that relies on co-occurrence and polarity cues, but no labeled information of word–colour associations. It obtains an accuracy of more than 60%. Comparatively, the random choice and most-frequent class supervised baselines obtain only 9.1% and 33.3%, respectively. Such approaches can be used to for creating similar lexicons in other languages.

2 Related Work

The relation between language and cognition has received considerable attention over the years, mainly on answering whether language impacts thought, and if so, to what extent. Experiments with colour categories have been used both to show that language has an effect on thought (Brown and Lenneberg, 1954; Ratner, 1989) and that it does not (Bornstein, 1985). However, that line of work does not explicitly deal with word–colour associations. In fact, we did not find any other academic work that gathered large word–colour associations. There is, however, a commercial endeavor—Cymbolism[3].

Child et al. (1968), Ou et al. (2011), and others show that people of different ages and genders have different colour preferences. (See also the online study by Joe Hallock[4].) In this work, we are interested in identifying words that have a strong association with a colour due to their meaning; associations that are not affected by age and gender preferences.

There is substantial work on inferring the emotions evoked by colour (Luscher, 1969; Xin et al., 2004; Kaya, 2004). Strapparava and Ozbal (2010) compute corpus-based semantic similarity between emotions and colours. We combine the word–colour and word–emotion association lexicons to determine the correlation between emotion-associated words and colours.

Berlin and Kay (1969), and later Kay and Maffi (1999), showed that often colour terms appeared in languages in certain groups. If a language has only two colour terms, then they are white and black. If a language has three colour terms, then they are white, black, and red. If a language has four colour terms, then they are white, black, red, and green, and so on up to eleven colours. From these groupings, the colours can be ranked as follows:

> 1. white, 2. black, 3. red, 4. green, 5. yellow, 6. blue, 7. brown, 8. pink, 9. purple, 10. orange, 11. grey (1)

We will refer to the above ranking as the *Berlin and Kay (B&K) order*. There are hundreds of different words for colours.[5] To make our task feasible,

[3]http://www.cymbolism.com/about

[4]http://www.joehallock.com/edu/COM498/preferences.html

[5]See http://en.wikipedia.org/wiki/List_of_colors

we needed to choose a relatively small list of basic colours. We chose to use the eleven basic colour words of Berlin and Kay (1969).

The MRC Psycholinguistic Database (Coltheart, 1981) has, among other information, the *imageability ratings* for 9240 words.[6] The imageability rating is a score given by human judges that reflects how easy it is to visualize the concept. It is a scale from 100 (very hard to visualize) to 700 (very easy to visualize). We use the ratings in our experiments to determine whether there is a correlation between imageability and strength of colour association.

3 Crowdsourcing

Amazon's Mechanical Turk (AMT) is an online crowdsourcing platform that is especially well suited for tasks that can be done over the Internet through a computer or a mobile device.[7] It is already being used to obtain human annotation on various linguistic tasks (Snow et al., 2008; Callison-Burch, 2009). However, one must define the task carefully to obtain annotations of high quality. Several checks must be placed to ensure that random and erroneous annotations are discouraged, rejected, and re-annotated.

We used Mechanical Turk to obtain word–colour association annotations on a large-scale. Each task is broken into small independently solvable units called *HITs (Human Intelligence Tasks)* and uploaded on the Mechanical Turk website. The people who provide responses to these HITs are called *Turkers*. The annotation provided by a Turker for a HIT is called an *assignment*.

We used the *Macquarie Thesaurus* (Bernard, 1986) as the source for terms to be annotated. Thesauri, such as the *Roget's* and *Macquarie*, group related words into categories. The *Macquarie* has about a thousand categories, each having about a hundred or so related terms. Each category has a *head word* that best represents the words in it. The categories can be thought of as coarse senses or concepts (Yarowsky, 1992). If a word is ambiguous, then it is listed in more than one category. Since a word may have different colour associations when used in different senses, we obtained annotations at word-sense level. We chose to annotate words that had one to five senses in the *Macquarie Thesaurus* and occurred frequently in the *Google N-gram Corpus*. We annotated more than 10,000 of these word–sense pairs by creating HITs as described below.

Each HIT has a set of questions, all of which are to be answered by the same person. We requested annotations from five different Turkers for each HIT. (A Turker cannot attempt multiple assignments for the same term.) A complete HIT is shown below:

Q1. Which word is closest in meaning to *sleep*?

- *car* • *tree* • *nap* • *olive*

Q2. What colour is associated with *sleep*?

• black	• green	• purple	• white
• blue	• grey	• pink	• yellow
• brown	• orange	• red	

Q1 is a word-choice question generated automatically by taking a near-synonym from the thesaurus and random distractors. The near-synonym also guides the annotator to the desired sense of the word. Further, it encourages the annotator to think clearly about the target word's meaning; we believe this improves the quality of the annotations in Q2. If a word has multiple senses, that is, it is listed in more than one thesaurus category, then separate questionnaires are generated for each sense. Thus we obtain colour associations at a word-sense level.

If an annotator answers Q1 incorrectly, then we discard information obtained from both Q1 and Q2. Thus, even though we do not have correct answers to Q2, likely incorrect annotations are filtered out. About 10% of the annotations were discarded because of an incorrect answer to Q1. Terms with less than three valid annotations were removed from further analysis. Each of the remaining terms had, on average, 4.45 distinct annotations.

The colour options in Q2 were presented in random order. Observe that we do not provide a "not associated with any colour" option. This encourages colour selection even if the annotator felt the association was weak. If there is no association between a word and a colour, then we expect low agreement amongst the annotators. The survey was approved by the ethics board at the authors' institution.

[6]http://www.psy.uwa.edu.au/mrcdatabase/uwa_mrc.htm

[7]Mechanical Turk: www.mturk.com

	white	black	red	green	yellow	blue	brown	pink	purple	orange	grey
overall	11.9	12.2	11.7	12.0	11.0	9.4	9.6	8.6	4.2	4.2	4.6
voted	22.7	18.4	13.4	12.1	10.0	6.4	6.3	5.3	2.1	1.5	1.3

Table 1: Percentage of terms marked as being associated with each colour.

4 Word–Colour Association

The information from multiple annotators was combined by taking the majority vote, resulting in a lexicon of 8,813 entries. Each entry contains a unique word–synonym pair (from Q1), majority-voted colour, and a confidence score—number of votes for the colour / number of total votes. (For the analyses in the rest of the paper, ties were broken by picking one colour at random.) A separate version of the lexicon that includes entries for all of the valid annotations by each of the annotators is also available.[8]

The first row, *overall*, in Table 1 shows the percentage of times different colours were associated with the target term. The second row, *voted*, shows percentages after taking a majority vote from multiple annotators. Observe that even though the colour options were presented in random order, the order of the most frequently associated colours is identical to the Berlin and Kay order (Section 2:(1)).

Table 2 shows how often the size of the majority class in colour associations is one, two, three, four, and five. Since the annotators were given eleven colour options to choose from, if we assume independence, then the chance that none of the five annotators agrees with each other (majority class size of one) is $1 \times 10/11 \times 9/11 \times 8/11 \times 7/11 = 0.344$. Thus, if there was no correlation among any of the terms and colours, then 34.4% of the time none of the annotators would have agreed. However, this happens only 15.1% of the time. A large number of terms have a majority class size ≥ 2 (84.9%), and thus more than chance association with a colour. One can argue that terms with a majority class size ≥ 3 (32%) have *strong* colour associations.

Below are some reasons why agreement values are much lower than those obtained for certain other tasks, for example, part of speech tagging:

- The annotators were not given a "not associated with any colour" option. Low agreement for certain instances is an indicator that these words have weak, if any, colour association.
- Words are associated with colours to different degrees. Some words may be associated with more than one colour in comparable degrees, and there might be higher disagreement for such instances.
- The target word is presented out of context. We expect higher agreement if we provided words in particular contexts, but words can occur in innumerable contexts, and annotating too many instances of the same word is costly.

[8]Please contact the author to obtain a copy of the lexicon.

majority class size						
one	two	three	four	five	$\geq$ two	$\geq$ three
15.1	52.9	22.4	7.3	2.1	84.9	32.0

Table 2: Percentage of terms in different majority classes.

Nonetheless, the term–colour association lexicon is useful for downstream applications because any of the following strategies may be employed: (1) choosing colour associations from only those instances with high agreement, (2) assuming low-agreement terms have no colour association, (3) determining colour association of a category through information from many words, as described in the next section.

5 Category–Colour Association

Words within a thesaurus category may not be strongly associated with any colour, or they may each be associated with many different colours. We now describe experiments to determine whether there exist categories where the semantic coherence carries over to a strong common association with one colour.

We determine the strength of colour association of a category by first determining the colour c most associated with the terms in it, and then calculating the ratio of the number of times a word from the category is associated with c to the number of words in the category associated with any colour. Only cate-

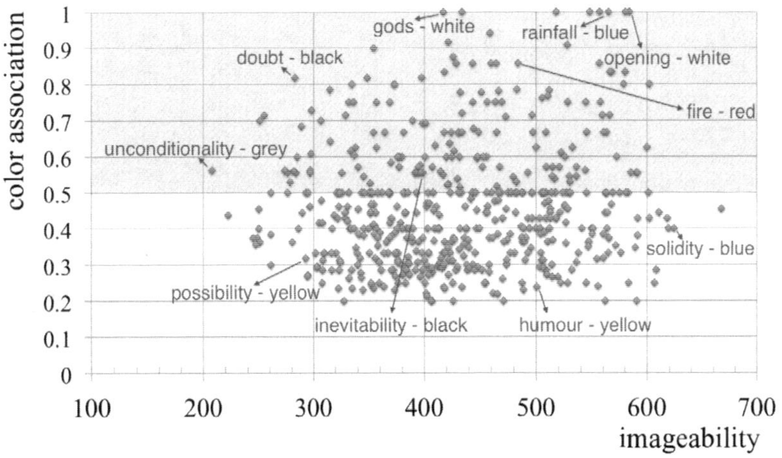

Figure 1: Scatter plot of thesaurus categories. The area of high colour association is shaded. Some points are labeled.

gories that had at least four words that also appear in the word–colour lexicon were considered; 535 of the 812 categories from *Macquarie Thesaurus* met this condition.

If a category has exactly four words that appear in the colour lexicon, and if all four words are associated with different colours, then the category has the lowest possible strength of colour association—0.25 (1/4). 19 categories had a score of 0.25. No category had a score less than 0.25. Any score above 0.25 shows more than random chance association with a colour. There were 516 such categories (96.5%). 177 categories (33.1%) had a score 0.5 or above, that is, half or more of the words in these categories are associated with one colour. We consider these to be strong associations, and a gold standard for automatic measures of association.

6 Imageability and Colour Association

It is natural for physical entities of a certain colour to be associated with that colour. However, abstract concepts such as *danger* and *excitability* are also associated with colours—red and orange, respectively. Figure 1 displays an experiment to determine whether there is a correlation between imageability and association with colour.

We define imageability of a thesaurus category to be the average of the imageability ratings of words in it. We calculated imageability for the 535 categories described in the previous section using only the words that appear in the colour lexicon. Figure 1 shows the scatter plot of these categories on the imageability and strength of colour association axes. The colour association was calculated as described in the previous section.

If higher imageability correlated with greater tendency to have a colour association, then we would see most of the points along the diagonal moving up from left to right. Instead, we observe that the strongly associated categories (points in the shaded region) are spread across the imageability axis, implying that there is only weak, if any, correlation between imageability and strength of association with colour. Imageability and colour association have a Pearson's product moment correlation of 0.116, and a Spearman rank order correlation of 0.102.

7 The Colour of Emotion Words

Emotions such as joy and anger are abstract concepts dealing with one's psychological state. Mohammad and Turney (2010) created a crowdsourced term–emotion association lexicon consisting of associations of over 10,000 word-sense pairs with eight emotions—joy, sadness, anger, fear, trust, disgust, surprise, and anticipation—argued to be the basic and prototypical emotions (Plutchik, 1980). We combine their term–emotion association lexicon and our term–colour lexicon to determine the colour signature of different emotions—the rows in Table 3. The top two most frequently associated colours with each of the eight emotions are shown in bold. For example, the "anger" row shows the percentage of

	white	black	red	green	yellow	blue	brown	pink	purple	orange	grey
anger words	2.1	**30.7**	**32.4**	5.0	5.0	2.4	6.6	0.5	2.3	2.5	9.9
anticipation words	**16.2**	7.5	11.5	**16.2**	10.7	9.5	5.7	5.9	3.1	4.9	8.4
disgust words	2.0	**33.7**	**24.9**	4.8	5.5	1.9	9.7	1.1	1.8	3.5	10.5
fear words	4.5	**31.8**	**25.0**	3.5	6.9	3.0	6.1	1.3	2.3	3.3	11.8
joy words	**21.8**	2.2	7.4	**14.1**	13.4	11.3	3.1	11.1	6.3	5.8	2.8
sadness words	3.0	**36.0**	**18.6**	3.4	5.4	5.8	7.1	0.5	1.4	2.1	16.1
surprise words	11.0	13.4	**21.0**	8.3	**13.5**	5.2	3.4	5.2	4.1	5.6	8.8
trust words	**22.0**	6.3	8.4	14.2	8.3	**14.4**	5.9	5.5	4.9	3.8	5.8

Table 3: Colour signature of emotive terms: percentage of terms associated with each colour. For example, 32.4% of the anger terms are associated with red. The two most associated colours are shown in bold.

	white	black	red	green	yellow	blue	brown	pink	purple	orange	grey
negative	2.9	**28.3**	**21.6**	4.7	6.9	4.1	**9.4**	1.2	2.5	3.8	**14.1**
positive	**20.1**	3.9	8.0	**15.5**	**10.8**	**12.0**	4.8	**7.8**	**5.7**	**5.4**	5.7

Table 4: Colour signature of positive and negative terms: percentage terms associated with each colour. For example, 28.3% of the negative terms are associated with black. The highest values in each column are shown in bold.

anger terms associated with different colours.

We see that all of the emotions have strong associations with certain colours. Observe that anger is associated most with red. Other negative emotions—disgust, fear, sadness—go strongest with black. Among the positive emotions: anticipation is most frequently associated with white and green; joy with white, green, and yellow; and trust with white, blue, and green. Thus, colour can add to the emotional potency of visualizations.

The Mohammad and Turney (2010) lexicon also has associations with positive and negative polarity. We combine these term–polarity associations with term–colour associations to show the colour signature for positive and negative terms—the rows of Table 4. We observe that some colours tend to, more often than not, have strong positive associations (white, green, yellow, blue, pink, and orange), whereas others have strong negative associations (black, red, brown, and grey).

8 Manifestation of Concept–Colour Association in WordNet and in Text

8.1 Closeness in WordNet

Colour terms are listed in WordNet, and interestingly, they are fairly ambiguous. Therefore, they can be found in many different synsets (see Table 5). A casual examination of WordNet reveals that some synsets (or concepts) are close to their associated colour's synset. For example, *darkness* is a hypernym of black and *inflammation* is one hop away from red. It is plausible that if a concept is strongly associated with a certain colour, then such concept–colour pairs will be close to each other in a semantic network such as WordNet. If so, the semantic closeness of a word with each of the eleven basic colours in WordNet can be used to automatically determine the colour most associated with the 177 thesaurus categories from the gold standard described in Section 5 earlier. We determine closeness using two similarity measures—Jiang and Conrath (1997) and Lin (1997)—and two relatedness measures—Lesk (Banerjee and Pedersen, 2003) and gloss vector overlap (Pedersen et al., 2004)—from the WordNet Similarity package.

For each thesaurus category–colour pair, we summed the WordNet closeness of each of the terms in the category to the colour. The colour with the highest sum is chosen as the one closest to the thesaurus category. Section (c) and section (d) of Table 8.2, show how often the closest colours are also the colours most associated with the gold standard categories. Section (a) lists some unsupervised baselines. Random-choice baseline is the score obtained when a colour is chosen at random (1/11 = 9.1%). Another baseline is a system that always chooses the most frequent colour in a corpus. Section (a) reports three such baseline scores obtained by choosing the most frequently occurring colour in three separate corpora. Section (b) lists a supervised baseline obtained by choosing the colour most commonly asso-

colour	white	black	red	green	yellow	blue	brown	pink	purple	orange	grey
# of senses	25	22	7	14	8	16	8	7	7	6	13

Table 5: The number of senses of colour terms in WordNet.

		white	black	red	green	yellow	blue	brown	pink	purple	orange	grey	ρ
	B&K rank:	1	2	3	4	5	6	7	8	9	10	11	
BNC	freq:	1480	3460	2070	1990	270	1430	1170	450	180	360	800	
	rank:	4	1	2	3	10	5	6	8	11	9	7	0.727
GNC	freq:	205	239	138	106	80	123	63	41	16	36	18	
	rank:	2	1	3	5	6	4	7	8	11	9	10	0.884
GBC	freq:	233	188	130	86	44	75	72	14	11	19	22	
	rank:	1	2	3	4	7	5	6	9	10	11	8	0.918

Table 6: Frequency and ranking of colour terms per 1,000,000 words in the *British National Corpus (BNC), Google N-gram Corpus (GNC),* and *Google Books Corpus (GBC).* The last column lists the Spearman rank order correlation (ρ) of the rankings with the Berlin and Kay (B&K) ranks.

ciated with a categories in the gold standard. The automatic measures listed in sections (c) through (f) do not have access to this information.

Observe that the relatedness measures are markedly better than the similarity measures at identifying the true associated colour. Yet, for a majority of the thesaurus categories the closest colour in WordNet is not the most associated colour.

8.2 Co-occurrence in Text

Physical entities that tend to have a certain colour tend to be associated with that colour. For example leaves are associated with green. Intuition suggests that these entities will co-occur with the associated colours more often than with any other colour. As language has expressions such as *green with envy* and *feeling blue*, we also expect that certain abstract notions, such as *envy* and *sadness*, will co-occur more often with their associated colours, green and blue respectively, more often than with any other colour. We now describe experiments to determine the extent to which target concepts co-occur in text most often with their associated colours.

We selected three corpora to investigate occurrences of colour terms: the *British National Corpus (BNC)* (Burnard, 2000), the *Google N-gram Corpus (GNC)*, and the *Google Books Corpus (GBC)* (Michel et al., 2011).[9] The *BNC*, a 100 million word corpus, is considered to be fairly balanced with text from various domains. The *GNC* is a trillion-word web coprus. The *GBC* is a digitized version of about 5.2 million books, and the English portion has about 361 billion words. The *GNC* and *GBC* are distributed as collections of 1-gram to 5-gram files.

Table 6 shows the frequencies and ranks of the eleven basic colour terms in the *BNC* and the unigram files of *GNC* and *GBC*. The ranking is from the most frequent to the least frequent colour in the corpus. The last column lists the Spearman rank order correlation (ρ) of the rankings with the Berlin and Kay ranks (1969) (listed in Section 2:(1)). Observe that order of the colours from most frequent to least frequent in the *GNC* and *GBC* have a strong correlation with the order proposed by Berlin and Kay, especially so for the rankings obtained from counts in the *Google Books Corpus*.

For each of the 177 gold standard thesaurus categories, we determined the conditional probability of co-occurring with different colour terms in the *BNC*, *GNC*, and *GBC*. The total co-occurrence frequency of a category with a colour was calculated by summing up the co-occurrence frequency of each of the terms in it with the colour term. We used a four-word window as context. The counts from *GNC* and *GBC* were determined using the fivegram files. Section (e) in Table 8.2 shows how often the colour with the highest conditional probability is also the colour most associated with a category. These numbers are higher than the baselines (a and b), as well as the scores obtained by the WordNet approaches (c).

From Table 5 in Section 7, we know that some

[9]The *BNC* is available at: http://www.natcorp.ox.ac.uk. The *GNC* is available through the Linguistic Data Consortium. The *GBC* is available at http://ngrams.googlelabs.com/datasets.

Automatic method for choosing colour	Accuracy
(a) Unsupervised baselines:	
- randomly choosing a colour	9.1
- most frequent colour in *BNC* (black)	23.2
- most frequent colour in *GNC* (black)	23.2
- most frequent colour in *GBC* (white)	33.3
(b) Supervised baseline:	
- colour most often associated with categories (white)	33.3
(c) WordNet similarity measures:	
- Jiang Conrath measure	15.7
- Lin's measure	15.7
(d) WordNet relatedness measures:	
- Lesk measure	24.7
- gloss vector measure	28.6
(e) Co-occurrence in text:	
- $p(colour \mid word)$ in *BNC*	31.4
- $p(colour \mid word)$ in *GNC*	37.9
- $p(colour \mid word)$ in *GBC*	38.3
(f) Co-occurrence and polarity:	
- $p(colour \mid word, polarity)$ in *BNC*	51.4
- $p(colour \mid word, polarity)$ in *GNC*	47.6
- $p(colour \mid word, polarity)$ in *GBC*	**60.1**

Table 7: Percentage of times the colour chosen by automatic method is also the colour identified by annotators as most associated to a thesaurus category.

colours tend to be strongly positive and others negative. We wanted to determine how useful these polarity cues can be in identifying the colour most associated with a category. We used the automatically generated Macquarie Semantic Orientation Lexicon (MSOL) (Mohammad et al., 2009) to determine if a thesaurus category is positive or negative.[10] A category is marked as negative if it has more negative words than positive, otherwise it is marked as positive. If a category is positive, then co-occurrence cues were used to select a colour from only the positive colours (white, green, yellow, blue, pink, and orange), whereas if a category is negative, then co-occurrence cues select from only the negative colours (black, red, brown, and grey). Section (f) of Table 8.2 provides results with this method. Observe that these numbers are a marked improvement over Section (e) numbers, suggesting that polarity cues can be very useful in determining concept–colour association.

[10]MSOL is available at http://www.umiacs.umd.edu/~saif/WebPages/ResearchInterests.html#semanticorientation.

Counts from the *GNC* yielded poorer results compared to the much smaller *BNC*, and the somewhat smaller *GBC* possibly because frequency counts from *GNC* are available only for those n-grams that occur at least thirty times. Further, *GBC* and *BNC* are both collections of edited texts, and so expected to be cleaner than the *GNC* which is a corpus extracted from the World Wide Web.

9 Conclusions and Future Work

We created a large word–colour association lexicon by crowdsourcing, which we will make publicly available. Word-choice questions were used to guide the annotators to the desired senses of the target words, and also as a gold questions for identifying malicious annotators (a common problem in crowdsourcing). We found that more than 32% of the words and 33% of the *Macquarie Thesaurus* categories have a strong association with one of the eleven colours chosen for the experiment. We analyzed abstract concepts, emotions in particular, and showed that they too have strong colour associations. Thus, using the right colours in tasks such as information visualization and web development, can not only improve semantic coherence but also inspire the desired emotional response.

Interestingly, we found that frequencies of colour associations follow the same order in which colour terms occur in different languages (Berlin and Kay, 1969). The frequency-based ranking of colour terms in the *BNC, GNC*, and *GBC* also had a high correlation with the Berlin and Kay order.

Finally, we show that automatic methods that rely on co-occurrence and polarity cues alone, and no labeled information of word–colour association, can accurately estimate the colour associated with a concept more than 60% of the time. The random choice and supervised baselines for this task are 9.1% and 33.3%, respectively. We are interested in using word–colour associations as a feature in sentiment analysis and for paraphrasing.

Acknowledgments

This research was funded by the National Research Council Canada. Grateful thanks to Peter Turney, Tara Small, and the reviewers for many wonderful ideas. Thanks to the thousands of people who answered the colour survey with diligence and care.

References

Satanjeev Banerjee and Ted Pedersen. 2003. Extended gloss overlaps as a measure of semantic relatedness. In *Proceedings of the Eighteenth International Joint Conference on Artificial Intelligence (IJCAI-03)*, pages 805–810, Acapulco, Mexico.

Brent Berlin and Paul Kay. 1969. *Basic Color Terms: Their Universality and Evolution*. Berkeley: University of California Press.

J.R.L. Bernard, editor. 1986. *The Macquarie Thesaurus*. Macquarie Library, Sydney, Australia.

Marc H. Bornstein. 1985. On the development of color naming in young children: Data and theory. *Brain and Language*, 26(1):72 – 93.

Roger W. Brown and Eric H. Lenneberg. 1954. A study in language and cognition. *Journal of Abnormal Psychology*, 49(3):454–462.

Lou Burnard. 2000. *Reference Guide for the British National Corpus (World Edition)*. Oxford University Computing Services.

Chris Callison-Burch. 2009. Fast, cheap and creative: Evaluating translation quality using amazon's mechanical turk. In *Proceedings of the Conference on Empirical Methods in Natural Language Processing (EMNLP-2009)*, pages 286–295, Singapore.

Stuart K. Card, Jock D. Mackinlay, and Ben Shneiderman, editors. 1999. *Readings in information visualization: using vision to think*. Morgan Kaufmann Publishers Inc., San Francisco, CA.

Wei-bin Chen. 2005. Comparative studies on cultural meaning difference of colors between china and western societies. *Journal of Fujian Institute of Socialism*.

Irvin L. Child, Jens A. Hansen, and Frederick W. Hornbeck. 1968. Age and sex differences in children's color preferences. *Child Development*, 39(1):237–247.

Richard E. Christ. 1975. Review and analysis of color coding research for visual displays. *Human Factors: The Journal of the Human Factors and Ergonomics Society*, 17:542–570.

Max Coltheart. 1981. The mrc psycholinguistic database. *Quarterly Journal of Experimental Psychology*, 33A:497–505.

John Gage. 1969. *Color and Culture: Practice and Meaning from Antiquity to Abstraction*. University of California Press, Ewing, NJ.

Jay J. Jiang and David W. Conrath. 1997. Semantic similarity based on corpus statistics and lexical taxonomy. In *Proceedings of International Conference on Research on Computational Linguistics (ROCLING X)*, Taiwan.

Paul Kay and Luisa Maffi. 1999. Color appearance and the emergence and evolution of basic color lexicons. *American Anthropologist*, 101:743–760.

Naz Kaya. 2004. Relationship between color and emotion: a study of college students. *College Student Journal*, pages 396–405.

Dekang Lin. 1997. Using syntactic dependency as local context to resolve word sense ambiguity. In *Proceedings of the 8th Conference of the European Chapter of the Association for Computational Linguistics (ACL/EACL-97)*, pages 64–71, Madrid, Spain.

Max Luscher. 1969. *The Luscher Color Test*. Random House, New York, New York.

Aaron Marcus. 1982. Color: a tool for computer graphics communication. *The Computer Image*, pages 76–90.

Barbara J. Meier. 1988. Ace: a color expert system for user interface design. In *Proceedings of the 1st annual ACM SIGGRAPH symposium on User Interface Software*, UIST '88, pages 117–128, New York, NY, USA. ACM.

Jean-Baptiste Michel, Yuan K. Shen, Aviva P. Aiden, Adrian Veres, Matthew K. Gray, The Google Books Team, Joseph P. Pickett, Dale Hoiberg, Dan Clancy, Peter Norvig, Jon Orwant, Steven Pinker, Martin A. Nowak, and Erez L. Aiden. 2011. Quantitative Analysis of Culture Using Millions of Digitized Books. *Science*, 331(6014):176–182.

Saif Mohammad and Peter Turney. 2010. Emotions evoked by common words and phrases: Using mechanical turk to create an emotion lexicon. In *Proceedings of the NAACL-HLT 2010 Workshop on Computational Approaches to Analysis and Generation of Emotion in Text*, LA, California.

Saif Mohammad, Cody Dunne, and Bonnie Dorr. 2009. Generating high-coverage semantic orientation lexicons from overtly marked words and a thesaurus. In *Proceedings of Empirical Methods in Natural Language Processing (EMNLP-2009)*, pages 599–608, Singapore.

Saif M. Mohammad. 2011. Even the abstract have colour: Consensus in wordcolour associations. In *Proceedings of the 49th Annual Meeting of the Association for Computational Linguistics: Human Language Technologies*, Portland, OR, USA.

Li-Chen Ou, M. Ronnier Luo, Pei-Li Sun, Neng-Chung Hu, and Hung-Shing Chen. 2011. Age effects on colour emotion, preference, and harmony. *Color Research and Application*, pages n/a–n/a.

Ted Pedersen, Siddharth Patwardhan, and Jason Michelizzi. 2004. WordNet::Similarity - Measuring the Relatedness of Concepts. In *Proceedings of the Nineteenth National Conference on Artificial Intelligence*

(Intelligent Systems Demonstrations), pages 1024–1025, San Jose, CA, July.

Robert Plutchik. 1980. A general psychoevolutionary theory of emotion. *Emotion: Theory, research, and experience*, 1(3):3–33.

Norma S. Pribadi, Maria G. Wadlow, and Daniel Boyarski. 1990. The use of color in computer interfaces: Preliminary research.

Carl Ratner. 1989. A sociohistorical critique of naturalistic theories of color perception. *Journal of Mind and Behavior*, 10(4):361–373.

Paul Sable and Okan Akcay. 2010. Color: Cross cultural marketing perspectves as to what governs our response to it. pages 950–954, Las vegas, CA.

Rion Snow, Brendan O'Connor, Daniel Jurafsky, and Andrew Ng. 2008. Cheap and fast - but is it good? Evaluating nonexpert annotations for natural language tasks. In *Proceedings of the Conference on Empirical Methods in Natural Language Processing (EMNLP-2008)*, pages 254–263, Waikiki, Hawaii.

Carlo Strapparava and Gozde Ozbal, 2010. *The Color of Emotions in Texts*, pages 28–32. Coling 2010 Organizing Committee.

J. H. Xin, K. M. Cheng, G. Taylor, T. Sato, and A. Hansuebsai. 2004. Cross-regional comparison of colour emotions part I: Quantitative analysis. *Color Research and Application*, 29(6):451–457.

David Yarowsky. 1992. Word-sense disambiguation using statistical models of Roget's categories trained on large corpora. In *Proceedings of the 14th International Conference on Computational Linguistics (COLING-92)*, pages 454–460, Nantes, France.

A Survival Analysis of Fixation Times in Reading

Mattias Nilsson
Department of Linguistics and Philology
Uppsala University
mattias.nilsson@lingfil.uu.se

Joakim Nivre
Department of Linguistics and Philology
Uppsala University
joakim.nivre@lingfil.uu.se

Abstract

Survival analysis is often used in medical and biological studies to examine the time until some specified event occurs, such as the time until death of terminally ill patients. In this paper, however, we apply survival analysis to eye movement data in order to model the survival function of fixation time distributions in reading. Semiparametric regression modeling and novel evaluation methods for probabilistic models of eye movements are presented. Survival models adjusting for the influence of linguistic and cognitive effects are shown to reduce prediction error within a critical time period, roughly between 150 and 250 ms following fixation onset.

1 Introduction

During reading, the eyes move on average four times per second with substantial variation in individual fixation times, reflecting, at least in part, momentary changes in on-line language processing demands. In psycholinguistics, it is commonly assumed that derivative measures of fixation times, such as first fixation duration and gaze duration, reflect cognitive processes during reading. It is less clear, however, how the distribution of *individual* fixation times in reading is affected by on-line processing activities. In eye movement oriented research, models that attempt to model the distribution of individual fixation times in reading typically assume that saccadic movements are executed relatively randomly in time, with cognition only occasionally influencing the timing of saccades (Feng, 2006; McConkie et al., 1994; Yang and McConkie, 2001; Yang, 2006). In the model by Yang and McConkie (2001), for example, it is assumed that cognitive control can have a direct influence over the timing of saccades only with very long fixations, after the normal saccade has been canceled due to processing difficulty. Distributional models have often made use of the hazard function in order to analyze fixation times in reading (Feng, 2006; Feng, 2009; Yang and McConkie, 2001). The hazard function, in general terms, is a function of time representing the instantaneous risk that an event (e.g., a saccade) will occur at some specified time t given that it has not occurred prior to time t.

In this paper, we model the distribution of fixation times in terms of a different but related quantity, namely the survival function, which defines the probability of being alive, i.e., the probability of the event not having occurred, at some specified time t. We use semiparametric regression for modeling the influence of linguistic and cognitive effects on the survival function, and we assess the results using survival-based time-dependent evaluation metrics. More specifically, our objectives are as follows. We first estimate the survival functions for ten different readers using the Kaplan-Meier method (Kaplan and Meier, 1958) in order to establish the general shape of the survival function for reading time data. Then, we estimate adjusted survival functions using Cox proportional hazards model (Cox, 1972) in order to examine the influence of stimulus variables on survival. Finally, we assess the adjusted survival models both with respect to the estimated effects of covariates and with respect to the predictive performance on held out data. The experiments we report in this paper are based on first fixation data (multiple refixations discarded) from the English section of the Dundee Corpus of eye movements in reading (Kennedy and Pynte, 2005).

The remainder of this paper is organized as follows. Section 2 introduces survival analysis and further motivates its use for modeling fixation durations in reading. Section 3 introduces and applies the Kaplan-Meier estimate, to compare the survival functions for the different readers in the corpus. Section 4 introduces the Cox proportional hazards model and section 5 outlines two methods for assessing the performance of survival models on new data. Section 6 presents the experimental evaluation of using Cox proportional hazards to model the survival function and summarize and discuss the results. Section 7, finally, concludes this paper.

2 Background

Survival analysis is the study and modeling of the time it takes for *events* to occur. Because methods for survival analysis originally were developed for studying the lifetime distributions of humans in an epidemiological context, the prototypical event in these studies is death and the primary variable of interest thus time until death occurs. The use of survival analysis, however, reaches beyond the clinical and medical sciences and survival methods apply to any study with a naturally identifiable starting point and a well-defined event of interest as end point. In non-medical contexts, survival analysis often goes by other names, such as *failure time analysis* or *reliability analysis* in engineering applications, *event history analysis* in sociology, or simply *duration analysis* in yet other contexts.

A defining characteristic of survival analysis is the ability to deal with censoring in a principled manner. Censoring is said to occur when only partial information about the survival time of an individual (human or other) is available. The most common type of censoring is referred to as right-censoring, which occurs when an individual is not subject to the event of interest during the course of the observation period. In this case, it is only known that the individual did not experience the event prior to the end of the study, but may perhaps do so at a later point in time and this piece of partial information about the censored survival time is included in the analysis.

There are, however, potentially good reasons for using survival analysis even in time-to-event studies that do not necessarily involve censored data, such as when measuring the brief periods of time elapsing between a stimulus appearance and a button-press in response-time studies, or when measuring the time between one saccade and the next during reading using eye-tracking. Such data is usually not normally distributed and even in the absence of censoring one may take advantage of the fact that survival data is almost never assumed to be normally distributed and the methods of survival analysis are designed to reflect this. Furthermore, if the correct parametric model for the data is not known, or one is not confident enough that a given parametric model is appropriate, the Cox proportional hazards model provides a robust[1] and widely used semiparametric regression method for time-to-event data. With respect to eye movement data, the Cox model appears appealing because, as pointed out by Feng (2006, 2009), several different types of distributions have been proposed as models of fixation times in reading at one time or another, suggesting there is indeed little agreement with respect to the correct parametric model.

2.1 Survival and Hazard

Survival data is commonly analyzed and modeled in terms of the survival and the hazard function.

The survival function describes the probabilistic relationship between survival and time. Let T be a random variable denoting an individuals' survival time ($T \geq 0$). The survival function, $S(t)$, defines the probability that the individual survives longer than some specified time t:

$$S(t) = P(T > t) \qquad (1)$$

The survival function is a monotonically decreasing function heading downward as t increases and has the following theoretical properties: $S(0) = 1$, the probability of surviving past time 0 is 1; and $S(\infty) = 0$, eventually nobody survives and $S(t)$

[1]Cox proportional hazards model is "robust" in the sense that the results will be reasonably close to those obtained using the correct parametric model.

falls to zero as t tends to infinity. Notice also that if $F(t)$ is the cumulative distribution function for T, the survival function, $S(t)$, is $1 - F(t)$.

In the present study, we let the event of interest be the occurrence of a saccade following a fixation period, and the most reasonable starting point for our measurements, at least in practice, appears to be the beginning, or the onset, of the fixation period. We will refer to the period onset-to-saccade interchangeably as the fixation time or the survival time. Thus, in this context, the survival function $S(t)$ simply expresses the probability that a given fixation lasts, or survives, longer than some specified time t.

The hazard function, $h(t)$, gives the instantaneous potential, per unit time, for an event to occur in some small time interval after t, given survival up to time t:

$$h(t) = \lim_{\Delta t \to 0} \frac{P(t \leq T < t + \Delta t \mid T \geq t)}{\Delta t} \quad (2)$$

The conditional probability in the formula for the hazard function expresses the probability that the survival time, T, will lie in the time interval between t and $t + \Delta t$, given that the survival time is greater than or equal to t, where Δt denotes an infinitesimally small interval of time. As already suggested, in this study the hazard function represents the instantaneous risk, or hazard, of a saccade occurring following a fixation at some specified time t, given that it has not yet occurred.

3 Kaplan-Meier Survival Estimate

The survival function for time-to-event data can be estimated from a sample of survival times, both censored and uncensored, using the Kaplan-Meier (aka Product-Limit) method. This is a non-parametric estimate of the survival function which orders the survival times, from the shortest to the longest, and adjusts, for each of the event times, the number of cases still alive according to the number of cases that were either subject to the event or censored in the previous time period.

Let d_j be the number of saccades that occur at time t_j, and let n_j be the number of fixations for which no saccade has yet occurred at time t_j. The Kaplan-Meier estimate of the survival function $S(t)$ is then given by:

$$\hat{S}(t) = \prod_{t(j) \leq t} (1 - \frac{d_j}{n_j}) \quad (3)$$

In the absence of censored observations, the Kaplan-Meier estimate is equivalent to the empirical distribution, and the cumulative survival probability at time t_j reduces to the number of surviving fixations at time t_j divided by the total number of fixations in the sample. The value of $\hat{S}(t)$ is constant between event times and the estimated function is therefore a step function that changes value only at times when one or more saccades occur.

3.1 Kaplan-Meier Survival of Reading Data

Feng (2009) estimated the hazard function for the distribution of fixation times for the readers of the Dundee corpus. Here, we give a complementary account by estimating the corresponding survival function for these readers using the Kaplan-Meier method. Figure 1 shows the survival functions for each reader plotted against time. Individual differences in the survival function emerge soon after 50 ms and at 100 ms we can spot different tendencies with respect to how fast or slow the curves decline. Overall, however, the behavior of the survival function appears similar across readers. Typically, the survival function begins with a slow decline up until about 150 ms and is then followed by a very rapid decline during the next 100 ms. Thus, we can see in figure 1 that the overall survival rates drop from about 80% to 20% in the time interval 150-250 ms. Thereafter, the function flattens again and at about 400 ms it appears to be converging between the readers. It is worth noting, however, that the reliability of the estimate decreases with time since the number of surviving fixations becomes fewer and fewer.

Median survival time is the point in time when 50% of the total number of fixations has been terminated by a saccade. It is thus read off the plot as the time where the probability of survival is 0.5. Median survival time ranges from 168 ms (reader *g*) to 220 ms (reader *b*). Mean median survival time across all ten readers is 191.4 ms with a standard deviation of 14.9 ms.

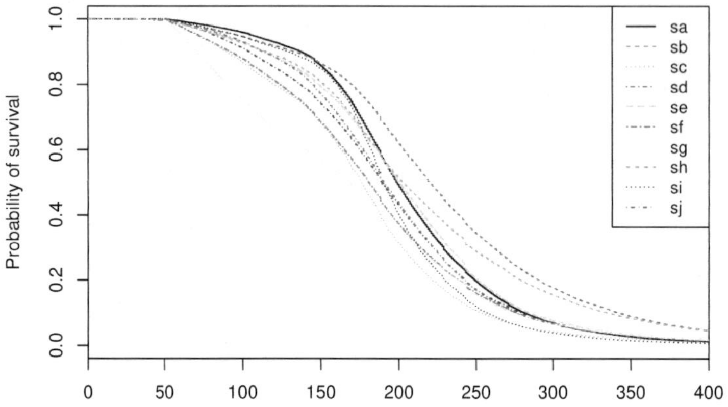

Figure 1: Kaplan-Meier curves for fixation durations showing the cumulative survival probability, following fixation onset, grouped by individual reader (subject a-j).

4 Cox Proportional Hazards Model

This section introduces the Cox proportional hazards model. We will later apply this model in the experimental part of the paper to obtain adjusted estimates of the survival function for the readers in the Dundee corpus.

The Cox proportional hazards model is a semi-parametric regression model for survival data relating survival time to one or more predictors or covariates. More precisely, the Cox model regresses the hazard function on a set of predictors, providing estimates of their effects in terms of hazard ratios. The Cox proportional hazards model has the following form:

$$h(t) = h_0(t) \exp\{\beta_1 x_1 + \beta_2 x_2 + \ldots + \beta_n x_n\} \quad (4)$$

where $h_0(t)$ is the baseline hazard function at time t, $x_1 \ldots x_n$ are the set of covariates or predictor variables, and $\beta_1 \ldots \beta_n$ are the corresponding coefficients to be estimated[2]. Thus, this model gives an expression for the hazard at time t for a particular individual with a given set of covariates.

The baseline hazard, $h_0(t)$, represents the value of the hazard function when all covariates are equal to zero, and in the Cox model this baseline hazard is left unspecified and varies as a function of time. Since no assumptions are made with respect to the form or distribution of the baseline hazard, this can be regarded as the nonparametric part of the Cox proportional hazards model. However, the Cox model assumes a parametric form with respect to the effect of the predictors on the hazard. In particular, as seen in equation 4, the predictors are assumed to multiply hazard at any point in time. This is an important assumption of the Cox model referred to as the assumption of proportional hazards. It means that the hazard functions for any two individuals at any point in time should be proportional. In other words, if a certain individual has a risk of the event at some initial point in time that is twice as high as that of another individual, then, under the proportional hazards assumption the risk remains twice as high also at all later times. There are a variety of different graphical and goodness-of-fit based procedures that can be used to evaluate the proportional hazards assumption for survival data (see Kleinbaum and Klein (2005) for an overview.).

The parameter estimates in a fitted Cox model are commonly interpreted in terms of their hazard ratios. If b_i is the value of the coefficient for predictor x_i, the exponentiated coefficient, e^{b_i}, gives the estimated hazard ratio for x_i. For continuous variables, the hazard ratio refers to the risk change associated with one unit increase in x_i, controlling for the effect of the other variables. A hazard ratio above one indicates a raised risk of the event occurring and the predictor is in this case thus negatively associated with survival. Correspondingly, a value below one indi-

[2]Parameter estimates in the Cox model are obtained by maximizing the "partial" likelihood, as opposed to the (full) likelihood. Details of procedures for parameter estimation can be found, for example, in Kalbfleisch and Prentice (1980).

cates a decreased risk and the predictor is thus positively associated with survival. Lastly, if the hazard ratio is equal to one, there is no indication of any associated risk change.

5 Assessment of Survival Models

Accurate prognoses are of critical importance in many areas where survival analysis apply, for instance in medical contexts where doctors have to estimate the expected remaining life time for terminally ill patients. Survival models are thus often assessed with respect to their predictive performance on novel data, in addition to the statistical significance of model covariates. We now briefly review two of the most commonly used measures for assessing the quality of survival models on independent data sets.

5.1 Prediction Error Curves

The prediction error for survival data is defined as a function of time and can be measured by the Brier score (Brier, 1950). Intuitively, if an individual is alive at time t, the predicted survival probability should be close to 1, and otherwise close to 0. The prediction error, or Brier score, at time point t is defined as the mean squared error between the observed survival status $Y_i(t)$ for the individual i at time t, which is equal to 1 if the individual is alive at t, and 0 otherwise, and the predicted survival probability for i at time t:

$$\hat{BS}(t) = \frac{1}{n}\sum_{i=1}^{n}\{Y_i(t) - S_i(t)\}^2 \tag{5}$$

The lower the Brier score, the lower the prediction error. Various benchmark values for the Brier score at time t exists. The values 0.25 and 0.33, for example, correspond to a constant predicted survival probability of 50% and to a randomly predicted value between 0 and 1, respectively. Often, however, the Kaplan-Meier estimate of the survival function over the training sample is used. In this case, the benchmark prediction at time point t corresponds to the proportion of individuals surviving past t, thus ignoring all available covariate information. By tracking the prediction error over time we get the prediction error curve (Graf et al., 1999) and a summary measure of the error for the whole observation period can be obtained by integrating over time (the integrated Brier score).

5.2 Concordance Index

The concordance index (Harrell et al., 1982), or *C*-index, estimates the probability that a given prediction agrees, or concurs, with the observed outcome. For uncensored data, the concordance index is given by the relative frequency of *concordant pairs* among all pairs of individuals. A pair is said to be concordant if the individual with the shorter survival time is also predicted by the model to have the highest risk of the two. Useful reference values for the concordance index are 0.5 which indicates that the predictions are no better than chance, and 1 which indicates that the model discriminates the pairs perfectly.

6 Experimental Evaluation

In order to study the influence of cognitive and linguistic effects on the survival function, the following experiment is performed. First, the Cox proportional hazards model is used to regress fixation times on five different stimulus variables associated with the current fixation, thus providing estimates of the hazard ratios for the effects of each variable adjusted for the other variables in the model. Second, we obtain adjusted survival functions, i.e. survival curves that adjust for the stimulus variables used as covariates, and we assess these curves with respect to the generalization error on held-out corpus data.

It is worth pointing out that regression studies on the Dundee Corpus of eye movements have been carried out before (e.g., Demberg and Keller, 2008; Pynte and Kennedy, 2006). Our experiment, however, differs from previous studies in at least three ways: (1) our goal is to model the survival function of fixation time distributions in reading, which means that we use the survival time of individual fixations as the unit of analysis; (2) we assess the survival model not only with respect to the estimated regression coefficients, but also with respect to the models' predictive performance on unseen data; (3) we use a semiparametric regression method for survival data which has not been previously applied, as far as we know, to reading-time data. It is also worth pointing out that although we believe that a

Table 1: Results of Cox proportional hazards model of fixation times in the Dundee Corpus section 01-16: hazard ratios (HR) and significance levels (p) for all covariates in the model, and for each individual model of reader a-j.

	a		b		c		d		e		f		g		h		i		j	
Variable	HR	p	HR	p	HR	p	HR	p	HR	p	HR	p	HR	p	HR	p	HR	p	HR	p
Word length	1.015	$< .001$	0.983	$< .001$	0.979	$< .001$	0.988	$< .001$	0.992	$< .05$	0.992	$< .01$	0.992	$< .01$	0.985	$< .001$	0.990	$< .01$	0.987	$< .001$
Word frequency	1.055	$< .001$	1.042	$< .001$	1.036	$< .001$	1.051	$< .001$	1.051	$< .001$	1.014	$< .001$	1.031	$< .001$	1.028	$< .001$	1.040	$< .001$	1.044	$< .001$
Bigram probability	1.108	$< .001$	1.196	$< .1$	1.092	$< .05$	1.006	$< .01$	1.013	$< .05$	1.014	$< .001$	0.953		1.011	$< .001$	1.003		1.005	$< .05$
Surprisal	1.001		0.986	$< .001$	0.994	$< .01$	0.984	$< .001$	0.998	$< .01$	0.991	$< .05$	1.002		0.994		0.993	$< .05$	0.996	$< .01$
Entropy	0.966	$< .001$	0.986	$< .01$	0.980	$< .001$	0.988	$< .01$	0.963	$< .001$	1.002		0.990	$< .05$	0.992	$< .05$	0.969	$< .001$	0.978	$< .001$

careful comparison of the results obtained using survival analysis to those reported for other regression methods would be useful and interesting, it is nevertheless beyond the scope of this paper.

Most of the stimulus variables included in the analysis have been shown to correlate with reading times in other regression studies: the number of letters in the word, the logarithm of the word's relative frequency (based on occurrences in the British National Corpus), the logarithm of the conditional (bigram) probability of the word (based on occurrences in the Google Web 1T 5-gram corpus (Brants and Franz, 2006)), the syntactic surprisal and entropy scores[3] (computed here using the probabilistic PCFG parser by Roark et al. (2009)). The surprisal (Hale, 2001) at word w_i refers to the negative log probability of w_i given the preceding words, computed using the prefix probabilities of the parser. A number of studies have previously established a positive relation between surprisal and word-reading times (Boston et al., 2008; Demberg and Keller, 2008; Roark et al., 2009). The entropy, as quantified here, approximates the structural uncertainty associated with the rest of the sentence, or what is yet to be computed (Roark et al., 2009).

In this experiment, we use the first 16 texts in the Dundee corpus for parameter estimation, and the following two texts, 17 and 18 for model assessment of the generalization error. To avoid introducing biases that may result from pooling distributional data together, we model each of the readers in the corpus separately. Prior to running the experiments, we also validated the Cox proportional hazards assumption using a goodness-of-fit approach based on the Schoenfeld residuals (Schoenfeld, 1982). The outcome of this test indicated a slight violation of the proportional hazards assumption. However, it is well-known that a slight violation may occur for large data samples, given that p-values can be driven by sample size (Kleinbaum and Klein, 2005).

6.1 Results

6.1.1 Hazard Ratios

Table 1 shows the results of the Cox proportional hazards regression models. The estimated hazard ratio for each covariate along with the corresponding significance level is reported for each reader. Recall that a hazard ratio above one indicates a worse survival prognosis, i.e. shorter fixation times, while a hazard ratio below one indicates better survival, i.e. longer fixation times.

Overall, the effects go in the directions expected for these variables based on previous research. There is a significant positive effect of *word length* on survival for all but one reader. The hazard ratio for the significant effects ranges between 0.979 and 0.992. Word length thus decreases the hazard by about 1-2% for each additional letter in a word when adjusting for the effects of the other covariates in the model. *Word frequency* is significantly and negatively related to survival across all readers. More frequent words have shorter survival times. The average hazard ratio among the readers is 1.0392 and the estimated risk of a saccade increases thus on average by a factor of 1.0392 for each unit increase in log word frequency. *Bigram probability* is negatively and significantly related to survival for eight readers with an average hazard ratio of 1.0569. *Surprisal* is significantly and positively related to survival for seven readers. Among these, the hazard decreases by 1% for each unit increase in surprisal. *Entropy* has a significant and positive effect on survival on all but one readers. The hazard ratios range between 0.963 and 0.992, corresponding to a de-

[3]To ease interpretation of the estimated hazard ratios, no interaction terms were included in this model.

	Brier score t									
	t.100		t.150		t.200		t.250		t.300	
Model	Cox	KM	Cox	KM	Cox	KM	Cox	KM	Cox	KM
a	0.05	0.05	0.14	0.15	0.24	0.25	0.14	0.15	0.05	0.06
b	0.05	0.05	0.12	0.13	0.23	0.25	0.21	0.23	0.12	0.13
c	0.13	0.13	0.23	0.24	0.17	0.18	0.06	0.07	0.02	0.02
d	0.07	0.07	0.17	0.18	0.23	0.25	0.15	0.16	0.06	0.06
e	0.05	0.05	0.15	0.15	0.23	0.25	0.14	0.15	0.05	0.05
f	0.09	0.09	0.21	0.21	0.22	0.23	0.12	0.12	0.06	0.06
g	0.16	0.16	0.23	0.23	0.24	0.25	0.12	0.13	0.07	0.07
h	0.07	0.07	0.15	0.15	0.24	0.25	0.20	0.20	0.12	0.12
i	0.04	0.04	0.13	0.13	0.23	0.25	0.10	0.10	0.03	0.03
j	0.06	0.06	0.18	0.19	0.23	0.25	0.12	0.12	0.05	0.05
Avg.	0.077	0.077	0.171	0.176	0.226	0.241	0.136	0.143	0.063	0.065

Table 2: Prediction error on held-out data between the observed survival status and the predicted survival probability at different times t, for Kaplan-Meier and Cox-model adjusted survival, and for all models of readers a-j.

creased risk by 1-4% per additional unit increase, after adjusting for the effects of the other predictors. While Frank (2010) recently showed that *sentence* entropy, i.e. non-structural entropy, accounts for a significant fraction of the variance in reading times, our results provide additional support for the influence of *structural* sentence entropy on reading times. Moreover, it is noteworthy that the effect of entropy appears reliably robust in individual first fixation times, suggesting that the effects of structural processing demands can be immediate rather than delayed in the eye movement record.

6.1.2 Adjusted Survival

We summarize the results of the evaluation of the adjusted survival function on held-out data in table 2 and in table 3. Table 2 shows the Brier score computed at different points in time in the interval 100 to 300 ms. Results are reported both for the Kaplan-Meier estimate of the survival function and for the fitted Cox-models. We present the results for each individual model. The bottom row gives the results obtained when averaging over all models at the specified time t.

Recall that the Brier score, or prediction error, at any specified time t, is computed over *all* fixations in the held-out set and gives the average of the squared distances between the actual survival status and the predicted survival probability at time t. Although the differences between the Cox-model and the Kaplan-Meier estimate are small overall, there are two subtle but notable results. First, the adjusted survival model is never underperforming the Kaplan-Meier survival estimate. The prediction error of the Cox model is consistently lower or equal to the Kaplan-Meier prediction error at each time point and for each reader. Second, in comparison to the Kaplan-Meier error, the prediction error of the adjusted model is systematically lower in the time window 150-250 ms, but essentially the same prior to, and after, this time period. This is readily reflected in the average scores, for example. One interpretation of these small but systematic differences suggests that there is a limited period, approximately no earlier than 150 ms. and no later than 250 ms. on average, during which the covariates in the model are primarily influencing the survival time. Before and after this period, the stimulus variables of the fixated word appear to have little or no influence on the time when saccades are generated. In other words, we observe an improved agreement to the observed data in the interval 150-250 ms. under the assumption that each individual fixation has an independent survival function whose value at time t is influenced by the specific values for the stimulus variables of the fixation. Recall that the benchmark, the Kaplan-Meier estimate, in contrast, assumes one and the same underlying survival function for all fixations, ignoring all available covariate information. By plotting the

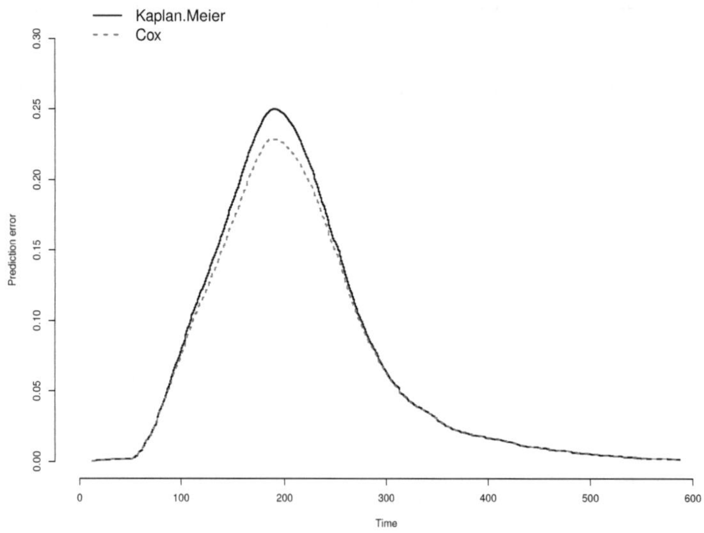

Figure 2: Prediction error curves on held-out data between the observed survival status and the predicted survival probability, for Kaplan-Meier and Cox-model adjusted survival, for the model of reader d.

Model	IBSC	C-index
Kaplan-Meier	0.041	0.582
Cox	0.043	0.598

Table 3: Integrated Brier score (IBSC) and Concordance index (C-index) on held-out data, for Kaplan-Meier and Cox-model adjusted survival, averaged over the results obtained for each model of reader a-j.

time-dependent prediction error, subtle differences in survival over the time course are more easily spotted. Figure 2 shows, as an example, the prediction error curve for one of the models.

Table 3 gives the integrated brier score, i.e., the prediction error obtained when integrating over all event times, and the concordance index C, for both the Kaplan-Meier estimate and the Cox model. These results are averaged over the results of the individual models. The integrated Brier score verifies that the Cox model fares somewhat better, although the impact of the model variables appears limited in time. The C-value for both the Kaplan-Meier and the Cox model is significantly better than chance (0.5). A C-value of 0.6 - 0.7 is a common result for survival data.

7 Conclusion

In this paper we applied survival analysis to model fixation times in reading. In particular, we modeled the survival function of fixation time distributions using the Kaplan-Meier estimate, and the Cox proportional hazards model to adjust for cognitive and linguistic effects on survival. The adjusted survival models were assessed with respect to the effect of covariates on hazard rates, and with respect to their predictive performance using evaluation metrics that are novel in the context of eye-movement and psycholinguistic modeling.

The results of the analysis suggests that: (1) structural sentence entropy influences survival, i.e., increasing structural uncertainty about the rest of the sentence decreases the risk of moving the eyes; (2) stimulus variables associated with the current fixation influence the survival of the fixation in a limited time frame, roughly between 150 and 250 ms following onset; and (3) linguistic and cognitive effects may influence the timing of saccades earlier than is sometimes assumed.

Looking ahead, important topics to be investigated in the future include *frailty models* and *competing risks survival analysis*. Frailty models are survival-based regression models with random effects, designed to account for variance due to individual-level factors otherwise unaccounted for.

Competing risks survival analysis apply to situations where a finite number of different types of events are possible, but only one of the events can actually occur per individual, e.g., dying from either lung cancer or stroke. In the current study we did not differentiate between different types of events following a fixation. A competing risks analysis, however, would let us differentiate between different types of saccades and study the influence of predictors on the survival function based on the type of the saccade following a fixation, e.g., whether it is a forward-directed saccade, refixation or regression. These and other issues will be addressed.

References

Marisa F. Boston, John Hale, Reinhold Kliegl, Umesh Patil, and Shravan Vasishth. 2008. Parsing costs as predictors of reading difficulty: An evaluation using the potsdam sentence corpus. *Journal of Eye Movement Reasearch*, 2:1–12.

Thorsten Brants and Alex Franz. 2006. Web 1T 5-gram Version 1. Linguistic Data Consortium.

Glenn W. Brier. 1950. Verification of forecasts expressed in terms of probability. *Monthly Weather Review*, 78:1–3.

David R. Cox. 1972. Regression models and life-tables. *Journal of the Royal Statistical Society. Series B (Methodological)*, 34:187–220.

Vera Demberg and Frank Keller. 2008. Data from eye-tracking corpora as evidence for theories of syntactic processing complexity. *Cognition*, 109:193–210.

Gary Feng. 2006. Eye movements as time-series random variables: A stochastic model of eye movement control in reading. *Cognitive Systems Research*, 7:70–95.

Gary Feng. 2009. Time course and hazard function: A distributional analysis of fixation duration in reading. *Journal of Eye Movement Research*, 3:1–23.

Stefan L. Frank. 2010. Uncertainty reduction as a measure of cognitive processing effort. In *Proceedings of the ACL Workshop on Cognitive Modeling and Computational Linguistics*.

Erika Graf, Schmoor Claudia, Sauerbrei Will, and Schumacher Martin. 1999. Assessment and comparison of prognostic classification schemes for survival data. *Statistics in Medicine*, 18:2529–2545.

John Hale. 2001. A probabilistic early parser as a psycholinguistic model. In *Proceedings of the second conference of the North American chapter of the Association for Computational Linguistics*, volume 2, pages 159–166.

Frank E. Jr Harrell, Robert M. Califf, David B. Pryor, Kerry L. Lee, and Rober A. Rosati. 1982. Evaluating the yield of medical tests. *Journal of the American Medical Association*, 247:2543–2546.

John D. Kalbfleisch and Ross L. Prentice. 1980. *The statistical analysis of failure time data*. Wiley.

Edward L. Kaplan and Paul Meier. 1958. Nonparametric estimation from incomplete observations. *Journal of the American statistical association*, 53:457–481.

Alan Kennedy and Joel Pynte. 2005. Parafoveal-on-foveal effects in normal reading. *Vision Research*, 45:153–168.

David G. Kleinbaum and Mitchell. Klein. 2005. *Survival analysis: A self-learning text*. Springer.

George W. McConkie, Paul W. Kerr, and Brian P. Dyre. 1994. What are normal eye movements during reading: Toward a mathematical description. In J. Ygge and G. Lennerstrand (Eds.), editors, *Eye movements in reading: Perceptual and language processes*, pages 315–327. Oxford: Elsevier.

Joel Pynte and Allan Kennedy. 2006. An influence over eye movements in reading exerted from beyond the level of the word: Evidence from reading english and french. *Vision Research*, 46:3786–3801.

Brian Roark, Asaf Bachrach, Carlos Cardenas, and Christophe. Pallier. 2009. Deriving lexical and syntactic expectation-based measures for psycholinguistic modeling via incremental top-down parsing. In *Proceedings of the Conference on Empirical Methods in Natural Language Processing (EMNLP)*, pages 324–333.

David Schoenfeld. 1982. Partial residuals for the proportional hazards model. *Biometrika*, 69:51–55.

Shun-nan Yang and George W. McConkie. 2001. Eye movements during reading: a theory of saccade initiation times. *Vision Research*, 41:3567–3585.

Shun-nan Yang. 2006. A oculomotor-based model of eye movements in reading: The competition/interaction model. *Cognitive Systems Research*, 7:56–69.

Author Index